Shadows of Things to Come: The Theological Implications of Intelligent Life on Other Worlds

Cynthia Anne Miller Smith

Cynthia Anne Miller Smith

Shadows of Things to Come:
The Theological Implications of Intelligent Life on Other Worlds

Fifth Estate, Post Office Box 116,
Blountsville, AL 35031

First Edition

Cover Designed by An Quigley

Printed on acid-free paper

Library of Congress Control No: 2010939578

ISBN: 9781936533022

Fifth Estate, 2010

Cynthia Anne Miller Smith

Table of Contents

Shadows of Things to Come: The Theological Implications of
Intelligent Life on Other Worlds
By
Cynthia Anne Miller Smith

Introduction

These are shadows of things to come; the reality belongs to Christ.
-- Colossians 2:17[1]

For what distances can love reach that are not in that vast sphere? What visions, what expectations and what presumptions can outsoar that flight? Like a giant oak tree covered with apple blossoms is the vast man in you. His might binds you to the earth, his fragrance lifts you into space, and in his durability you are deathless.
-- Khahlil Gibran, *The Prophet*[2]

Now is the time for all of us to start making the necessary mental preparations for the revelation that we are not alone in the universe.
– Father Kenneth J. Delano, *Many Worlds, One God*[3]

Let us now consider the real God, the genuine God, the great God, the sublime and supreme God, the authentic Creator of the real universe, whose remotenesses are visited by comets only comets unto which incredible distant Neptune is merely an outpost, a Sandy Hook to homeward-bound specters of the deeps of space that have not glimpsed it before for generations—a universe not made with hands and suited to an astronomical nursery, but spread abroad through the illimitable reaches of space by the flat of the real God just mentioned, by comparison with whom the gods whose myriads infest the feeble imaginations of men are as a swarm of gnats scattered and lost in the infinitudes of the empty sky.
-- Mark Twain, 1906[4]

Is there intelligent life on other planets? This book does not presume to know the answer or to argue one way or the other but rather assumes for the sake of argument that inhabitants of other

---

[1] All Scripture translations are, unless otherwise noted, from the New American Bible for Catholics. Iowa Falls, Iowa: Catholic World Press, 1987.
[2] Page 85 (112th printing, 1985)
[3] Page xiii (New York: Exposition Press, 1977)
[4] Chapter 295 of Albert Bigelow Paine's biography

worlds do exist and explores the theological ramifications thereof. The answer to the question about the existence of inhabitants of other worlds has profound implications for the Christian concepts of sin and redemption.[5] Did the Incarnation of Christ (that is, Jesus taking on human flesh) happen on one planet -- Earth -- and one species -- humans -- or did an event like the Incarnation occur in every world where intelligent inhabitants have evolved? Or is it the case that only humans fell from grace and are inflicted with original sin because our first parents sought God-like wisdom? The concept of intelligent life evolving on other planets is a scientific view held by the majority of the world's scientists, but what about the world's theologians and ordinary Christians? What indeed do Star Trek, Star Wars, Alien, and E.T. have to do with Christian theology? In a sense, science and religion dance together in a way that allows each to inform the other and balance the other in the minds of people who think about such things. If you are reading this book, then you have been and are thinking about such things.

There are two possibilities: Yes, there are intelligent inhabitants of other worlds, or no, there are not intelligent inhabitants of other worlds. As we progress through the book, we will see that the questions about the incarnation, sin, redemption, and salvation of people throughout the universe profoundly affected the thought of Christian theologians and apologists and ordinary folks for over a thousand years. Many scholars embrace a broad range of religious ideas disseminated and presented by Catholic and Protestant authors about the theological implications of intelligent life on other worlds. In this book, I am examining the ideas of various authors, many Catholic, some not, in an attempt to grasp the basic religious ideas surrounding inhabitants of other worlds, in an effort to present cogent theories about our possible reactions to the very real possibility of discovering intelligent life elsewhere in the universe.

---

[5] In economic language, redemption refers to the practice of purchasing an item for a price; in Christian theology, Jesus purchased sinful human beings, and the price was his own blood. In other words, Christ ransomed, liberated, and freed us from bondage, captivity, and punishment for our sins. Thus, redemption for Christians generally means deliverance from sin. Christ rescues, saves, and delivers us from our sins and their consequences.

How likely is it that we will discover life on other worlds, any kind of life, intelligent life or animal life or even just plant life? The odds have very recently increased as I write this sentence on Thursday, 30 September 2010: Through very careful calculations, astronomers have discovered a planet called Gliese 581g which is in the Goldilocks Zone -- that is, a distance from a sun at which the planet is capable of retaining liquid water, a factor many scientists believe is not only requisite for life but which one astronomer, Professor Steven Vogt at the University of California, Santa Cruz, claims practically guarantees life (http://www.foxnews.com/scitech/2010/09/29/odds-life-newfound-earth-size-planet-percent-astronomer-say/?test=latestnews). This is because on the one planet with life that we know about, our own Earth, where there's water, there's life, so it stands to reason that on Gliese 581g, where there's water, there's life also (http://www.scientificamerican.com/article.cfm?id=habitable-exoplanet-gliese-581). Gliese 581g orbits a red dwarf star, Gliese 581, and red dwarfs are known to be cooler than yellow suns like our own sun, Sol. Thus, the planet in question is much closer to its star than the Earth is to our sun (it is six million miles away as opposed to the Earth which is an average of 149,600,000 kilometers or 92,960,000 miles away from Sol or one A.U.), so that its year is only 37 Earth days, but scientists claim that its status as a red dwarf makes the location of the planet's orbit likely to allow life to develop. The sun in question, Gliese, found in the constellation Libra, is approximately 20 light-years away from the Earth, a distance that is quite close in astronomical terms. Gliese 581g's diameter is about 1.2 -- 1.4 times the Earth's, its mass is 31. -- 4.3 times the Earth's, its average surface temperature is between -24 Fahrenheit and 10 degrees Fahrenheit, its composition is rocky with an atmosphere and liquid water, and it is one of six planets to orbit its star. Some day Gliese may not be an insurmountable distance away, so we may at some time in the future send a spaceship to Gliese 581g to determine for sure whether it harbors life. Traveling at a tenth the speech of light, a spaceship from Earth could reach Gliese 581g in about two hundred years, while at close to the speed of light it would take twenty years (http://www.dailymail.co.uk/sciencetech/article-1316538/Gliese-581g-mystery-Scientist-spotted-mysterious-pulse-light-direction-newEarth-planet-year.html). The astronomer Dr. Ragbir Bhhathal at the University of Western Sydney claims he detected a signal from around the Gliese star system around 2008, but the signal has not been detected again yet (as of this writing). Homo sapiens are now a step closer to answering one of the most profound questions we know how to ask: Are we alone? How likely is Gliese 581g to harbor intelligent life? The scientists in the articles do not address this question, but, if the planet does harbor intelligent life, then the theological issues involved in the discovery of such intelligent life become more immediate and pertinent.

The question of how the existence of inhabitants of other worlds affects us is one of the oldest problems in philosophy as well as science and religion, and the answer has profound implications for our worldview. If we presume the reality of universal sin, then we thus presume the need of a universal savior. Whether the Christ taking on human flesh (Incarnation) requires as context the history of the Hebrew people is an open question. Now we will take a look at the arguments and discussions surrounding this open question, and one place to begin exploring the implications of that question is to examine and analyze past approaches of theologians to the possibilities of life on other worlds.

Frederick William Cronhelm, a member of the 19th century British congregation of Rev. Dr. Charles Musgrave, argues in his short book entitled *Thoughts on the Controversy As to a Plurality of Worlds* (London, 1858) that the universe cannot be strewn with a plurality of worlds[6] lest we have "a Bethlehem in Venus, a Gethsemane in Jupiter, a Calvary in Saturn" (cited in Crowe 334). However, other Christian authors from recent centuries argue the opposite is the case, claiming that the Logos (the "Word" in the Gospel of John 1:1) becomes incarnate (as in John 1:14a: "And the Word became flesh....") on inhabited worlds throughout the cosmos (i.e., Christ is born as an extraterrestrial on every inhabited world in the universe). Still others like Rev. Josiah Crampton (1809 – 1883)

---

[6] Historically, the plurality of worlds theory refers to the belief that a multiplicity of universes exists, each with its own Earth and its own sky (the ancients including the Greeks lacked the idea of different planets orbiting other stars, not having a clear idea of the nature of stars), or the later belief that a multiplicity of planets orbit not only our sun but other stars (which are also suns).

argue that "the material heavens [are] places of habitation" because Jesus ascended into heaven (cited in Crowe 335). Ernan McMullin of Notre Dame University writes that theologians have been largely silent on the issues of whether the work of Christ extends to inhabitants of other worlds or whether the Logos has become or will become incarnate on a multiplicity of worlds, but John Jefferson Davis writes that McMullin seems to be unaware of the research of Steven Dick and Michael Crowe, both of whom indicate clearly that such speculations have been going on at least since the third century A.D. (J.J. Davis 22). Since a number of Christians believe that Jesus is physically in heaven, some speculate that it follows that he has become or may yet become incarnate in many worlds. Is this position theologically sound, or does Christian theology demand that the Incarnation be unique to the Earth?

For millennia, people gazing up at the starry heavens have asked questions and speculated about the possibility of life on other planets, the nature of the universe, and the place of human beings in it. There are a series of interesting theological implications to the existence of extraterrestrials, leading to a series of questions regarding the significance of Jesus, the salvific (leading to salvation) effects of the Incarnation on inhabitants of other worlds in terms of the redemption purchased by the blood of Christ, as well as issues of justification, sanctification, and resurrection. These issues ultimately raise the question: if extraterrestrials are creations of God, can they be redeemed, justified, sanctified, and saved by the earthly Incarnation of the Logos (i.e., Jesus Christ)? The redemption and salvation of extraterrestrials pose significant theological questions deserving of serious study by scholars and the faithful alike because an understanding of the effects of the actions of the Logos on inhabitants of other worlds tells inhabitants of the Earth as much about ourselves as about God.

It should be noted that this book is written within the context of a Christian and pre-Christian Jewish framework encompassing both Old Testament and New Testament theologies while taking into considerations the religious beliefs of ancient Greeks and Romans in terms of the way in which they influenced first-century and later Christianity. While the beliefs of other religions are interesting and certainly worthwhile subjects of study, I have limited my investigation to the Christian and pre-Christian Jewish context since the primary topic is the theological implications of intelligent life on other worlds with respect to the Incarnation of the Logos, a specifically Christian idea influenced by pre-Christian Greek theological thought on the Logos, which the Greeks defined as the organizing force through which the universe was created. The Greek word Logos means "reason" or "speech" or "word." Philosophically, to the pre-Christian Greeks, it means universal reason providing order and sensibility to the *kosmos*, a Greek word, ὁ κόσμος, meaning "an orderly array" or "adorning" or perhaps "an orderly universe." The word *kosmos* may have taken on the meaning "an orderly universe" from what the ancients regarded as the orderly arrangement of the stars which moved so consistently in the sky from night to night and from season to season that calendars were based on their movements. The words *kosmos, Logos*, and other technical terms will be discussed more extensively in Chapter 1.

Another important word is "catholic" meaning "universal." Is the salvation of Christ truly universal, extending throughout the universe? The Catholic Church teaches that Christ offers his grace to everyone freely. Does that mean Christians should spread the Gospel in order to make that offer known to inhabitants of other worlds? This book will suggest that, for all its complexities, the question of the salvation of inhabitants of other worlds is not qualitatively distinct from the question of the salvation of humans. C.S. Lewis (1898 – 1963), a British scholar, Christian apologist, Anglican, and novelist, writes in his science fiction works that inhabitants of other worlds, like humans, are *hnau,* that is, sentient conscious beings (*Space Trilogy)*. For some Christians, the greatness of God implies that the greatness of his universe include other minds and souls who quest for the ultimate reality, just as do humans. This position is consistent with those of a wide range of Christian theologians, not only Aurelius Augustine and Thomas Aquinas but also William of Vorilong, Thomas Chalmers, Sir David Brewster, and others. The idea that inhabitants of other worlds can experience the salvation of Christ is not an official teaching of the Catholic Church[7], but it is not heresy either. I believe it is consistent with Catholic teaching including Scripture as well as Protestant doctrines that inhabitants of other worlds can be saved, and I will attempt to show that, although neither the Catholic Church nor any Protestant body has yet issued any official proclamations about the matter, important Catholic and non-Catholic theologians have speculated on the question throughout the ages, and many have arrived at similar conclusions.

In this book, I demonstrate that, prior to the twentieth century, the vast majority of intellectuals in the West express the belief that a plurality of populated worlds exists, and many Christians attempt to reconcile Christianity with such pluralism[8]. I believe it is consistent with Catholic teachings as well as the teachings of many Protestant churches, including the beliefs and writings of both Catholic and Protestant authors and theologians discussed in this book, to believe that inhabitants of other worlds, like human beings, are creatures with souls made in the spiritual image of God whose spiritual essence and physical forms of *hnau* are incidental to their relationship to his true image.

Some Greek philosophers argue that the notion of an exclusively singular world is ludicrous, and the myths of many ancient peoples populate the heavens with gods and goddesses who are certainly extraterrestrial in origin. Some Medieval scholars fight charges of heresy to argue that the heavens are teeming with inhabited worlds, while some Renaissance scholars believe that all of the planets in our solar system contain intelligent beings more or less like humans. Northrop Frye, in *The Great Code,* discusses the development of humanity's understanding of the sky:

---

[7] "ROMAN CATHOLIC is the designation known to English law; but 'Catholic' is that in ordinary use on the continent of Europe, especially in the Latin countries; hence historians frequently contrast 'Catholic' and 'Protestant', especially in reference to the continent; and, in familiar non-controversial use, 'Catholic' is often said instead of Roman Catholic." Source: OED.

[8] The word "pluralism" in this book follows the usage of various theologians and authors of the subject of this book on extraterrestrials and Christianity to mean the belief that a plurality of worlds in the universe exists and that it is possible that intelligent beings inhabit those worlds.

The nature around us is permeated by death and corruption, but we can discern within it the original "good" creation. The symbol of this original nature, and all that is now really left of it, is the sky. The stars give out, according to legend, a music or harmony that expresses the sense of perfected structure. The two levels of nature thus make up for man a purgatorial order, a means whereby he attains his own "true nature."

This symbolic structure wore out in the eighteenth century for two main reasons. First the images of the sky's perfection disappeared: the stars were not made out of immortal quintessence, and the planets did not revolve around the earth in perfect circles. The sky joined the rest of nature as an image of alienation, often in fact as the most extreme form of it. Second, there was no real evidence that the "natural" on the upper human level really was natural to man except the assertions of custom and established authority. The Lady in Milton's *Comus* regards her chastity as natural on her level of nature, but the arguments used are circular: she wishes to remain chaste, and that is that. For us, human creativity is still thought of as purgatorial, as a way of raising the level of human nature. But that it imitates or restores an original divine creation of nature is not a principle now defended with much confidence. The essential meaning of the creation story, for us, seems to be as a type of which the antitype is the new heaven and earth promised in Revelation 21:1. (113 – 114)

It would seem, then, that as the centuries progress, humanity's view of the heavens changes to reflect the evolving science of the day. When the sky becomes something other than the abode of God, and heaven becomes spiritualized as a relationship with God, albeit on some kind of aethereal plane (in the sense of "a level of existence, consciousness, or development" (Webster)), then humanity's understanding of the *kosmos* evolves to include beings in it which are not necessarily any less fallen than humanity. With the myth of the perfection of the heavens shattered, scientists and theologians alike are freed from the fetters of its dogma to speculate about other worlds which some theorize may not be all that different theologically from our own.

In the eighteenth century, intelligent design supporters (usually those favoring Saint Thomas Aquinas's Fifth Proof for the Existence of God[9]) attempt to explain the design of the universe in terms of Newtonian physics, but, when the theory then in vogue became outdated, later supporters attempted to explain design in terms of quantum theory, and no doubt in the future supporters will attempt to explain design in terms of whatever new theory, perhaps the T.O.E. (Theory of Everything), that will then be in fashion. The problem, as I see it, is that some scientists and some theologians attempt to yoke together then-current interpretations of scientific theories with then-current interpretations of theology so that, when the scientific theories lose their vigor, the practice is to simultaneously reject the theological interpretation to which it is yoked. For this reason, the Catholic Church at one time rejected new interpretations of scientific theories of the *kosmos* because its theology was linked to the older Aristotelian science. When the scientific ideas of Aristotle (384 B.C. – 322 B.C.) were thrown out, the Church scrambled to save its theology from being thrown out with it. Since Vatican II, the Catholic Church more openly supports scientific research and proclaims that scientific theories such as evolution and quantum theory, which explain the construction of the universe and the development of life, do not contradict Catholic teachings including the Bible. As scientific explanations increase in number and clarity, so do theological explanations of the *kosmos* and the place of intelligent beings like humans within it. While scientific theories often are very successful at explaining the process of cosmic

---

[9] Saint Thomas Aquinas, *Summa Theologica*, Question 2, Article III (Whether God Exists?), "I answer that, The existence of God can be proved in five ways....The fifth way is taken from the governance of the world. We see that things which lack intelligence, such as natural bodies, act for an end, and this is evident from their acting always, or nearly always, in the same way, so as to obtain the best result. Hence it is plain that not fortuitously, but designedly, do they achieve their end. Now whatever lacks intelligence cannot move towards an end, unless it be directed by some being endowed with knowledge and intelligence; as the arrow is shot to its mark by the archer. Therefore some intelligent being exists by whom all natural things are directed to their end; and this being we call God." Most people today call this Saint Thomas's "Intelligent Design" argument. See Chapter 6 for more discussion of this proof. See Appendix B for Saint Thomas's more complete argument surrounding these proofs.

evolution and hylology (theory of matter or the stuff of which the universe is made), they often explain hylogenesis (theory of the origin of matter or origin of the stuff of which the universe is made) very poorly, if at all. In this book, we will see that, as scientific views of the *kosmos* are updated over the centuries, the views of many theologians and authors are updated as well.

Perhaps unfortunately, the twentieth century initially rejects the heady ideas of the Renaissance and other earlier enthusiasts of intelligent life in the universe, and many modern scholars denounce the idea of a universe populated with intelligent creatures, arguing that the probabilities are quite low (despite the famous Drake Equation[10]) for their existence. Scholars risk losing their respectability for speculating on the possibility of extraterrestrial life, much less discussing the theological implications of inhabitants of other worlds. However, since the 1950s, when some reputable scientists expressed support for the notion of inhabitants of other worlds, some daring theologians are joining the fray.

Indeed, many of these theologians reveal a fascinating and provocative set of questions surrounding the Incarnation of the Logos (or Christ) with respect to inhabitants of other worlds, and this book will examine the various arguments scholars and theologians have put forth in response. The primary thrust of this book is to discuss the Incarnation of Christ, his death and resurrection, and the meaning of

---

[10] The Drake Equation is a formula developed by Frank Drake to determine the probability of intelligent life in the universe. The Drake Equation states that:

$$N = R^* \times f_p \times n_e \times f_\ell \times f_i \times f_c \times L$$ where:

N is the number of civilizations in our galaxy with which communication might be possible; and
R^* is the average rate of star formation in our galaxy
f_p is the fraction of those stars that have planets
n_e is the average number of planets that can potentially support life per star that has planets
f_ℓ is the fraction of the above that actually go on to develop life at some point
f_i is the fraction of the above that actually go on to develop intelligent life
f_c is the fraction of civilizations that develop a technology that releases detectable signs of their existence into space
L is the length of time such civilizations release detectable signals into space.

these events, all of which are equally pertinent to salvation, whether for inhabitants of Earth or inhabitants of other worlds. I will argue that the Incarnation is unique to the Earth, even while putting forth arguments to the contrary, because the resurrection of the Logos is distinct from the practice of Jesus of raising people from the dead. Lazarus, whom Jesus raised from the dead, would die again, but Jesus, after being resurrected, did not and does not die again, according to basic Christian theology. Therefore, because Jesus does not die again, I will argue that it is incongruous with Christian theology to suppose that he, after becoming incarnate on other worlds, ever dies again; i.e., one incarnation, one death, and one resurrection are sufficient for salvation. Although some of the authors examined in this book disagree, I will suggest that Scripture and tradition strongly support the view that Jesus transcends and permeates the universe he created, that he is immanent inside that universe, and that he panentheistically maintains and subsists within the *kosmos* (i.e., Christ is in everything and everything is in Christ, although it is not true that the universe is God, a view known as pantheism).

Chapter 1

Scripture and Inhabitants of Other Worlds and Christ

For God so loved the *kosmos* that he gave his only Son, so that everyone who believes in him might not perish but might have eternal life.
    – John 3:16

Any sufficiently advanced technology is indistinguishable from magic.
    – Arthur C. Clarke (Clarke's Third Law), "Profiles of the Future" (1962)

Christ, His Cross shall be my speed!
Teach me, Father John, to read:
That in Church on Holy Day
I may chant the Psalm and pray.

Let me learn that I may know
What the shining windows show:
Where the lovely Lady stands,
With that bright Child in her hands.

Teach me the letters A B C
Till that I shall able be
Signs to know and words to frame
And to spell sweet Jesus' Name.

Then, dear Master, will I look
Day and night in that fair book
Where the tales of Saints are told
With their pictures all in gold.

Teach me, Father John, to say
Vesper-verse and Matin-lay:
So when I to God shall plead,
Christ, His Cross shall be my speed!
    -- Robert Stephen Hawker, "A Christ-Cross Rhyme"

Section 1. *Kosmos*: The Extent of Redemption

Does Scripture support the idea that the redemptive work of Christ extends to inhabitants of other worlds throughout the *kosmos*? In this chapter, I will argue that the Scriptural usage of the term *kosmos* may be viewed as implying that the message of Christ, the Gospel, applies to all intelligent beings throughout the universe. If the Incarnation is an event unique to the Earth yet with universal effects, then it follows that Scripture should support this view. I will argue that the Greek word *kosmos* is a term which has a history of specific meanings depending on the scientific level of the time and culture in which the word appears. In New Testament times, *kosmos* means more than simply the world which today we call the Earth but means everything in what we now call the universe or cosmos. To argue, therefore, that Scripture attests to the universality of the Incarnation and redemptive work of the Logos is more than probable. The word "Logos" is a technical term in Greek which will be explored more fully in this chapter. Furthermore, since the Incarnation and redemptive work of Christ have universal effects, I will argue that these events effect the salvation of not only human beings but also of inhabitants of other worlds who have souls in need of redemption just like inhabitants of the Earth. We will discuss the meaning of "soul" later in this chapter to determine the nature of the beings purportedly saved by the Logos. In other words, is it theological plausible to assert that extraterrestrials, if they exist, have souls and that these souls of inhabitants of other worlds can be saved just like human souls?

 Torah, a Hebrew word meaning "teaching" or "instruction" but later "law," is a word with broad meanings but generally refers to either the first five books of Moses (the Pentateuch) or the entire Hebrew Bible (the Christian Old Testament) or, for Jews, both the Written Law (Hebrew Bible) and the Oral Law (Mishnah and Gemara, that is, the Talmud), and for Christians Oral Tradition (teachings of the Catholic Church) and Written Tradition (the Old Testament and the New Testament). Jesus speaks of the Torah in this way when he said "Do not think that I have come to abolish the law [Greek *nomos* or Hebrew *Torah*] or the prophets. I have come not to abolish but to fulfill" (Matthew 5:17). People thought that Jesus brought a new *didache* or teaching: "All were amazed and asked one another, 'What is this? A new teaching with authority. He commands even the unclean spirits and they obey him" (Mark 1:27). The Hebrew Bible and the New Testament are an interwoven green wreath of poetry and mystery flowing like waves on the ocean with rhythmic principles and precepts expressed in pithy truths and mellifluous maxims of universal import and cosmic power.

From a Christian perspective, one might maintain that the authors of Scripture may not have fully comprehended the extent of the meaning of their words when they wrote them since the Bible contains many prophecies that did not become apparent and faithful people did not understand until later in history. For example, prophecies of the Messiah in the Old Testament did not become comprehensible to certain religious commentators until the coming of Jesus Christ. I will consider the possibility that prophecies about the mission of Christians to spread the Gospel throughout the *kosmos* did not or perhaps will not become apparent until human beings encounter living extraterrestrials.

I will take a look at some passages from the Bible in a moment. For Christians, these passages may mean more than has traditionally been perceived. Before we can appreciate the significance of the Greek *kosmos*, we need to arrive at a definition of the term.

How scholars define the words "cosmos" or "world" or "universe" has direct bearing on the theological discussion surrounding Christ's redemptive work with respect to both humans and inhabitants of other worlds. Examination of the meanings of words often directly impacts our interpretation of Scripture. The notion that the world or universe is an ordered and harmonious and perfect system dates back to the ancient Greeks. (I should briefly note at this point that I am relying here on the expert opinions of the cited authors for the definitions of many classical language words.)

The Greek word *kosmos* means "world" or "universe" or "known sphere of existence" or "realm of existence" (Strong). The word *world* means to the ancient Greek astronomers, particularly the Epicureans, a system with its own earth, sun, planets, and stars. The ancient Greeks think of heaven (or the sky) as the Source of infinite nature. Later theologians interpret the Source as being an all-powerful Creator-God. (Zeus is the god of the sky.) The ancient Israelites, according to some scholars, thought of the sky as a physical vault holding back a watery chaos, and when God opened the sluice-gates water fell through in a process we call rain. So, *kosmos* is a combination of the Earth and the sky along with the heaven's contents. Many scholars believe that both the Israelites and the

Greeks thought of the sky as one-dimensional though vaulted or dome-shaped, although the ancient Greeks knew that the Earth was round (more about this shortly). Moreover, the Friberg lexicon defines *kosmos* as follows:

> 16161 ho kosmos means basically *something well-arranged*;
> (1) *adornment, adorning* (1P 3.3); (2) as the sum total of all
> created beings in heaven and earth *world, universe* (AC
> 17.24); (3) as all human beings *mankind, humanity, all people*
> (MK 16.15); (4) as this planet inhabited by mankind *world,*
> *earth* (MT 16.26; JN 11.9); (5) morally, mankind as alienated
> from God, unredeemed and hostile to him *world* (1J 5.19); (6)
> *sum total* of particulars in any one field of experience, *world,*
> *totality* (JA 3.6)

This spatial definition of *kosmos,* however, does not account for all of its signification. The notion of *kosmos* developed over the years and is defined differently at different times. For instance, Anaximenes of Miletus (d c 525 B.C.) "envisioned the sky as a 'crystal sphere' to which the stars were 'nailed...'" (cited in Robert Newman 1). The early Greeks apparently held the notion that the *kosmos* was a system ordered by destiny or the Fates. This view was held until Plato (c. 428 B.C. – 348/347 B.C.) and Aristotle (384 B.C. – 322 B.C.) who developed the idea that the *kosmos* is an ordered system designed by an intelligent principle, specifically, *nous* (mind, reason), which governed the divine concept of justice and determined the harmony of the spheres. Plato, in *Philebus* (30c), insists: "...there exist in the universe much 'unlimited' and abundance of 'limit,' and a presiding cause of no mean power, which orders and regulates the years, the seasons, and the months, and has every claim to the names of wisdom and reason." Aristotle, in *Physics* (8.1; 252a), writes: "nature *(physis) is* everywhere the cause of order." This cosmological conviction was a critical idea for the Stoics and their system of metaphysics that was later adopted by medieval philosophers and theologians as the system by which God governs and orders the universe through providence (here *kosmos* signifies order).

The pre-Socratic philosophers disseminated (that is, spread abroad and made known by public declaration) and perlustrated (that is, traversed completely to examine and review) cosmological principles and problems and their theories. Plato dissects, rearranges, modifies, and expands these views in the *Timaeus*. Aristotle reviewed and systemized these views in his *Physics*. In *On the Heavens* Aristotle expands his view that the *kosmos* is unique as an orderly structure:

> Either, therefore, the initial assumptions must be rejected, or there must be only one center and one circumference; and given this latter fact, it follows from the same evidence and by the same compulsion, that the world must be unique. There cannot be several worlds. (cited in Dick, *Plurality of Worlds* 6)

By contrast, Epicurus (341 B.C. – 270 B.C.) in the fourth century B.C. writes:

> There are infinite worlds both like and unlike this world of ours. For the atoms being infinite in number, as was already proved, are borne on far out into space. For those atoms which are of such nature that a world could be created by them or made by them, have not been used up either on one world or a limited number of worlds....So that there nowhere exists an obstacle to the infinite number of worlds. (cited in Dick, *Plurality of Worlds* 6)

So, it would seem that, for Aristotle, one world system exists, whereas for Epicurus, innumerable world systems exist. This does not mean that Epicurus was speaking of other planets around other stars because the Greeks lacked this idea. Rather, Epicurus felt that more than one *kosmos* in the sense of world system or world unit exists on what might best be termed other aethereal planes of existence. In his "Letter to Pythocles," Epicurus further writes:

> A world (*kosmos*) is a circumscribed portion of the sky (*ouranos*), containing heavenly bodies and an earth and all the heavenly phenomena, whose dissolution will cause all within it to fall into confusion: it is a piece cut off from the infinite (*apeiron*) and ends in a boundary either rare or dense, either revolving or stationary: its outline may be spherical, or three-

cornered, or any kind of shape. (cited in Dick, *Plurality of Worlds* 6)

Epicurus, then, appears to believe that the Earth and the sky are intimately connected in a way suggestive of modern science, although he departs from modern scientists in failing to recognize the sky as three-dimensional. It is perhaps unfortunate that Aristotle's view held sway over Christendom for over a thousand years because his understanding of the nature of the *kosmos* was so badly flawed that, like other Greeks of his time, he was unable to visualize other star systems. Since his science limited him to believing that the sun, Sol, was the only great light in the sky with enough power to illumine the Earth, Aristotle, again like other Greeks, believed this *kosmos* to be the only sphere of existence. Even so, it should be noted that, due to the definition of *kosmos* as "universe," it may be that Aristotle was right in asserting that there is only one universe, although Epicurus could also be right in terms of the multiple universes theories.

Although many Greeks differed among themselves about the technical niceties of the nature of the universe, most of them agreed on several principles, among which are that the *kosmos* is finite (in a spatial sense) with no beginning and no ending (in a temporal sense) in what modern scientists would call the steady state theory, is governed by a group of immutable laws which give it a precise and consistently repetitious rhythm, and is ordered by divine principles giving it an unalterable integrity (Runes 68 – 69). By contrast, medieval philosophers and theologians, broadly speaking, interpreted the Scriptures in such a way that they thought of the *kosmos* as having a beginning (*creatio ex nihilo* or creation from nothing*)* and an ending (teleology and apocalypticism), as being a system in which laws were not necessarily immutable on the theory that God can change laws by divine will (miracles), and as being providential in the sense of both God's foresight and divine right to rule (Runes 69).

These ancient Greek ideas seem echoed by Josephus (c. A.D. 37/38 – A.D. 100), the famous Jewish historian, who makes the following observation in his *Antiquities* (1.1.1) regarding the creation of the *kosmos*:

After this, on the second day, he placed the heaven over the whole world, and separated it from the other parts; and he determined it should stand by itself. He also placed a crystalline [firmament] round it, and put it together in a manner agreeable to the earth, and fitted it for giving moisture and rain, and for affording the advantage of dews. (cited in Newman 1)

Similarly, the Babylonian Talmud also indicates that the Jews believed the sky to be a physical dome, although different from the beliefs of the Gentiles of the same era:

The Sages of Israel say: the sun travels beneath the sky during the day, and above the sky during the night, while the Sages of the world maintain that the sun travels beneath the sky by day and beneath the earth by night. It seems that their opinion is better than ours, because during the day the wells are cool, but at night they are warm [!]. (cited in Newman 1)

Moreover, the early Catholic teachers also believed the sky to be a physical dome. The second century bishop of Antioch, Theophilus, writes: "The heaven, therefore, being like a dome-shaped covering, comprehended matter, which was like a clod" (cited in Newman 1). Indeed, the fourth century Catholic Father Chrysostom writes:

Waters embrace the back of the visible heaven on all parts; and yet they neither flow down, nor are moved out of their place....Besides the water hath not quenched the sun; nor hath the sun, which hath gone on his way beneath for so long a time, dried up the water that lies above. (cited in Newman 2)

These views of the nature of the sky prevailed for many centuries, although they were not necessarily held by all people of all cultures. Anaxagoras (d 428 B.C.) thought the sky was a "whirling, airy 'ether,' which swept the sun, moon and stars around the earth" (Newman 2). I am citing these authors to indicate that the ancient science of the Greeks and Israelites reflected an imperfect understanding of nature, although one need not agree with their understanding of nature to appreciate either their science or their theology. In other words, the Biblical cosmology reflects a scientifically inaccurate view of the universe, but the scientific beliefs of Biblical authors do not necessarily adversely affect later interpretations of the texts in favor of different scientific explanations of the nature of the universe. As for the science of the Bible, Harry Emerson Fosdick, an American minister of the twentieth century, gives his understanding of the Biblical view of the *kosmos*:

> In the Scriptures the flat earth is founded on an underlying sea; it is stationary; the heavens are like an upturned bowl or canopy above it; the circumference of this vault rests on pillars; the sun, moon and stars move within this firmament of special purpose to illumine man; there is a sea above the sky, "the waters which were above the heavens," and through the "windows of heaven" the rain comes down; within the earth is Sheol, where dwell the shadowy dead; this whole cosmic system is suspended over vacancy; and it all was made in six days, each with a morning and evening, a short and measurable time before. This is the world-view of the Bible. (cited in Newman 2 – 3)

I am noting this worldview of the Bible because it is a view that was held to be literally true by many devout Christians and is the primary reason why many Christian leaders, Catholic and Protestant alike, took such a dim view of Renaissance and later science which appeared to deny the centrality of humanity's place in the *kosmos*.

The cosmological ideas of Decartes, Lebniz, and Newton diverge from the medieval view to accord more harmoniously with the Greeks, while Kant regarded the difficulties associated with cosmology to be inherently unsolvable and inexplicable – what we might call mysterious (Runes 69). Post-Kantian analysis of cosmological principles yielded a mesh of scientific ideas with metaphysical ones, leading to an attempt to develop a unified theory of everything hinging on the most basic principles and more resilient argumentation (Runes 69). Those opposed to this view hold that the *kosmos* is more complex, and, indeed, its complexities are the most powerful argument for its radical nature as a system and not a unit, despite all the ancient and modern cosmogonies (theories of the generation or creation of the existing universe) to the contrary (Runes 69).

Now, with a reasonably sufficient understanding of the meaning of the word *kosmos* to different peoples in different cultures, we can begin to explore issues involving not only the contents of the *kosmos* but also its creation and creator. Whether souls populate the *kosmos* within the bodies of inhabitants of other worlds is a question significant to this book. The notion of what the soul is developed over millennia. Most of the Fathers of the Church (with the exception of Tertullian) argue the nature of the soul is comprised of a simple substance (i.e., consisting of one substance or element that is uncompounded or unmixed as opposed to a complex or composite substance) that is essentially spiritual; that is, the essence or essential nature of the soul is atemporal, noncorporeal, and a separate and distinct being that is self-subsistent (as designed by the divine) with properties originating in the ethereal plane as opposed to originating as temporal accidents (properties or qualities or attributes not essential to substances) in the material realm (cf. Runes 296). In other words, the soul is real and gives the material body character since it is the essence of the corporeal and is as essential to its function as the mind. Moreover, after ensoulment in the body takes place at conception, the soul becomes infused with accidents as time progresses and the child engages in activities in the material realm. In other words, the faculties of the soul grow as the body and mind grow (Saint Thomas). Traducianism is the belief that the soul stems from the parents (Runes 296). Creationism is the belief that the soul is created by God and is today a doctrine of the Catholic faith (ibid.). Saint Augustine and his later followers in the Middle Ages argue that the soul enters the body by an act of God and achieves a unity with the body so that the two become one (ibid.). Augustinianism on this point is a kind of modification of Platonic Dualism because the spiritual substance that is the soul is independent of the body until it merges with the body when it becomes inseparable until the death of the body. The Aristotelian/Thomistic view, known as the hylemorphic (changeability of the first matter or substance of the universe) theory, is that the soul is in essence not so much a substantial extension of the body but the very substance of the body itself (ibid.). Later Scholastics believe a *forma corporeitatis* (the corporeal nature of a body the essence of which is the principle of life and the existence of which cannot subsist or be vital without matter) independent of the soul exists – that is, the essence of a being is a *soma* (a Greek word usually meaning a living body), which is naturally and essentially the foundation of life (ibid.). In terms of later medieval alchemists, the soul is comprised of a spiritual substance that is laden with "accidents" that are infused in the soul as the result of experiences in the earthly life (ibid.). When the soul is in union with the body, it is the substance of the body, but when the soul is separated from the body, it is substantially deficient and fragmentary. How do these understandings of the nature of the soul relate to inhabitants of other worlds?

I will suggest that, by the standards of Catholic theology, it is consistent to hold that inhabitants of other worlds have souls that are the substantial parts of their bodies. The modern Catholic Church teaches that ensoulment of humans takes place at conception. Assuming that inhabitants of other worlds reproduce with seeds and eggs or their equivalents, then ensoulment of extraterrestrial bodies takes place at the equivalent of conception also. Unlike the perishable souls of animals and plants (sensitive and vegetative), *hnau*,[11] one may assume, have sensitive and vegetative and immortal souls. On the theory that inhabitants of other worlds have souls, one may assume that something happens to the immortal souls of extraterrestrials upon the deaths of the bodies, just as is true of human souls. As we will see, some Christian authors and theologians maintain that the souls of extraterrestrials do not sin and thus have no need of redemption, while others maintain that all souls have sinned and need redemption regardless of the shape of their physical bodies.

Spirit, from the Latin *spiritus* meaning "breath, life, soul, mind or spirit," was originally conceived by the Stoics to be a fire-like principle (*pneuma* or spirit) that animated and gave energy to the *kosmos* (Runes 299). The Greeks often speak of the soul in a manner similar to the way they refer to the mind. Generally, a spirit is an *hnau* capable of intellectual thought and willful behavior. Spirit, like soul, is immaterial yet conscious. Classical spiritualism is the belief that Spirit is the "ultimate reality in the" *kosmos,* that is, that *Pneuma*

---

[11] *Hnau* is a word invented by C.S. Lewis in his novel *Out of the Silent Planet* to refer to sentient beings on any planet including Earth and is often used by writers to mean intelligent beings on other worlds as opposed to nonsentient life like animals or plants. The word *hnau* also implies intelligent creatures with faith in God or who are members of societies that do express some kind of belief in the divine realm.

(spirit), *Nous* (mind), *Logos* (Reason), or an Over-Mind is immanent in the *kosmos* (as opposed to materialism, which in its pure empirical form rejects the notion that anything spiritual or an aethereal plane exists) (Runes 300). Plutarch once said, "The mind is not a vessel to be filled but a fire to be kindled." George Berkeley, the philosopher, takes the interesting but unusual position that the material realm is not real and that only the spiritual realm is real. Spiritual aspects of the body are supersensuous, representing a perfect order of existence or demesne (in the sense of domain) of the mind. Spirit is not only intellectual, rational, and noetic (that is, pertaining to the mind or intellect) but also moral and divine. For the author of the Gospel of John, worship is the process of the human spirit communing with the Holy Spirit (Runes 300). For writers of the Hebrew[12] Scriptures, that is, the Israelites, the body cannot be clearly distinguished from the soul, whereas for the authors of the New Testament, body and soul and spirit comprise a complete unit such that soul and spirit can be differentiated but not separated (cf. 1 Thessalonians 5:23: "May the God of peace himself make you perfectly holy and may you entirely, spirit, soul, and body, be preserved blameless for the coming of our Lord Jesus Christ"; and Hebrews 4:12: "Indeed, the word of God is living and effective, sharper than any two-edged sword, penetrating even between soul and spirit, joints and marrow, and able to discern reflections and thoughts of the heart"). Paul in the previous passage in 1 Thessalonians is not necessarily promoting an anthropological interpretation of human nature or even a philosophical or Stoic

---

[12] The word "Hebrew" is used to designate both the language and the people who are either "the descendents of Eber" (Genesis 10:21; 10:24-25; and 11:14-16; cf. NAB note for 11:16: "Eber: the eponymous ancestor of the Hebrews, 'descendants of Eber' (Gn 10, 21.24-30); see note on Gn 14, 13") or who are members of the religion that has come to be known as Judaism. This book uses the term "Hebrew" according to its usage in the Old Testament (or Hebrew Scriptures along with the Deuterocanonicals) and New Testament as referring to either the language, the people, or the religion, but the NAB note on Genesis 14:13 reads: "Abram the Hebrew: elsewhere in the Old Testament, until the last pre-Christian centuries, the term 'Hebrew' is used only by non-Israelites, or by Israelites in speaking to foreigners, since it evidently had a disparaging connotation – something like 'immigrant.' The account in this chapter may, therefore, have been taken originally from a non-Israelite source, in which Abraham, a warlike sheik of Palestine, appears as a truly historical figure of profane history."

analysis of the tripartite soul (vegetative, sensitive, and rational) but is rather making a positive comment about the combination of the natural with the supernatural qualities of all people in the way that they worship and obey God. This position seems to be borne out in the maxim that, as Scripture also attests, "So, too, it is written, 'The first man, Adam, became a living being [the Greek phrase is *psuche zwsan* which can be translated "a living soul"],' the last Adam a life-giving spirit" (the Greek phrase is *pneuma zwopoioun*) (1 Corinthians 15:45), implying that God through Christ gives a life-giving spirit to the faithful that is to be distinguished from the soul. Harry L. Poe and Jimmy H. Davis, twenty-first century authors of *Designer Universe: Intelligent Design and the Existence of God*, remark:

> The ancient Hebrews described the interplay of the human body and spirit as the *nephish hayah* (living being). It was a concept quite different from Plato's view of the *psyche* (life principle). It is most unfortunate for Western civilization that centuries ago scholars translated both words as *soul*. For the Hebrew, the soul represented the unity of life that involved both a physical and a spiritual dimension. For Plato, the soul was the life principle of the universe that became embodied in flesh until it could cast off the physical shell. Physical life was a hindrance to the soul. Aristotle reacted to his teacher and suggested that the spirit had nothing to say to the body. Unfortunately, philosophers and theologians for over two thousand years have played off Plato and Aristotle while paying little heed to the ancient Hebrew understanding of the relationship between physical and spiritual reality. The Hebrew concept of the Creator and the Christian concept of the Incarnation of God in Jesus Christ affirm the dynamic relationship between the spiritual and physical realms. (229 – 230)

Many Christian authors who believe extraterrestrial intelligent beings exist maintain that they have souls and spirits as well as bodies which will resurrect on Judgment Day. This belief is elementary to the Incarnation of Jesus, his death and resurrection. The reason many Christians embrace this belief is because they believe God chose to enmesh the stuff of which he is comprised with the stuff of which the *kosmos* is made. The entire intelligent design movement is an effort to reestablish the relationship between the material realm and the spiritual realm via communication between science and theology, a dialogue that culminates in an attempt to understand the mystery of the incarnate Logos who is Jesus Christ (John 1:1: "In the beginning was the *Logos* (Word), and the *Logos* (Word) was with God, and the *Logos* (Word) was God").

Closely related to the ancient understanding of *kosmos* is the meaning and function of the *logos*, meaning "word" or "speech" or "reason," which has a definite history that is worth mentioning at this point, although Henri Frankfort remarks that "*Logos*...[is] a term so heavily laden with associations as to be an embarrassment whether we translate it or not" (256). A discussion of the meaning of the Logos is important because this book is about the Incarnation of the Logos, and it is logical to define just what it is that Christians believe became incarnate to effect the salvation of human beings and inhabitants of other worlds. The ancient and scholarly understanding of the nature of the Logos is important because the Logos is the crux of the argument concerning the nature of God and God's Incarnation. The Logos is what became, according to Christians, incarnate on Earth, and what many Christians believe became incarnate on other worlds, so a discussion about exactly what the Logos is seems to be in order.

Heraclitus ("The Obsure") of Ephesus (536 – 470 B.C.) is the first to use the word *logos* to mean a principle governing the physical universe as well as the principle governing human law (Runes 183 – 184). Heraclitus believes that the stuff of which the universe is made is in a constant state of flux so that the changing nature of things represents the only true reality (Runes 184). Thus, Heraclitus argues, the *kosmos* is like an everlasting fire, continuously burning and consuming via the guidance of the *Logos*: "This world (*kosmos*) which is the same for all, no one of the gods or men has made; but it was ever, is now, and ever shall be an ever-living fire, with measures of it kindling, and measures going out" (cited in Frankfort 256). The Stoics developed this idea more completely, arguing that the *kosmos* is essentially one, and this living oneness contains infinitely many parts that fit together perfectly much like pieces of a puzzle, and the thing that gives the *kosmos* its life is the Logos, which abides within the *kosmos* and is itself perfect and immutable with divine purpose (Runes 184). The *kosmos-Logos* union is a kind of seed from which the creative impulse stemmed (*logos spermatikos* or "word seed"). The creative impulses yielded a multitude of *logoi spermatikoi* which individually function in the creation as the causes of ideas or forms with intelligence and purpose (Hyman & Walsh 17). Since the Logos governs everything in creation, it is also regarded by some as equivalent to *heimarmene* (fate). Since the Logos leads everything in creation to the *agathos* (good), it is also regarded by some as *pronia* (providence). Finally, the Logos, because it is identified with the universal order of things, is sometimes regarded as *physis* (nature) (Runes 184).

Philo Judaeus (also known as Philo of Alexandria) (ca. 20 B.C. – A.D. 50), who mixes Greek and Jewish thought, regards the Logos as the spiritual director, or the individual agent, through which the universe was created and ordered and governed by the transcendent God. Northrop Frye in *The Great Code* remarks:

> The Biblical terms usually rendered "word," including the *logos* of the Gospel of John, are solidly rooted in the metaphorical phase of language, where the word was an element of creative power. According to Genesis 1:4, "God said, Let there be light; and there was light." That is, the word was the creative agent that brought the thing into being. This is usually thought of as characteristically Hebrew in approach, although in Heraclitus the term *logos* is also essentially metaphorical, and still expresses a unity of human consciousness and physical phenomena. In the metonymic phase *logos* takes on rather the meaning of an analogical use of words to convey the sense of rational order. This order is thought of as antecedent to both consciousness and nature. Philo and the author of John combine the two traditions, and John's "In the beginning was the *logos*" is a New Testament commentary on the opening of Genesis, identifying the original creative word with Christ. (18)

Philo (some give his dates as c 15-10 B.C. -- A.D. c 45-50) is a Neoplatonic[13] philosopher and Jewish theologian who holds that

---

[13] Neoplatonism consists of the beliefs of such Neoplatonists as Plotinus (A.D. 205 -- A.D. 270), Porphyry (A.D. 234 -- A.D. 305), and Proclus

Greek philosophy ultimately stems from Mosaic theology, thus justifying his syncretistic[14] blending of the two disciplines in order to apply Greek philosophy to new spiritual interpretations of the Old Testament (Runes 234). His fame is a mark of his success in his task. Philo believes that the Logos dwells in the hearts of all people whose purpose is to unite with God by the process of renouncing self, a view Jesus himself makes use of when he says that his disciples must renounce self and take up their cross to follow him (cf. Mark 8:34 – 35; Matthew 10:38 – 39; 16:24 – 25). James C. Vanderkam writes:

> An interesting concept for Philo is the Logos of God, the power in which all the others are summed up. In one sense the Logos is God's thought as he planned to create the world -- a world that is divided into two parts: the intelligible world (Gen. 1) and the sensible world. The former resembles Plato's world of ideas or pure forms, while the latter is what is perceptible to the senses. The powers of God, such as the Logos, belong to the intelligible world but influence the sensible world. The influence of the Logos came especially through Moses and Aaron. Philo spoke of the Logos in other senses as a divine being separate from God himself, as the firstborn of God (like lady Wisdom), and as the beginning. Since the Logos is the mental power of God in creating the universe, it remains in the universe as a natural law, governing the operation of the universe. The Logos also manifested itself in the biblical patriarchs and became wisdom or virtue in the matriarchs -- that is, through them a natural, unwritten law

---

(A.D. 419 -- A.D. 485) who combined Platonic ideas with Oriental mysticism. Platonists are followers of the Greek philosopher Plato (429 B.C. -- 347 B.C.) or those who hold to Platonic philosophy or doctrine or beliefs. The Neoplatonists considered themselves just Platonists, but later scholars have called them Neoplatonists to distinguish them from earlier philosophers.

[14] The word "syncretism" is a technical term in religious studies referring to the blending of ideas from one religion with the ideas of another religion. Thus, the author of the Gospel of John engaged in syncretism when he blended the pagan Greek idea of the Logos with the Christian concept of the Incarnation of that Logos in the person of Jesus Christ.

came to expression before the law was revealed to Moses.
(140 -- 141)

Many Christians regard Philo's writings as a precursor to Christian
theology, though he is actually a Greek-speaking Diaspora Hellenized
Jew who apparently before anyone else synthesized Hellenistic
philosophy including the concept of reason with the revealed theology
of Judaism.

Plotinus (A.D. 205 – 270) develops his theology by calling the
initial three Hypostases the One (the eternal source of all Being), the
Mind (*Nous*), and the Soul (*Psyche*). Plotinus gives the Logos the
important task of creating and providing shape to *Nous*
(Intelligence/Mind), which conceptually leads to the hypostatic[15]
union of the Christian Trinity, although, for Plotinus, the initial three
Hypostases function as the chaotic operations of nature rather than the
deliberate organizing order of a god since Plotinus is not monotheistic
(Runes 240), but, like many Greeks, uses the word "God" in the
singular to refer to all the gods in the same way that English speakers
use the word "Man" to refer to all human beings. Although Plotinus
took no notice of Christianity, many Christians of his era and later
eras took notice of him and his ideas, such as Boethius, the last of the
Romans, as well as medieval and renaissance philosophers and
Kabbalists (practitioners of traditional Jewish mysticism which began
approximately in the 9th century A.D. with the publication of the
Zohar).[16] The point I'm making is that, for Plotinus, the Logos

---

[15] In Greek, hypostasis refers to the substance, essence, existence,
subsistence, reality, or personality of a creature or created thing, as
opposed to a creature's or created thing's "accidents" meaning that which is
distinguished from true reality because it lacks substance such as a
reflection in a mirror or a shadow on the ground, with the "hypostatic
union" being a technical expression for the union of the divine and human
natures of Jesus Christ; that is, the fundamentally consubstantial unity of
the three "hypostases" of the Godhead with "consubstantial" meaning,
literally, "together substance" or that which is the same substance or
essence such as the three consubstantial persons of the Christian Trinity.
In other words, in terms of substance, the Son by identity is both 100%
substantially human and 100% substantially God.

[16] "Zohar" is from a Hebrew word meaning "light" or "splendor" and is an
esoteric text probably written by Rabbi Moses de Leon in 9th century
Spain, although he attributed it to the second century A.D. Rabbi Simeon

performs the function of providing an order to the lower realities and governing them, while the One is the absolute Source needing nothing but which allows the Logos to act as a kind of go-between for the three Hypostases and their product the *kosmos* and everything in it.

For Christian philosophers, the Logos is the Second Person of the Trinity, functioning as not only the creative impulse of God but also the enlightenment and redemption of disciples of Jesus Christ. Again, for Christians, the syncretistically borrowed concept of the Logos is the organizing force through which God created the *kosmos*. For the Israelites, the *kosmos* is a combination of a flat table underneath a physical vault (the sky) which holds back a watery chaos and below which is a subterranean ocean (what the Greeks called Okeanos) leading to Sheol (the world of the dead). Thayer's Lexicon says:

> In several passages in the writings of John *ho logos* denotes the essential Word of God, i.e. the personal (hypostatic) wisdom and power in union with God, his minister in the creation and government of the universe, the cause of all the world's life both physical and ethical, which for the procurement of man's salvation put on human nature in the person of Jesus the Messiah and shone forth conspicuously from his words and deeds: John 1:1, 14. (1 John 5:7 Rec.) (cited in BibleWorks 6.0)

Robert C. Newman, by contrast, suggests that the Biblical firmament is not a vault but vapor: "Now I am not suggesting that the ancient Jews and Christians may not have believed that the sky was a solid dome, but only that the Bible does not teach such a view." (13) Newman further notes on the word normally translated "firmament" or "expanse":

> The use of the noun *raqia* seems to be consistent with either a two-dimensional or three-dimensional expanse. The object to which this term is applied may be rigid (as, perhaps, in Ezekiel

---

bar Yohai (it was customary for authors to attribute works to more ancient authors to lend them more respectability and authority, and this is also true of certain authors of the Bible such as pseudo-Paul).

1), but it may also be non-material (as probably in Psalm 150:1). Regarding the particular application of *raqia* to that object created in Genesis 1 which separates the lower and upper waters, we have noted that the text gives no evidence that anything but the "firmament" intervenes between these two waters, suggesting that this "expanse" may be the air. If the upper water is in the form of vapor or small droplets, there is no physical problem with the air supporting a quantity of water of the same order of magnitude as that presently in our atmosphere. (16)

The word *raqia* may mean an immaterial expanse consistent with our understanding of the atmosphere while the word *shamayim* is usually translated "heavens" or "sky" as opposed to "atmosphere." It is thus possible to argue that Biblical Jewish cosmology is roughly consistent with modern science, even if not exactly. Again, Newman writes:

> Basically, the word *shamayim* seems to involve a twofold division into visible and invisible regions, with the visible further subdivided into lower and upper regions which we would probably call the "atmosphere" or "sky" and "outer space." Such a twofold division of the visible heavens was not unknown in antiquity, as the Greeks spoke of the "sublunary" and "superlunary" regions.

> The term "heaven" is occasionally used for all three regions taken together (probably Psalm 148:1 and Jeremiah 23:24), and sometimes as a synonym for "upward" (...Genesis 15:5). In other cases, two of the regions may be spoken of as one (perhaps in Deuteronomy 30:12, 1 Samuel 2:10 or Job 38:29). Likewise several stereotyped phrases such as "heaven and earth" or "host of heaven" clearly cross the boundaries of the three suggested categories. Nevertheless, there are clear signs of this distinction in addition to 2 Corinthians 12:2 or modern attempts to harmonize the Bible with science. (19)

Newman also suggests that "'heaven' is the atmosphere, 'the heaven of heavens' is outer space, and 'heaven, God's dwelling place' is the invisible realm" (20). He also implies that God's presence transcends all these places (20). Newman finally claims that translations like the Septuagint and Jerome's Latin Vulgate use terms that are specifically geared to coincide with ancient science rather than actual Biblical meanings so that the Bible's expressions for various natural phenomena such as heaven and earth are actually consistent with modern science (44 – 45).

Accordingly, this discussion illuminating the history of the development of science from ancient Jewish science to modern science serves to illustrate that interpretations of Scripture can be regarded as consistent with modern science, while scientific theories based on imperfect understandings of Scripture developed over millennia sometimes must be taken with a grain of salt. The point is that the meaning of words like *kosmos* and Logos that changed over the centuries directly affected Christian theology in terms of, to use Kenneth J. Delano's term, astrotheology (literally, "theology of the stars" but implying a modern understanding of space and the place of God and people, whether human or extraterrestrial or both, in it). How scholars interpret the meanings of these terms today directly impacts the whole theory of the uniqueness of the Incarnation of the Logos. Saint Augustine's science was much poorer than his theology, for example, because he lacked modern understandings of ancient terms like Logos and *kosmos.*

The concepts of the Logos and the *kosmos* are so heavily laden with philosophical and theological overtones that we must be cautious when using these terms, especially since their definitions vary from one culture and time to another. To believe that Jesus is the incarnate Logos who came to a planet in the *kosmos* called Earth is the focus of Christian belief.

Jesus, the focus of Christian faith, is believed by many Christians to be the universal savior, although what constitutes "universal" varies from one Christian to another. In looking at the teachings of Jesus, one may argue that the message of Jesus originally was addressed to the Jewish people and only later expanded to the Gentiles. For example, Jesus says to a Canaanite woman who asks him to heal her daughter of demonic possession, "I was sent only to the lost sheep of the house of Israel" (Matthew 15:24), although, moved by her persistence, confrontation, and argument rooted in an obvious trust and faith, he grants her request. Jesus later expands his ministry to both the Samaritans and the Gentiles, and the Apostle Paul successfully expands the new faith to include as many Gentiles as possible. In this sense, the expansion of the Gospel message to include inhabitants of other worlds throughout the *kosmos* seems a logical progression from Jew to Gentile to extraterrestrial. Indeed, many passages from Scripture can be similarly more broadly interpreted to suggest that the Gospel message is divinely intended to be universal in the widest sense of the term.

In examining the following Scripture verses, I am using the translation of the New American Bible for Catholics while using the transliterated Greek word *kosmos* instead of "world" or "universe." The idea of the universality of God's message is implied in the usage of the word *kosmos* in these passages, although this interpretation is, as far as I know, original with me. Newman notes, "I do not believe Scripture is misleading, though it is capable of being misunderstood. I think the Christian has nothing to fear from a thorough and honest investigation of Scripture, as it will eventually vindicate itself as the Word of God" (5). For Christians, Scripture is the Word of God and is its own vindication. On the other hand, how do scholars understand the Bible in terms of modern views of the nature of the *kosmos* and the message of Jesus?

For one, the author of the New Testament Gospel and letters of John regards Jesus as a universal savior. By universal, the author means everyone in the entire cosmos, although, as I said earlier, *kosmos* means to John (who is writing for an audience of Gentiles who are Greek-speakers since Greek is the lingua franca of the first century A.D.) the Earth and the sky with all its one-dimensional contents. Since many passages in the Bible imply things to later generations that were not obvious to the original authors, it could be that the usage of the word *kosmos* in the Bible implies a larger, more complex universe than that originally envisaged by the authors. References to the *tebel* (world) as "stand[ing] in place, never to be moved" (Psalm 93:1b) should be understood as imperfect Biblical Jewish science and not Biblical Jewish theology. The Septuagint translation translates the Hebrew word tsaba' with the Greek word *kosmos*, though perhaps the Hellenized Jews who translated the Septuagint held a different view of *kosmos* than later Jewish and Jewish Christian as well as Gentile Christian authors and theologians. Carol Newsom, a professor of Hebrew Bible at Emory University, writes in a personal email to the author of this book (18 March 2004):

In Genesis 2:1 pas ho kosmos autwn translates the hebrew word tsaba', which means "host" in the sense of "military personnel, troops." It is also often used in the expression "host of heaven" to refer to the heavenly bodies or stars. Occasionally, it also is used to refer to the entourage around Yahweh. The standard reference dictionary, the 3d edition of Koehler-Baumgartner lists the expression "all their hosts" in Genesis 2:1 and notes the ways in which it has been interpreted in recent scholarship. "Either the beings surrounding God or alternatively the stars, or the totality of what is denoted in the individual works [of creation]." [vol. 3, p. 995] You are right that in Isa 13:10 the Septuagint's reading is not attested in the Masoretic text of the Hebrew, but it seems to refer to a similar conception.

Ancient Israelites did assume that Yahweh was surrounded by various divine beings who served in the heavenly court and as a heavenly army. Even when one gets the development of something recognizably like monotheism in the post-exilic period, the belief in these other divine beings continues to flourish and indeed in the Hellenistic period they become much more vivid and individuated, receiving names and descriptions. At that point they tend to be referred to as "angels" or "watchers" or "holy ones" but can sometimes be called "gods" especially in the Dead Sea Scrolls). So, although the conception of these beings changes over time, there is a clear trajectory from the older conceptions into the ones that flourished at the time of the New Testament writings. I must admit I was a bit surprised to realize that the Greek translators were using kosmos for the term tsaba', but I'm less familiar with the nuances of Greek.

So, for the Israelites, like the Greeks, *tsaba'* is a very orderly array like an army or host with the soldiers perfectly lined up and marching in unison, just like *kosmos* is an orderly array of the host of heaven (i.e., the stars and planets) marching across the sky in a regular and predictable way. Let's take a look at some passages from John the evangelist and epistolary:

1 John 2:2:   *He is expiation for our sins, and not for our sins only but for those of the whole* kosmos.

This verse is commonly read to mean that Jesus expiates the sins of human beings but can also be interpreted to mean that Jesus expiates the sins of all intelligent beings throughout the "whole *kosmos.*" Is the crucifixion a universal event with universal effects? Again, we may interpret this passage to have a greater meaning than that which was originally intended by the human author, John, because God may have intended a meaning, filtered through John, beyond John's limited understanding of the *kosmos*, so that the notion of Jesus saving both humans and extraterrestrials by his crucifixion and resurrection is consistent with scholarly hermeneutics.[17] La Peyrére says:

> That mystery, is the force and power of the Spirit of Christ, by which the Gentiles are changed into spiritual Jews, and into the true sons of *Abraham*, not according to the nature of the flesh, but according to the nature of Promise and Spirit, which is the true adoption and election of the Gentiles. Yea, Promise is that election, by which alone the Jews are what they are; by which the Jews themselves are the sons of *Abraham*, true Israelites, and true Jews, not according to the flesh, but according to Promise and to Spirit. *For all those that descended of Israel, are not Israelites, nor those who are the seed of* Abraham *all his sons: but in* Isaac *shall thy seed be call'd; that is to say, not the sons of the flesh, or the Jews, but those that are called sons of the Promise in his seed*, Romans 9. I say, that promise is it which makes true Israelites, and true sons of God. (86 – 87)

It would seem, then, that inhabitants of other worlds can also be children of God through being or becoming children of the Promise

---

[17] Hermeneutics refers to the art or science of interpretation, particularly scholarly interpretation of the Bible, in the sense of studying methods or principles of interpretation, as opposed to exegesis, which is a critical interpretation of a text or an explanation of meaning based on original intent.

regardless of the nature of their flesh because Scripture says that people who are the descendents of Israel are not necessarily Israelites while those who are not Israelites of the flesh may be Israelites of the Promise. In other words, extraterrestrials scattered throughout the *kosmos* may be children of God by adoption via the Promise even while not being the sons of Adam or the daughters of Eve.

Other passages with Eucharistic overtones lead to interesting questions:

John 6:33   *For the bread of God is that which comes down from heaven and gives life to the* kosmos.

John 6:51   *I am the living bread that came down from heaven; whoever eats this bread will live forever, and the breadthat I will give is my flesh for the life of the* kosmos.

The reference by Christ to the Eucharist in these passages implies that Christians need to bring their celebrations of Communion to inhabitants of other worlds throughout the *kosmos*, so that they too can participate in the sacred mysteries of the Christian faith. Many Christians may wish extraterrestrials to participate in their own salvation and experience the unity of the Communion of Saints by receiving the Eucharist. A major problem I foresee is the possibility that the physiology of inhabitants of other worlds might not allow them to receive the accidents of bread and wine when consuming the body and blood of Christ. For humans of many cultures, bread is the staff of life, but for some inhabitants of other worlds bread might be poison. This may be extremely problematic in that the Church regards the elements of bread and fermented wine to be essential to the celebration, since Jesus used bread made from wheat and fermented wine in his original Last Supper. Thus, a passage such as this one indicating that the incarnate Logos is the food we need to sustain us spiritually may lend support to the view that inhabitants of other worlds may need other economies of salvation since they may need foodstuff other than bread to experience communion with God on the grounds that the "bread of heaven" is to be distinguished from earthly bread. In such a case, "bread" may have a larger meaning than the Christian Eucharist and may mean that inhabitants of other worlds who embrace Christ spiritually consume "the living bread that came down from heaven" to effect their salvation. What is important is that a transubstantiation takes place so that the bread becomes the living flesh of the incarnate Logos, and, on other worlds, other foodstuff may transubstantiate into the body and blood (or their equivalents in terms of the real presence of the Logos). While Catholic teaching is that bread from wheat and fermented wine are essential for the transubstantiation to take place, the Church may recognize the transubstantiation of other elements for the purpose of spiritually feeding inhabitants of other worlds. Since other elements may be necessary, it is possible that other economies of salvation are necessitated by different evolution of different species with different sustenance requirements.

Another passage from the Gospel of John has Jesus say:

John 9:5   *While I am in the* kosmos, *I am the light of the* kosmos.

Genesis tells us that light was the first of all things created, but this light is a supernal light that does not come from the sun and other stars, since the Logos created the sun and the stars on the fourth day. For Christians, the Logos is the true light which illumines our souls and enlightens our minds and brightens our spirits. Scripture also asserts, "God is light, and in him there is no darkness at all" (1 John 1:5b). Also, "The true light, which enlightens everyone, was coming into the *kosmos*" (John 1:9). If, as Christians believe, Jesus is the Logos who is the light illuminating the human race, then it is consistent with Christian theology that, by bringing the good news to inhabitants of other worlds, the light may well illumine them also.

Now let us take a look at the Gospel of Mark:

Mark 16:15   *He said to them, "Go into the whole* kosmos *and proclaim the gospel to every creature."*

According to Scripture, the so-called Great Commission tells Christians to spread the Gospel to every "creature," a word meaning "creation of God." If creatures as creations of God exist throughout the *kosmos*, Scripture passages such as this one may indicate that it is a Christian duty to develop new ways of exploring space so that humans can go to other worlds and spread the Gospel to their inhabitants. Mark also suggests that the Second Coming of Christ will be universal, extending to planetary inhabitants throughout the *kosmos*:

> Mark 13:26-*27 And then they will see "the Son of Man coming in the clouds" with great power and glory, and then he will send out the angels and gather (his) elect from the four winds, from the end of the earth to the end of the sky.*

Here, the word translated "Earth" is from the Greek *ges* and the word translated "sky" is *ouranon* (often translated "heaven"). For the Greeks and Jews, the earth and the sky collectively make up the *kosmos*. According to the Christian tradition, both Catholicism and some aspects of Protestantism, Jesus will come again at the Parousia (a technical term in Greek referring to the practice of the town elders going outside the city gates to welcome to their city a visiting dignitary but often used in the New Testament to refer to the Second Coming of Jesus when certain people will be "raptured" to greet Jesus in the air as he is coming on the clouds of heaven in order to escort him to the Earth) to gather his elect from all over the Earth, and the text may imply everywhere in space. All over the Earth may mean he will gather all the chosen human beings, while everywhere in the sky may mean all chosen extraterrestrials.

The tradition of some Christian groups would seem to imply that Scripture passages such as those cited above support the notion that Christ is not only a universal savior but also that the benefits of his work on Earth apply to inhabitants of other worlds. In John and Mark, the authors imply that humans are not the only creatures subject to Christ's salvific work.

Section 2. Scripture and Other Sheep in the
Universe/Heavens/Sky/*kosmos*

Next, I will examine other Scripture passages which point to
the possibility of God including inhabitants of other worlds among the
people whom Christ must lead.

> John 10:16   *I have other sheep that do not belong to this
> fold. These also I must lead, and they will hear
> my voice, and there will be one flock, one
> shepherd.*

A. Durwood Foster cites John 10:16 to support the contention that the
"other sheep" referred to may be inhabitants of other worlds, saying,
"[t]he love of God manifest in Jesus Christ has surely not remained
unknown wherever there is spiritual receptivity" (cited in Peters,
"Contemporary Theology" 2). Jesus may lead these inhabitants of
other worlds through the activity of the Church throughout the
kosmos. The Church's mission, as stated above, may be to bring the
good news to otherworldly populations so that they can be led by
Christ. It is possible that Christ himself appeared to inhabitants on
their own worlds, but that does not necessarily mean that he would
appear in human form. The disciples did not recognize the
resurrected Jesus until he revealed himself to them in the breaking of
the bread. A book called *Faces of Jesus* features pictures of Jesus as
black, white, Japanese, Indian, and so forth. We all see Jesus in terms
of our own cultural upbringing, and it may be no different with
inhabitants of other worlds. We just do not know. As Jesus said,
"When the Son of Man comes, will he find faith on Earth?" (Luke
18:8b). This may be the primary concern of Christians – before
Christians can bring the faith to inhabitants of other worlds, they must
first be examples of faith on Earth. Then, seeing their faith,
inhabitants of other worlds may come to recognize the truth that
Christians believe Jesus taught.

The Pauline and pseudo-Pauline epistles also speak of the
universality of the creator who made the Earth and all the planets in
the cosmos:

Hebrews 1:2   *In these last days, he spoke to us through a son, whom he made heir of all things and through whom he created the universe* [Greek aiwnas, an accusative masculine plural meaning "world" or "material universe," as opposed to elsewhere in Scripture where it often means "eternity"].

Hebrews 11:3   *By faith we understand that the universe* Greek aiwnas] *was ordered by the word of God, so that what is visible came into being through the invisible.*

Psalm 90:2   *Before the mountains were born, the earth* [Hebrew eretz, a (89:2) common feminine singular absolute noun meaning "ground, piece of land, territory, land, earth"; and Greek gen, accusative feminine singular common from he ges, tes ges meaning "soil, earth, round, dry land, land, region, country," or even "the inhabited earth"] *and the world* [Hebrew tebel, a common feminine singular absolute noun meaning "world"; Greek oikoumene, an accusative feminine singular common noun meaning "inhabited" with ge (earth) understood, i.e., "the inhabited earth, the world," and sometimes later the Roman Empire"] *brought forth, from eternity to eternity* [olam to olam, a common masculine singular absolute noun meaning "long time, for all time, forever, eternity"] *you are God.*

The Greek word *aiwn aiwnos* (age, world order, eternity) is used in both Psalm 90:2 (Septuagint) and Hebrews 1:2 and 11:3. The Hebrew *owlam* or *olam* means, according to Strong's dictionary, "long duration, antiquity, futurity, for ever, ever, everlasting, evermore, perpetual, old, ancient, world, ancient time, long time (of past or of future), for ever, always, continuous existence, everlasting, indefinite or unending future, eternity." The Hebrew word *tebel* means "world" or "habitable part" (Strong). The Greek word *oikoumene* in Psalm 90:2 means "world, inhabited earth, mankind" and sometimes "the Roman Empire." The Hebrew *eretz* means, according to Strong, "land, earth, whole earth (as opposed to a part), earth (as opposed to heaven), earth (inhabitants), country, territory, district, region, tribal territory, piece of ground, land of Canaan, Israel," etc. These passages indicate that God made all the worlds in the universe, creating both the material universe and the spiritual universe. Since God made all the worlds, it follows that he made any inhabitants upon them and that he is just as concerned about their salvation as he is about the salvation of the inhabitants of the Earth. Since God lives in eternity, he has all of time to effect the salvation of the peoples of the universe, and it is consistent with Christian theology to believe that the redemptive work of Christ has efficacy for humans and inhabitants of other worlds alike.

The author of the Gospel of Matthew supports this contention when Matthew's Jesus speaks of the salvation of the good and punishment of the evil.

> Matthew 13:37-39   *[Jesus] said in reply, "He who sows good seed is the Son of Man, the field is the* kosmos, *the good seed the children of the kingdom. The weeds are the children of the evil one, and the enemy who sows them is the devil. The harvest is the end of the age and the harvesters are angels.*

Since some Biblical authors imply that Jesus is the universal savior, this passage may be interpreted to mean that Jesus sows children of the kingdom throughout the *kosmos* and will separate the good from the evil among both humans and inhabitants of other worlds at the end of the age. The text presupposes the resurrection of Christ since God the Father will grant to him "all power in heaven and on earth" (Matthew 28:18), implying that the resurrection is a universal event affecting both humans and inhabitants of other worlds. Father Delano writes in *Many Worlds, One God*, "Several theologians, including C.S. Lewis, have pointed out that a remark made by St. Paul in the Epistle to the Romans could be interpreted as meaning that the human race has been given by God the mission of evangelizing the entire universe" (118). Delano cites Romans 8:19-21, which in the NAB translation Paul writes:

> For creation awaits with eager expectation the revelation of the children of God; for creation was made subject to futility, not of its own accord but because of the one who subjected it, in hope that creation itself would be set free from slavery to corruption and share in the glorious freedom of the children of God.

Delano continues: "Four other passages from the New Testament: Col. 1:20; Eph. 1:10; 2 Peter 3:13; and Rev. 21:15 also speak of everything in the heavens and on Earth as being reconciled to God through Christ" (119). In terms of covenant[18] theology, while the covenants made with Adam and Eve and Noah are with all human beings, some authors suggest that, while these covenants were specific to the inhabitants of the Earth, they nevertheless imply that the covenant established by Jesus applies universally on the grounds that the Incarnation on Earth is actually a cosmic event with cosmic implications.

Various Scriptural passages assert that God made the heavens, which reflect his glory, and that he lives there:

Psalm 19:1-2   *The heavens declare the glory of God; the sky proclaims its builder's craft.*

Sirach 43:9   *The beauty, the glory, of the heavens are the stars that adorn with their sparkling the heights of God,...*

Habakkuk 3:3   *God comes from Teman, the Holy One from Mount Paran. Covered are the heavens with his glory, and with his praise the earth is filled.*

---

[18] Covenant, Hebrew beriyth (Gen 6:18 WTT), Greek diatheken (Gen 6:18 BGT) or diatheke, means an agreement, an alliance, a treaty, a pledge, an arrangement, a pact, a testament, a contract, theologically between God and his creatures.

Acts 7:55   *But he, filled with the holy Spirit, looked up intently to heaven and saw the glory of God and Jesus standing at the right hand of God,...*

Rev. 14:7   *He said in a loud voice, "Fear God and give him glory, for his time has come to sit in judgment. Worship him who made heaven and earth and sea and springs of water."*

Edward Nares, in his *EIP HEOP, EIP ΛΕΡΙΣΓΡ*; or "An Attempt to Shew How Far the Philosophical Notion of a Plurality of Worlds Is Consistent, or Not So, with the Language of the Holy Scriptures" argues that the Hebrew and Greek words typically translated "heaven(s)" and "world(s)" allow for a more expansive interpretation. For example, he translates Nehemiah 9:6: "Thou, even thou, art God alone; thou hast made the WORLDS, the UNIVERSE OF WORLDS; with ALL THEIR INHABITANTS; the EARTH, with all things that are therein; and thou fillest the whole with life; and THE INHABITANTS OF THE WORLDS worship thee" (cited in Crowe 173) (emphasis with caps Nares). The NAB translates this verse: "Then Ezra said: 'It is you, O LORD, you are the only one; you made the heavens, the highest heavens and all their host, the earth and all that is upon it, the seas and all that is in them. To all of them you give life, and the heavenly hosts bow down before you.'"

Kenneth Delano, a Catholic priest, in a personal letter to the author of this book, writes:

Concerning the question of whether the Bible does or does not offer any evidence or clues concerning the existence of ET's, I regard the Bible pretty much as did Abbe Georges Lemaitre (b. 1894). He was a Belgian astrophysicist, cosmologist, and Catholic priest renowned for his hypothesis of the expanding universe. When asked about an opposing theory, the steady state theory, Abbe Lemaitre replied: "Religion has no bearing either on my theories or that of the steady state. An atheist or a Christian could logically support either one of them. I do not believe that the Bible was intended to explain such things as cosmology. I do not believe that God ever intended to disclose to man what man could find out for himself." (Delano 1)

Certainly, there are statements and words (e.g., *kosmos*) in the Bible that can be understood as referring to all intellectual beings throughout the universe, but not with any certainty. So, in effect, the Bible leaves open the questions of inhabitants of other worlds and their possible need for redemption (Delano 2). Once again in *Many Worlds, One God,* Delano writes:

> The Bible has only this much to tell us about ETI[19]: that God would have to be their Creator too, since the Sacred Scriptures clearly state that the God we worship is the Creator of the entire universe and of all that is in it. Any further information about ETI we will have to find out for ourselves in the course of our and their endeavors to explore space. (121 – 122)

I am attempting to prove that the Incarnation is unique to the Earth with its effects spreading out across the entire universe; it seems consistent with many authors, especially Thomas Chalmers and Sir David Brewster, that inhabitants of other worlds probably have a literature and a revelation that inclines them to quest among the stars for the birthplace of their savior. Christians should be prepared to receive any pilgrims searching for knowledge of their creator, just as Christians should be prepared to receive knowledge from pilgrims about the creator. It will be of interest to scholars to inquire if they have a salvation history and whether it gibes with the earthly counterpart. Christians should no more expect information about extraterrestrials from the pages of Scripture than they should expect information about chemistry or particle physics from the lips of Jesus; his listeners had a hard enough time understanding the parable of the wheat and the tares (Delano 3).

A Catholic can only be sure that the *kosmos* is united in the glory of Christ (Levine 1). Furthermore, as Al Levine writes,

---

[19] Extraterrestrial Intelligences

> It occurred to me on a relativistic basis alone there are
> parts of the cosmos, temporally speaking, in which the
> Sacrifice has not yet happened. If there are domains
> outside our light cone – which there might very well be
> – then there are domains about which we know nothing
> whatsoever. The knowledge of the inspired writers
> must be limited by their assumption of absolute time,
> as in much else. All that they need to know is Easter,
> and that is what they experienced. Yet if God is
> literally 'light from light,' then in Him there is no
> passage of time as we know it, but one eternal present.
> I think it's best not to try to inspect the mysteries too
> closely, because we have no intellectual access to their
> contents, and to keep our options open. (personal
> email to the author, 7-27-2003, 1)

Indeed, many Christians believe Scripture not only gives knowledge
of the divine but also enables one to experience the mysteries of God.
Because it is written in the Bible that Jesus is the *monogenes*
(literally, "the only-begotten") of God (John 1:18), it seems contrary
to Scripture to suggest that God begets other incarnations of the
Logos throughout the universe. Furthermore, it is written in the
Christian Credo, "We believe in one God, the Father, the Almighty,
maker of heaven and earth, of all that is, seen and unseen. We believe
in one Lord Jesus Christ, the only begotten Son of God, eternally
begotten of the Father, God from God, light from light, true God from
true God, begotten, not made, of one being with the Father, through
him all things were made." Thus, it seems also inconsistent with
Catholic Tradition including Scripture as well as general Protestant
theology that Christ ever dies again on other worlds or rises again.
While many Christians believe the mystery of the Incarnation cannot
be scientifically explained but only mystically experienced, it seems
consistent with Catholic teachings and Protestant doctrines to believe
that the Incarnation is a unique universal event with universal effects
spreading out across all of space and time yet which God sees as one
ever-present now.

Conclusion to Sections 1 and 2

Since, according to Christianity, God created the heavens, it follows that God may have created inhabitants of the worlds in the heavens. Since Christians believe that God is good, it is unlikely that God does not care about inhabitants of other worlds in the same way he cares about inhabitants of the Earth. Scripture explicitly states that the actions of God affect the *kosmos* and not just the Earth, so it is consistent with Scripture to state that God became incarnate to redeem not only sinful human beings but sinful inhabitants of other worlds as well (if they exist).

The view that God is in the universe and the universe is in God is known as panentheism.[20] From the panentheistic viewpoint, all creatures naturally yearn for the God who is inside them. It is consistent with Christian theology to aver that God is the creator of all creatures, great and small, and all intelligent creatures, human and extraterrestrial, because it is consistent with Christian Scripture. While for Saint Thomas the souls of animals perish with their bodies whereas the souls of human beings are immortal, it is possible to theologize, as a form of astrotheology, that the souls of intelligent inhabitants of other worlds are also immortal as a function of the very nature of the intellect of sapient beings since it is the intellectual soul which, according to some philosophers, including Aquinas, is made in the image of God.

Inhabitants of other worlds may have their own theologies based on God's intervention in the history of their worlds, but what about the Logos? Did the Logos become incarnate only once on Earth for the salvation of all intelligent beings throughout the cosmos? Some theologians I will discuss in this book hold the belief that Christ became incarnate on every world with intelligent beings throughout the *kosmos*, that he lived and died and rose again over and over again...poor Jesus! According to my interpretation of mainstream Christian theological principles, the Logos became incarnate only once, and that Jesus suffered on the cross only once

---

[20] Panentheism comes from the Greek *pan* meaning "all" and *en* meaning "in" and *theos* meaning "God." In other words, "all in God" or "God in all."

and rose again only once, and also that the redemptive effects of Christ apply to inhabitants of other worlds. To say that Jesus dies and rises over and over again is quite different from the belief, according to Scripture, that "Christ, raised from the dead, dies no more; death no longer has power over him. As to his death, he died to sin once and for all; as to his life, he lives for God" (Romans 6:9-10). It seems more consistent with Scripture and Christian theology to say that Christ, the incarnate Logos, lives continuously without interruptions of death and subsequent risings. Many authors make this conclusion because many of the Scripture passages examined in this book support the notion that the Incarnation of the Logos along with the crucifixion and resurrection of Christ transcend and permeate all of space and time in order to effect the salvation of inhabitants of the many worlds.

Chapter 2

The Debate over How the Incarnation and Redemptive Work of Christ Affects Inhabitants of Other Worlds

And the Logos became flesh
And pitched his tent among us,
And we saw his glory,
The glory as of the Father's only Son,
Full of grace and truth.
      – John 1:14

He is the Ancient Wisdom of the World,
The Word Creative, Beautiful and True,
The Nameless of Innumerable Names,
Ageless forever, yet Forever New.
      -- Charles Carroll Albertson, "The Holy Child"

The idea that *we* are the only intelligent creatures in a cosmos of a hundred million galaxies is so preposterous that there are very few astronomers today who would take it seriously. It is safest to assume, therefore, that *They* are out there and to consider the manner in which this fact may impinge upon human society.
– Arthur C. Clarke, *Report on Planet Three and Other Speculations*[21]

Section 1. Thomas Chalmers, William Whewell, and Sir David Brewster et al. and the Public Debate over the Theological Implications of Plurality of Worlds Theory and of Intelligent Life on Other Worlds

Long before the twentieth century, public debates raged about whether inhabitants populate other worlds and, if so, how this hypothesis affects Christianity, Christians, and Christian theology, particularly the doctrines of the Incarnation and redemption of Christ. William of Vorilong (1390 – 1463), a Franciscan theologian and author of a widely quoted commentary on the *Sentences* of Peter Abelard (1079 – 1142), believes that inhabitants of other worlds would not sin after the manner of Adam:

---

[21] In the chapter, "When the Aliens Come," New York, 1972, pages 89 – 102. Cited in Dick, *The Biological Universe* 256.

> If it be inquired whether men exist on that [other] world, I answer no, for they would not exist in sin and did not spring from Adam. As to the question whether Christ by dying on this earth could redeem the inhabitants of another world, I answer that he is able to do this even if the worlds are infinite, but it would not be fitting for Him to go into another world that he must die again (cited in Dick, *Plurality of Worlds* 88).

A little more than a century later, Philip Melanchthon (1497 – 1560), a German disciple of Martin Luther, espouses the early Protestant view that a plurality of worlds violates Scripture, and since in his belief Scripture is the sole rule of faith, God would not have made other worlds without saying so in the Bible (cited in Dick, *Plurality of Worlds* 88). Since the Bible describes the creation of one world with the sun, the moon, and the stars, it follows that he created nothing else, certainly not other *kosmoi*, in his view. As a result, Melanchthon contends that the Incarnation of the Logos is unique to the Earth on the grounds that other worlds do not exist.

A generation later, Galileo Galilei (1564 – 1642), an Italian astronomer, mathematician, and natural philosopher, expresses concern about how his Catholic Church might react to the speculation of the effects of the Incarnation and redemption on inhabitants of other worlds and so denies that otherworldly beings exist, though it is not clear what beliefs he would have asserted without such constraints. Galileo's friend, the Jesuit Giovanni Ciampoli (1589 – 1643), a brilliant Latinist, warns Galileo in 1615 that ideas about inhabitants on other worlds have profound consequences when taking into consideration the view that such inhabitants are not descendents of Adam nor descendents of Noah (Dick, *Plurality of Worlds* 90). To solve this problem, Tommaso Campanella (1568 – 1634), an Italian philosopher and writer, attempts to reconcile Catholic teachings with Renaissance humanism and defends Galileo, speculating about the plurality of worlds theory by insisting that such theories do not violate Catholic teachings including Scripture but merely the teachings of Aristotle. Campanella disbelieves that "men" in other worlds had sinned and needed redemption, asserting therefore that Jesus did not have to die for them. This idea implies that Christ needed to die and rise again for the people populating the antipodes[22] of the Earth. However, for these reasons, Campanella seems unconcerned with the theological ramifications of this issue and is unclear as to how theology would be affected if extraterrestrials did inhabit other worlds and had sinned (Dick, *Plurality of Worlds* 92 – 93).

Thus begins one of the most important historical debates over whether the Incarnation is unique to the Earth or whether it was necessary for Christ to become incarnate on other worlds to redeem their inhabitants in the same way that earlier theologians believed another Incarnation on Earth was necessary to save the people of the antipodes. Since most of the authors discussed in this book support the notion that other worlds may be inhabited, the question arises if the redemptive work of Christ on Earth applies universally to inhabitants of other worlds without multiple incarnations or if the redemptive work of Christ applies only to humans through his unique Incarnation? Put another way, does Christ save a multiplicity of inhabitants of other worlds via a multiplicity of incarnations or is his Incarnation unique to the Earth because inhabitants of other worlds are not fallen like human beings are and thus do not need to be redeemed or is his Incarnation unique to the Earth while his work in this world incurs the salvation of inhabitants of other worlds? Before we can answer these questions, let us review the principal positions.

A prominent position we will examine is that of Thomas Chalmers (1780 – 1847), a Presbyterian reverend, theologian, writer, and social reformer who first moderated the Free Church of Scotland. He wrote *Astronomical Discourses* in which he preaches fervently on the doctrines of Christ's Atonement and the sinfulness of human beings who, he believes, desperately need grace. He also argues in favor of pluralism, although he does not believe that Christ became incarnate on other worlds but believes his redemption extends to other planets (Crowe 186 – 187). Chalmers believes it is acceptable to reinterpret Scripture according to modern knowledge of science and astronomy. For example, he interprets Scripture to mean that possible

---

[22] The "Antipodes," a word meaning literally "opposite foot," refers to the people on the opposite side of the spherical Earth; in medieval and later thought those on the opposite side of the world with respect to Europe, an idea leading to popular discussions about their salvation.

inhabitants of other worlds rejoice over the repentance and conversion of one sinner along the lines of Luke 15:7:

> I tell you, in just the same way there will be more joy in heaven over one sinner who repents than over ninety-nine righteous people who have no need of repentance.

Chalmers's sermons and writings were instrumental in the debate about pluralism and extraterrestrials (Crowe 190). Chalmers argues that:

> For anything he can tell, the eternal Son, of whom it is said, that by him the worlds were created, may have had the government of many sinful worlds laid upon his shoulders; and by the power of his mysterious word, have awoke them all from that spiritual death, to which they had sunk in lethargy as profound as the slumbers of non-existence. (73)

Chalmers asserts that nonbelievers cannot accept extraterrestrial redemption because they believe an omnipotent God would never bother to visit our paltry planet or take on human form, let alone die or redeem insignificant man (*Discourse III* 89 – 90). Yet, for Chalmers, that is exactly what happened: He writes that God does not let a single world become lost, especially if evangelists bring its inhabitants back from the errors of their ways (94). The position of Chalmers is that no world is too small or too mean for God to care for its inhabitants, and the way God cares for the inhabitants of all worlds is through the mediation of his Son (Chalmers 107 – 112). He also writes, "Let us put forth an effort, and keep a steady hold of this consideration – for the deadness of our earthly imaginations makes an effort necessary – and we shall perceive, that though the world we live in were the alone theatre of redemption, there is something in the redemption itself that is fitted to draw the eye of an arrested universe" (*Discourse IV* 130). Chalmers seems to imply that the greatness of the Incarnation and redemptive work of Christ suffuses the universe and all its inhabitants, earthly and extraterrestrial. Chalmers continues:

Now, though it must be admitted that the Bible does not speak clearly or decisively as to the proper effect of redemption being extended to other worlds, it speaks most clearly and most decisively about the knowledge of it being disseminated among other orders of created intelligence than our own. But if the contemplation of God be their supreme enjoyment, then the very circumstance of our redemption being known to them may invest it, even though it be but the redemption of one solitary world, with an importance as wide as the universe itself. (134 – 135)

For Chalmers, inhabitants of other worlds are aware of the Incarnation and events surrounding the redemptive work of Christ (135 – 136). He writes:

[God] does not tell us the extent of the atonement; but he tells us that the atonement itself, known as it is among the myriads of the celestial, forms the high song of eternity – that the Lamb who was slain is surrounded by the acclamations of one wide and universal empire – that the might of his wondrous achievements spreads a tide of gratulation over the multitudes who are about his throne; and there never ceases to ascend from the worshippers of Him who washed us from our sins in his blood, a voice loud as from numbers without number, sweet as from blessed voices uttering joy, when heaven rings jubilee, and loud hosannas fill the eternal regions. (139 – 140)

Chalmers cites Revelation 5:11-13 to support his contention that all creatures throughout the universe praise the name of the Lamb:

I looked again and heard the voices of many angels who surrounded the throne and the living creatures and the elders. They were countless in number, and they cried out in a loud voice: "Worthy is the Lamb that was slain to receive power and riches, wisdom and strength, honor and glory and blessing." Then I heard *every creature in heaven and on earth and under the earth and in the sea, everything in the universe*, cry out: "To the one who sits on the throne and to the Lamb be blessing and honor, glory and might, forever and ever." [Chalmers 140; emphasis mine]

If the expression "every creature" means every living thing created by God, then the possible implication is that inhabitants of other worlds are aware of the messianic events that have taken place on the earth.

The second primary position examined in this book is that pluralism in and of itself, along with its spinoff, the salvation of extraterrestrials, contradicts basic Christian theology. While this book primarily argues in favor of pluralism and the salvation of extraterrestrials, it is important to discuss the opposite view espoused by William Whewell since his arguments, along with the responses of Sir David Brewster, set the tone for the whole debate. The discussion surrounding the theology of a plurality of worlds and the Incarnation of the Logos continues in this famous debate in the nineteenth century between William Whewell (1794 – 1866), an English philosopher and historian and ethics author (who is largely responding to Chalmers), and Sir David Brewster (1781 – 1868), a Scottish physicist known for his optics and polarized light experiments (who is responding to Whewell). Whewell, a Christian, was once a pluralist but later writes a book in which he declares that believing that inhabitants live on a plurality of worlds violates Christian teachings for a variety of reasons, while Brewster, also a Christian, reaches the opposite conclusion.

The debate between these two Protestant men was followed closely by the educated community of the day with many of the people supporting the view that otherworldly inhabitants exist (Crowe 351 – 352) and that their existence does not denigrate Christian theology, essentially Brewster's position; fifty-six percent of religious writers of the era as well as seventy-one percent of Anglican authors and non-Anglican Protestants and eighty-three percent of the scientists supported pluralism in opposition to Whewell (Crowe 352). Some debaters of the period argue that Christ needs to become incarnate on a variety of worlds, while others suggest that the Incarnation is unique to the Earth with its benefits extending to inhabitants of other worlds. Still others suggest that extraterrestrial populations may not have fallen and so are in no need of redemption. Sir David Brewster opposes Whewell, engaging in a vigorous debate that was followed closely by the public. Brewster falls back on the traditional belief that Christ died and rose again for all people on the Earth -- past, present, and future -- as well as the people of the antipodes, claiming that extending the benefits of the atonement to inhabitants of other worlds is simply a logical progression (Crowe 304 – 305). Whewell's beliefs along with the beliefs of Chalmers and Brewster constitute a lengthy argument which sets the tone for the entire public debate.

Whewell argues that the very nature of the Incarnation on Earth indicates the special quality of our planet as the unique habitation of intelligent beings in the universe. Thus, for Whewell, precisely because of the uniqueness of the Incarnation and the Christian message, Christianity is not compatible with the notion that intelligent beings populate other worlds even though these worlds are also governed by God.

The heart of the theological dispute historically lies in whether life on other worlds expatriates[23] human beings as the most important creations in the universe on the theory that humans alone were made in the image of God (Genesis 1:27 – 30). The notion that creatures other than humans may also have been made in the image of God has, for authors like Whewell, deleterious effects on the previously conceived unique relationship of human beings to their Creator inasmuch as Christ became incarnate on Earth precisely because of that unique relationship. The notion that the Incarnation of the Logos may not be unique to the Earth may have, for many people, deleterious effects on the redemption, justification, sanctification, and salvation of inhabitants of the Earth. The question becomes whether inhabitants of other worlds are also made in the image of God? Are they crowns of God's creation for their particular worlds as humans are for the Earth (Psalm 8:5-9)? It also raises the issue as to whether inhabitants of other worlds are tainted with original sin and need to be redeemed by the death and resurrection of Jesus. The contemporary commentator and author Steven J. Dick asks, "Was Jesus Christ to be seen as a planet-hopping Savior in the new cosmology? Moreover, extraterrestrial inhabitants were nowhere to be found in the pages of Scripture. Such a Pandora's box of puzzling questions and implications was sufficient to give even many Copernicans, especially in Catholic countries, cause for grave concern" (Dick, *Plurality of*

---

[23] "Expatriates" literally means to withdraw from one's citizenship in a particular country; in this sense, expatriates refers to the act of withdrawing from our citizenship in heaven as the apple of God's eye or perhaps simply banishment or exile from our former status as the very epitome of God's creation.

Worlds 89). These questions should give all Christians, Catholic and Protestant alike, cause for serious apprehension over the consequences of discovering intelligent life on other worlds because the response now may strongly impact human/extraterrestrial relations in the future.

Section 2. Five Categories of Opinion on the Incarnation and
Redemptive Work of Christ Debate

The nineteenth century debate among Chalmers, Whewell, and
Brewster rests upon the theological arguments of a host of earlier
figures and continues with a series of later figures. Rev. Charles
Louis Hequembourg, who cites Whewell's essay (not by name),
suggests that the whole argument of the Incarnation with respect to
other worlds is a difficult one. Hequembourg feels that, "No
difficulty…was ever made a source of skeptical opposition of half
such formidable magnitude" (cited in Crowe 344). The authors and
theologians whose ideas I describe below relate, whether occurring
before or after, to the Chalmers/Whewell/Brewster debate and fall
into five categories, which I have grouped according to my research,
representing the leading theological positions in the debate:

1. Those who hold that there are multiple incarnations
   despite sinless inhabitants of other worlds who need no
   redemption.
2. Those who hold that there are multiple incarnations to
   achieve multiple salvations for sinful inhabitants of other
   worlds who need redemption.
3. Those who hold that there was an Incarnation unique to
   the Earth that applies only to humans and not to
   inhabitants of other worlds who have not sinned and thus
   need no redemption.
4. Those who hold that there was an Incarnation unique to
   the Earth that applies only to humans and not to
   inhabitants of other worlds whether they have sinned or
   not.
5. Those who hold that there was an Incarnation unique to
   the Earth whose effects permeate the universe and save not
   only sinful humans but also sinful inhabitants of other
   worlds.

Category 1 Authors: Multiple Incarnations Despite Sinless
Inhabitants of Other Worlds

Abbe Jean Terrasson (1670 – 1750), a French priest, Cartesian
commentator, and influential novelist, (probably) writes *Traite de
l'infini cree* (written before 1746, published 1769) in which he
fundamentally changes the arguments regarding the Incarnation and
redemption so that man becomes one with God, i.e., "man in the
plural, God in the singular, because the hommes-Dieu [God/man]
would be several in number as to human nature, but only one as to
Divine nature" (cited in Dick, *Plurality of Worlds* 139 and Crowe
135). Terrasson suggests that God became incarnate even on worlds
which had not fallen, claiming such inhabitants would deserve the
honor even more than sinful beings (Crowe 135). Indeed, "[a]dmitting
that Christ's terrestrial incarnation and redemption have sufficient
merit for the entire universe, he nonetheless suggests that because
Christ has a role both as savior and as teacher, his incarnation as
teacher on sinless planets is fully appropriate" (Crowe 135). In 1876
Jules Boiteux published *Lettres a` un materialiste sur la pluralite des
mondes habites et les questions qui s'y rattachent* in which he attacks
the pluralism of popular astronomer Camille Flammarion (1842 –
1925) and writes "in the spirit of an orthodox Catholic" (cited in
Crowe 415). While maintaining that inhabitants of other worlds may
not have fallen, he argues that it does not preclude the possibility of
multiple incarnations and suggests that Christ's redemptive work on
Earth extends to inhabitants of other worlds.

The view that the Logos becomes incarnate on multiple worlds
seems to imply that there are benefits other than redemption from sins
for numerous local incarnations. It may be that Earth would not be
swaying in the balance had our first father and mother not eaten the
apple. However, the Bible says that Adam and Eve did eat the apple,
and their descendants experience the consequences of original sin.
What if free will inevitably results in a fall from grace? This question
leads us to Category 2 authors who maintain that every inhabited
world has the equivalent of our Adam and Eve who inevitably fall
from grace via sin and need grace via multiple incarnations of the
Logos.

Category 2. Multiple Incarnations for Multiple Salvations of Sinful Inhabitants of Other Worlds

Rene Descartes (1596 – 1650), a Catholic philosopher, theologian, and author, largely popularizes the idea of a plurality of worlds in the 17th century. He writes to Chanut on 6 June 1647: "It seems to me that the mystery of the incarnation and all the other advantages which God bestowed on man do not preclude the possibility that he may have granted infinitely many others, very great, to an infinity of other creatures" (Dick, *Plurality of Worlds* 106). In 1753, William Hay (1694 – 1755), a layman, politician, popular essayist in theology, barrister, and poet, published in London *Religio Philosophi: or, The Principles of Morality and Christianity Illustrated from a View of the Universe, and Man's Situation in It* in which he argues that Jesus saves only human beings while inhabitants of other worlds need other incarnations of the Logos on their planets in order to gain salvation (Crowe 87). Hay says that human beings should love inhabitants of other worlds "not as our own Species, but as our Fellow-creatures, and as Members of the same Church and Communion…" (cited in Crowe 86) He further asserts that "…Praise and Thanksgiving are continually ascending to [God's] Throne…from every Quarter of the Universe," making as a result "a general Religion, a joint Communion, a Universal Church" (cited in Crowe 86 – 87).

Alice Meynell (1847 – 1922), an English Catholic poet and essayist, also writes poetry apparently favoring the notion of multiple incarnations and multiple gospels (Crowe 444 – 445). The vision of a universe permeated by the ever-acting, ever-working, and potentially explicit self-expression of the divine Word/Logos was never better expressed than in her poem "Christ in the Universe":

Christ in the Universe

With this ambiguous earth
His dealings have been told us.
These abide:
The signal to a maid, the human birth,
the lesson and the young Mancrucified.

But not a star of all
The innumerable host of stars has heard
How he administered this terrestrial ball.
Our race have kept their Lord's entrusted Word...
No planet knows that this
Our wayside planet, carrying land and wave,
Love and life multiplied, and pain and bliss,
Bears, as chief treasure, one forsaken grave.

Nor, in our little day,
May his devices with the heavens he guessed,
His pilgrimage to thread the Milky Way,
Or his bestowals there be manifest.

But, in the eternities,
Doubtless we shall compare together, hear
A million alien Gospels, in what guise
He trod the Pleiades, the Lyre, the Bear.
(cited in Peacocke 114-115.)

O, be prepared, my soul!
To read the inconceivable, to scan
The million forms of God those stars unroll
When, in our turn, we show to them a Man.
(cited in Crowe 445.)

Meynell and others like her, then, suggest that Christ has one voice but many faces in the sense of one substance but many appearances. Such a view is supported by Scripture's indication that the disciples did not recognize the risen Christ until he made himself known to them by word or deed such as speaking their names or breaking bread. I am citing this poem and others in the belief, as Miguel de Unamuno (1864 -- 1936), a Spanish philosopher and educator, writes, that "poet and philosopher are twin brothers, if not even one and the same -- " (*Tragic Sense of Life* 7). Sometimes poetry expresses truths which prose only dreams about.

John Foster (1770 – 1843), an English essayist and Baptist minister, responds to Chalmers by suggesting that the Incarnation may have occurred on other planets while disagreeing with Chalmers that other planets know about the religious events that have occurred on the Earth (Crowe 191). Reverend Baden Powell (1796 – 1860), a devout Christian who embraces Darwinism, writes *The Unity of Worlds and of Nature: Three Essays on the Spirit of Inductive Philosophy; the Plurality of Worlds; and the Philosophy of Creation* in 1856 in which he states: "If it be an inscrutable mystery *wholly beyond human comprehension* that God should send His Son to redeem this world, it cannot be a *more* inscrutable mystery...that He should send His Son to redeem ten thousand other worlds" (cited in Crowe 310). R. M. Jouan, a French Catholic who in his voluminous *La question de l'habitabilite des mondes etudiee au point de vue de l'historoire, de la science, de la raison et de la foi* (ca. 1900) tries to prove that pluralism is consistent with the teachings of the Catholic Church (pp. 305 – 392), also writes in favor of multiple incarnations (cited in Crowe 420).

Rev. Father Joseph Pohle (1851 – 1922), a Catholic priest from Germany who was one of the founding professors of the Catholic University of America and a pluralist, wrote *Stellar Worlds and Their Inhabitants* (Koln 1840) in which he argues that a universe populated with intelligent beings on other worlds achieves a higher perfection than a universe consisting of "unadorned deserted wastelands" (cited in Crowe 433). He also supports multiple incarnations, writing in the last chapter of his book *Die Sternenwelten* entitled "The Plurality of Inhabited Worlds before the Tribunal of Christianity":

> Concerning the dogma of the Redemption of fallen men through the God-man Christ, it is not necessary to assume as probable also the fall of species on other celestial bodies. No reason...obliges us to think others as evil as ourselves. However even if the evil of sin had gained its pernicious entry into those worlds, so would it not follow from it that also there an Incarnation and Redemption would have to take place. God has at his disposal many other means to remit a sin that weighs either on an individual or on an entire species....(cited in Crowe 433 – 434)

Such authors seem to imply that multiple economies of salvation are not only possible but should be respected as applying to each world upon which intelligent inhabitants live. It seems, in this view, that the saviors of these worlds are exclusively the saviors of the inhabitants of these worlds and not of other worlds (including the Earth), just as the savior of the Earth does not save inhabitants of other worlds. This is apparently the reason for multiple incarnations.

Rev. Father Kenneth J. Delano, a Catholic priest and author of *Many Worlds, One God* in which he suggests the possibility of multiple incarnations of the Logos, agrees with Tillich that the Incarnation may have occurred (and may occur in the future) on other planets. Delano reacts to a writer who claims that, if human beings are not the epitome of God's creation, then Scripture is completely wrong in its estimation of the relationship of human beings to God, by suggesting that God may have declined to mention inhabitants of other worlds in Scripture because during the time and in the culture in which the text was written, it did not theologically or morally edify the faith community (cited in Dick, *Life on Other Worlds* 250). Father Delano writes a personal letter to the author of this book (17 June 2003) in which he denies that one must hold that the Logos became incarnate only once effecting the salvation of humans and inhabitants of other worlds alike, claiming that, while such a conclusion is consistent with the teachings of the Catholic Church, one should be open to the possibility of other economies of salvation (1). Delano writes:

> In my opinion, intelligent beings on other worlds are <u>probably</u> <u>not</u> sinless and so, like us, can please God by showing a growth in virtue....It could very well be that Christ's sacrifice on Calvary redeemed all ET's as well. But maybe the Logos chose to be incarnated and even suffer and die on other planets to redeem their inhabitants. It's not unthinkable that He would do so, when you consider what motivated Him to do that here, i.e., to show how very much God loves His children, made in His own image. (Delano 2)

Delano continues that the vast distances of space preclude humanity's spreading the Gospel of Jesus Christ to inhabitants of other worlds, so he is "inclined to believe that God must have made other provisions for ET's – other revelations and other redemptions perhaps" (Delano 3).

If intelligent beings throughout the rest of the universe either, as Chalmers suggests, know about the Incarnation and redemptive work of Christ on Earth, or, as other authors suggest, know about local Incarnations and redemptive work of the Logos on their worlds, then why are they not here discussing the issue with human beings? Perhaps, in the view of Category 2 authors, intelligent beings on other worlds have no need to visit the Earth because they have already experienced the salvation of either Christ or the local Incarnation of the Logos in their lives. Perhaps for the same reason, as I see it, in this view, human beings need not visit other worlds to learn anything theologically new. It is possible that God made the great distances among planets impossible to traverse in order to maintain the uniqueness of each world's intelligent beings or for theological reasons we do not yet comprehend. This view contrasts with Category 1 authors who maintain that Christ becomes incarnate on multiple worlds despite the sinlessness of their inhabitants. While the authors of Category 2 maintain that multiple incarnations of the Logos are necessary to redeem sinful inhabitants of other worlds, Category 3 authors maintain that the Incarnation is unique to the Earth because inhabitants of other worlds are sinless so that they need no redemption.

Category 3 Authors: Incarnation Unique to Earth with Effects Applying Only to Humans Due to Sinless Inhabitants of Other Worlds

As mentioned above, William of Vorilong believes that inhabitants of other worlds did not sin after the manner of Adam, and that the Incarnation of the Logos is unique to the Earth (Crowe 8 – 9). Monseigneur de Montignez (ca. 1865 – 1866) publishes "Theorie chretienne sur la pluralite des mondes" in which he argues that Christ became incarnate on the Earth because it is insignificant and its people worthless in order to show forth more grandly the power of God. Nevertheless, Montignez seems a bit inconsistent in that he argues that the benefits of the Incarnation extend throughout the universe even upon intelligent beings who, being sinless, have no need of redemption (Crowe 411 – 413).

Friedrich Gottlieb Klopstock (1724 – 1803), the German epic and lyric poet, writes enthusiastically about a universe created by God with Christ at the center while maintaining that "only the inhabitants of the earth have fallen into sin and they alone need salvation through a divine mediator" (cited in Crowe 145). Even so, Klopstock believes that Christ brought goodness that permeates the universe (ibid.). Delano, while a Category 2 author, nevertheless entertains the possibility that Category 3 authors may be correct, writing in a personal letter to the author of this book:

> When St. Paul wrote to the Romans: "All have sinned and fallen short of the glory of God (Rom. 3:23), he must have been referring only to human beings, since there are angels who never sinned and enjoy the glory of God. If God created pure spirits who never sinned, perhaps He also saw fit to create embodied spirits that live without sinning on other worlds. And if the Logos became incarnated on their worlds, it would not be for the purpose of redemption but to inspire them to even higher virtues, as well as to honor them and to demonstrate His love for them. (Delano 4)

The notion of sinless inhabitants of other worlds is, according to Delano, consistent with Catholic teachings. The Christian apologist C.S. Lewis, an Anglican, writes in his *Space Trilogy*, particularly the second volume *Perelandra*, that each world may have its First Parents who are tempted and yet do not fall from grace as did Adam and Eve of Earth, so that their children do not inherit original sin and yet rejoice in their relationship with God and look forward to what Lewis calls "the Great Dance" at the end of time.

Ellen White (1827 – 1915), an American religious leader of the Seventh Day Adventists whose prophecies greatly facilitated its growth, is a pluralist who writes that Christ became incarnate only once on Earth and that the inhabitants of other solar systems, although evil has not extended beyond the Earth, rejoiced when Jesus cried out, "It is finished!" She writes in *The Story of Patriarchs and Prophets:*

> It was the marvel of all the universe that Christ should humble himself to save fallen man. That he who has passed from star to star, from world to world, superintending all…[took] upon himself human nature, was a mystery which the sinless intelligences of other worlds desired to understand. When Christ came to our world…, all were intensely interested in

following him as he traversed…the bloodstained path from the manger to Calvary….And as Christ in his expiring agony upon the cross cried out, "It is finished!" a shout of triumph rung through every world…(cited in Crowe 240 – 241)

Moreover, Al Levine, a modern Catholic poet, writes in a personal letter to the author (27 July 2003) that he is unsure of his position but thinks he probably falls into Category 3 and composed the following poem posted on the Free Catholic Mailing List (Catholic@freecatholic.net) entitled "The Mouth of God":

THE MOUTH OF GOD

They live so far away,
these people on other worlds
And if they signal to us
By radio, by laser light
We think: how sad

For if they use such primitive
Such mean technology
It means they are the same as us
They'll never reach us

But if they use the means of those
Who understand the world much more than we
Then how are we to read their signals
Or even know that they exist?

Why should they condescend to us
Or why should we think them knowable -
And yet
God condescends, God speaks

To them as well?
Neither microwaves, nor infrared
Nor even waves of gravity come forth
From the mouth of God.

For Levine, contact with God is more important than contact with inhabitants of other worlds, though God precludes neither. It is possible that the more we learn about other worlds and their possible inhabitants, the more we learn about the nature of God. It seems that, for Category 3 authors, even if inhabitants of other worlds are sinless, they are still capable of comprehending the nature of sin enough to rejoice at Christ's conquering of sin on Earth.

Walter Miller, a Catholic science fiction writer of a novel entitled *A Canticle for Leibowitz*, suggests that one who has "preternatural[24] innocence" has no need of the sacrament of baptism, a rite necessary only for those tainted with original sin as well as personal sin. So, in any possible encounters with inhabitants of other worlds, it may be that such inhabitants do not need to receive the sacraments because the sacraments are necessary to infuse the grace of Jesus Christ to forgive sins, and their inhabitants have theoretically committed no sins requiring forgiveness. Then, some authors maintain that, even though inhabitants of other worlds have fallen from grace via sin, because the Incarnation is unique to the Earth, its effects apply only to natives of this world, so that intelligent beings populating other worlds cannot be saved. These are Category 4 authors.

---

[24] Preternatural means that which is outside the normal operations of nature. Preternatural innocence is to be distinguished from prelapsarian innocence, which is the innocence of Adam and Eve before the Fall, that is, before they ate the fruit of the Tree of the Knowledge of Good and Evil (original sin), when they lost their innocence and their natures were damaged so that their descendants inherited a state of deprivation of original holiness or loss of prelapsarian innocence. In essence, postlapsarian human beings inherit a genetic predisposition towards committing sins. Preternatural innocence is a postlapsarian innocence in which the grace of Jesus Christ was imputed to the Virgin Mary at the instant of her conception in the womb of her mother, Good Saint Anne, so that she was cleansed of original sin and remained sinless throughout her life and after her earthly life into eternity. An argument in this section is that extraterrestrials may be in a state of prelapsarian innocence because their first parents may not have sinned after the manner of Adam and Eve and thus their natures would not have been damaged so that they are not deprived of original holiness.

Category 4 Authors: Incarnation Unique to Earth with Effects Applying Only to Humans Whether Inhabitants of Other Worlds Have Sinned or Not

The French writer Bernard le Bovier de Fontenelle (1657 – 1757), a nephew of Corneille and a specialist in interpreting science, in *Conversations on the Plurality of Worlds*, a popular work in 1686 depicting a fictional conversation in which he supports the notion that inhabitants exist on other worlds, claims that their existence does not violate Scripture or the human faculty of reason. De Fontenelle claims that, because they are not descendents of Adam and Eve, then the concepts of the Incarnation of Christ and redemption are not applicable (Dick, *Plurality of Worlds* 124). Rev. Dr. Richard Bentley (1662 – 1742), a British clergyman and classical scholar who corresponds with Sir Isaac Newton (1642 – 1727) on how the latest scientific theories support the notion of the intelligent design of the universe, assures us that otherworldly inhabitants are not necessarily human in order to allay the fears of theologians that the relationship of extraterrestrials to the Incarnation and redemption does not apply since they are not the descendents of Adam and Eve. Brewster notes that Dr. Bentley asserts that, simply because Scripture mentions only the creation of creatures upon the Earth, it does not follow that God did not create inhabitants of other worlds. Bentley notes that the Pentateuch does not mention the creation of angels, but faithful Christians are certain that angels were created (Brewster 139 – 140). Bentley continues, "Neither need we be solicitous about the condition of those planetary people, nor raise *frivolous disputes how far they may participate in* Adam's *fall or in the benefits of Christ's incarnation*" (Brewster 140).

Timothy Dwight (1752 – 1817), an American theologian, poet, minister, and Yale president from 1795 to 1817, writes a series of sermons collected as *Theology Explained and Defended* in which he argues that Christ's Incarnation and redemption are not only unique to Earth but that redemption applies only to human beings, even though he is a pluralist in favor of worlds whose inhabitants Christ rules. Johann Heinrich (John Henry) Kurtz (1809 – 1890), a German Lutheran theologian, university professor, and prolific writer of popular books, writes against the Incarnation of God on other worlds, claiming that either their inhabitants are not fallen and therefore have no need of redemption or, if they are fallen, then Christ does not save them (Crowe 261 – 262). This, I think, is a rather bleak outlook for intelligent beings on other worlds.

The Canadian curé of Fort Kent, Maine, Abbe Francois Xavier Burque (1851 – 1923), in his *Pluralite des mondes habites consideree au point de vue negatif* (Montreal), suggests that pluralism cannot be reconciled with the Incarnation and redemption of Christ (Crowe 420 – 421). He claims that Christ being crucified numerous times on other planets to save intelligent beings contradicts Hebrews 9:26 (Crowe 421), to wit: "Not that he might offer himself repeatedly, as the high priest enters each year into the sanctuary with blood that is not his own; if that were so, he would have had to suffer repeatedly from the foundation of the world. But now once for all he has appeared at the end of the ages to take away sin by his sacrifice." Burque does not address, as far as my research can tell, whether the benefits of the work of Christ extend to intelligent beings on other worlds, though he avers that, if they exist, they must have sinned, leading to his conclusion that they probably do not exist. Rev. William Leitch, D.D. (1818 – 1864), a Scottish Presbyterian minister and Principal of Queen's University in Kingston (1860-1864), writes *God's Glory in the Heavens* (1862) in which he argues that the Incarnation is unique to the Earth because "Scripture…declares that He will forever bear His human nature" (Crowe 452). He also rejects the idea that the merits of Christ's atoning sacrifice applies to inhabitants of other worlds (Crowe 452).

Category 2 and 4 authors maintain that inhabitants of other worlds are sinners in need of redemption while Category 1 and 3 authors maintain that they are sinless. This leads us to Category 5 authors who maintain, like 2 and 4, that inhabitants of other worlds are sinners in need of redemption but particularly the redemption purchased by the blood of Jesus Christ, the Messiah of Earth, the God-Human.

Category 5 Authors: Incarnation Unique To Earth Applies
Universally to Inhabitants of Other Worlds

Dick says in *Plurality of Worlds* that a Cartesian author[25]
wrote *Traite de l'infini crée* (written before 1746, published 1769) in
which he fundamentally changes the arguments regarding the
Incarnation and redemption so that man becomes one with God, "man
in the plural, God in the singular, because the hommes-Dieu
[God/man] would be several in number as to human nature, but only
one as to Divine nature" (139). The notion that the Incarnation is a
universal event rather than one that pertains exclusively to the Earth
challenges us to new heights of thought that are not for the faint of
heart (Dick, *Plurality of Worlds* 139). Henry More (1614 – 1687), an
English poet and philosopher of religion, reared a Calvinist but
converted as a youth to the Anglican Communion, was the most well
known of the Cambridge Platonists, and writes in *Divine Dialogues*
(1668) speculation that extraterrestrials are saved by God's revelation
to them of the Incarnation and redemptive work of Christ on Earth
(cited in Crowe 17). In other words, More argues that God himself
reveals to inhabitants of other worlds the nature of the Incarnation and
redemption of Christ in order to effect their salvation.

Isaac de La Peyrère in his *Men Before Adam* asserts that,
according to the two creation narratives in Genesis, God created men
before Adam, and Adam's descendents are the Jews whereas all other
people are the descendents of the men who were created before. The
author believes that the sin of Adam is imputed not only to Adam's
descendents but is also "imputed backwards unto those first men, that
were created before Adam: and that the condemnation of death
reigned backward upon them by reason of that sin" (Chapter XIX;
EEBO image 32). This would seem to imply that the sin of Adam can
be imputed also, forwards and backwards, to inhabitants of other
worlds who were created both before and after Adam. This would
also seem to imply that the benefits of Christ's Incarnation, work on

---

[25] Dick in *Plurality of Worlds* writes: "Vartania, *Didero and Descartes*,
asserts that the treatise was not written by Malebranche but was 'almost
certainly composed by the abbé Jean Terrasson who, with Fontenelle and
Mairan, was reputed one of the eighteenth century's leading Cartesians'"
(215).

the cross, and resurrection are also imputed to inhabitants of other worlds both before and after the death and resurrection of Christ. For this author, it would appear that Christ's work not only transcends time and space but also permeates time and space – an argument I will develop in Chapter 3.

Pierre Courbet, a French Catholic theologian, in an 1894 essay in *Cosmos,* writes that the Logos may have become incarnate on Earth because "the human race is perhaps…the most guilty of all [and had] the greatest need to profit directly from the redemption" (cited in Crowe 416). Courbet denies that Christ became incarnate elsewhere arguing in favor of the uniqueness of the Incarnation on Earth even while favoring the extension of the benefits of Christ's redemptive work to inhabitants of other worlds. Courbet writes that perhaps inhabitants of other worlds benefit from the redemptive work of Christ without knowing it in the same way that a baby benefits from baptism without knowing how or why (Crowe 417). His intent is, as a Catholic, to combat the view that pluralism somehow stands in direct opposition to the Christian faith (ibid.).

Januarius De Concilio (1836 – 1898), "priest, professor, pastor, and even playwright" (Crowe 454) writes that God made inhabitants of other worlds "in and through Christ" and that Christ's redemptive work is universal although his Incarnation is unique to the Earth, so that inhabitants of other worlds who have fallen may also be saved (Crowe 455). To the criticism of Thomas Hughes (1849 – 1939), a Jesuit, who argues against De Concilio's arguments but not his conclusions, De Concilio, in his *Harmony between Science and Revelation* in 1889, writes, "when Christ died and paid the ransom of our redemption, He included [extraterrestrials] also in that ransom, the value of which was infinite and capable of redeeming innumerable worlds" (cited in Crowe 456).

Wolfhart Pannenberg (1928), a German theologian, called an "eschatological[26] realist," and an interdisciplinary thinker, asserts the possibility of inhabitants of other worlds in solar systems of the Milky

---

[26] Eschatological means relating to the Apocalypse or the end of the world. Eschatology, from the Greek eschaton (last or final thing), is the branch of theology dealing with the end of the world or the ultimate destiny of human beings in terms of hell, purgatory, and heaven, and also dealing with the Parousia, the Second Coming of Jesus Christ, the resurrection of the dead, and/or the Final Judgement.

Way or other galaxies. Pannenberg does not follow Tillich's line, arguing that the Incarnation of the Logos is Jesus Christ alone through whom the entire created universe came into existence. Through Christ alone, God has chosen to bring the entire universe, all of space and time, into a unified whole (Peters, "Contemporary Theology" 4).

James Beattie (1735 – 1803), a prominent Scottish poet, and professor of moral philosophy and logic at Marischal College, Aberdeen, writes concerning the redemption that inhabitants of other worlds

> will not suffer for our guilt, nor be rewarded for our obedience. But it is not absurd to imagine, [sic] that our fall and recovery may be useful to them as an example; and that the divine grace manifested in our redemption may raise their adoration and gratitude into higher raptures and quicken their ardour to inquire…into the dispensations of infinite wisdom." (cited in Crowe 102)

Beilby Porteus (1731 – 1808), bishop of Chester and subsequently of London, writes in favor of the plurality of worlds theory and redemption, remarking, "on what ground is it concluded, that the benefits of Christ's death extend no further than to ourselves?" Moreover, in support of his theory that the crucifixion's benefits extend to inhabitants of other worlds, in his work *Redemption* (79), he cites the Apostle Paul:

> We are expressly told, that as "by him were all things created that are in heaven and that are on earth, visible and invisible [Colossians 1:16a]; and by him all things consist: so by him also was God pleased (having made peace through the blood of his cross) to reconcile *all things unto himself, whether they be things on earth, or things in heaven* [Colossians 1:20]: that in the dispensation of the fullness of times, he might gather together in one *all things in Christ, both which are in heaven, and which are on earth, even in him*" [Ephesians 1:10]. (cited in Crowe 103)

Porteus goes on to assert that "if the Redemption wrought by Christ extended to other worlds, perhaps many besides our own, if its virtues penetrate even into heaven itself; if it gathers together *all things* in Christ; who will then say, that the dignity of the agent was disproportioned to the magnitude of the work...?" (cited in Crowe 103). Porteus supports my contention that it is consistent with Christian theology to say that Jesus saves inhabitants of other worlds by his incarnation, life, crucifixion, and resurrection. Since the efficacy of the redemption Jesus acquired for us extends to all, humans and extraterrestrials alike, it follows that it is incumbent upon Christians to spread this good news not only to other human beings but also to inhabitants of other worlds.

George Adams (1750 – 1795), a British astronomer, writes *Lectures,* vol. IV in which he remarks:

> ...since the inhabitants of...other planets...must equally be objects of the Divine favour with ourselves; and since the rational inhabitants of some few or more among so many myriads may have been found disobedient; is a man to blame for thinking that if they stand in need of restoration, they must be fully as worthy of it as ourselves; and may for anything that we know, have been already redeemed, or may yet to be redeemed...?"   (cited in Crowe 105)

This implies that either Christ has redeemed inhabitants of other worlds as a result of his earthly Incarnation or will redeem their inhabitants if and when humans evangelize them.

Andrew Fuller (1754 – 1815), an English Baptist minister and theologian, in *The Gospel Its Own Witness* in 1799 – 1800, argues against Tom Paine's *Age of Reason*. Fuller claims that the doctrine of a plurality of worlds is consistent with Christianity and Scripture. He further writes that the idea of our redemption by Christ is "strengthened and aggrandized" by pluralism, that human beings and angels are not necessarily the only beings who have Fallen from grace, and that inhabitants of other worlds who have fallen from grace may be comforted to know that the Incarnation and redemption brought to us by Christ "are competent to fill all and every part of God's dominions with everlasting and increasing joy" (cited in Crowe 172). Fuller agrees that Christ's Incarnation is unique to the Earth while his redemption spreads across the entire universe, averring, "The consistency of the Scripture doctrine of Redemption with the modern opinion of the Magnitude of Creation" (i.e., pluralism) and "the credibility of the redemption is not weakened by this doctrine, but, on the contrary, is, in many respects, strengthened and aggrandized" (cited in Brewster 162).

   Rev. Edward Nares D.D. (1762 – 1841), an English clergyman and professor of modern history and modern languages at Merton College, Oxford, writes "Eis Theos, Eis Mesites" (1803) in which he discusses how the notion that other worlds are inhabited by intelligent beings is consistent with Scripture. Believing that the Incarnation is unique to the Earth, Nares writes that Jesus is "the ONE GREAT manifestation…to accomplish the redemption of *all flesh*…." Yet Nares maintains that the effects of the redemptive work of Christ extends and is manifest "in some way inscrutable to us, to every rational creature throughout the mighty firmament…." (cited in Crowe 173). Nares believes that God somehow, we do not know how, spread the knowledge of Christ's crucifixion and resurrection throughout the universe (ibid.).

   Comte Joseph de Maistre (1754 – 1821), a devout French Catholic moralist, diplomat, polemical author, and conservative politician, criticizes theologians who reject pluralism on the grounds that it somehow damages redemption dogma, claiming that believing God has created the vast universe with innumerable stars and planets without inhabitants does a disservice to God's omnipotence (Crowe 181). De Maistre writes:

> If the inhabitants of other planets are not like us guilty of sin, they have no need of the same remedy, and if, on the contrary, the same remedy is necessary for them, are the theologians of whom I speak then to fear that the power of the sacrifice which has saved us is unable to extend to the moon? The insight of Origen is much more penetrating and comprehensive when he writes: "The altar was at Jerusalem, but the blood of the victim bathed the universe." (cited in Crowe 181)

Sir John Herschel (1792 – 1871), English astronomer and the famous son of the famous astronomer William Herschel, favors pluralism, as did his father, but his reasons are religious and metaphysical rather than scientific (Crowe 217). Sir William Rowan Hamilton (1805 –

1865), an Irish mathematician who contributes significant work to the fields of optics, dynamics, and algebra (particularly quaternions), leading to further progress in quantum mechanics, favors pluralism and, according to Robert Perceval Graves's *Life of Sir William Rowan Hamilton*, vol. II, speculates that Christ's ascension and Pentecost may have consisted of visiting other planets one by one: "May not [Christ's] transit from the cloud to the throne have been but one continued passage, in long triumphal pomp, through powers and principalities made subject? May not the only begotten Son have then been brought forth into the world, not by a new nativity, but as it were by proclamation and investiture, while the Universe beheld its God, and all the angels worshipped Him?" (cited in Crowe 221 – 222). This idea implies, to my thinking, that Christ's transit from his earthly life to heavenly life may be more literal than spiritual – that is, Jesus literally travels from planet to planet spreading the Gospel. This idea contrasts with the notion that all of the inhabited worlds came to know Christ when the Gospel permeated the universe at the resurrection of Jesus so that the Lord need not necessarily literally travel physically to other worlds in order to make known to their inhabitants the message of the cross and the resurrection. On the other hand, it is possible that humans are destined to be the medium by which inhabitants of other worlds come to know the risen Lord.

Samuel Noble (1779 – 1853), a minister of the New Jerusalem Church, who, after reading Paine's *Age of Reason*, becomes a Christian pluralist, writes *Astronomical Doctrine of a Plurality of Worlds* in which he attempts to assert that pluralism is consistent with Christianity. After reading Swedenborg, he becomes convinced that Yahweh (Jehovah) became incarnate on the Earth because humans were the worst sinners in the universe while Christ's salvific work extends to inhabitants of other worlds (Crowe 228). Philip James Bailey (1816 – 1902), a British poet, composes a poem in 1839 called *Festus* in which Christ speaks to the angel in charge of the *hnau* on Earth:

> Think not I lived and died for thine alone,
> And that no other sphere hath hailed me Christ:
> My life is ever suffering for love.
> In judging and redeeming worlds is spent
> Mine everlasting being.

(cited in Crowe 232)

Thus, it seems that for this Category 5 author inhabitants of other worlds are familiar with the work of Christ on earth because they are aware of their own need for redemption.

Rev. Thomas Rawson Birks (1810 – 1883), a Fellow and Professor of Moral Philosophy at Trinity College at Cambridge and hymn composer, writes *Modern Astronomy* in which he suggests that two contradictory possibilities exist with respect to the redemption and the insignificance of the Earth in the vast universe: Either "ours is the only world where sin has entered," an idea that violates "the plainest lessons of moral probability" (pp. 53 – 54), or the Advent of Jesus is the only one of a "series of revelations" (cited in Crowe 296 – 297). Birks denies the second assertion because the Incarnation has "the plainest impress of eternity…Christ…is the Son of God and the Son of man, in two distinct natures and one person, forever" (cited in Crowe 297). Birks writes an imaginary comment by Christ during the Wedding at Cana:

> My hour to people these worlds of light with myriad worshippers is not yet come. Your planet, little though it is…is the Bethlehem where I now choose to reveal the mystery of my love to sinners, the guilty and despised Nazareth of the wide universe from which streams of light and heavenly wisdom shall go forth to gladden the countless worlds I have made. (cited in Crowe 297)

Birks implies that "when the work of redemption is complete, a celestial emigration may begin from our little planet…It may be, that as fresh planets are prepared…to receive a race of inhabitants, unborn patriarchs may be sent forth, like Noah, to people its desolate heritage…" (cited in Crowe 297).

Hugh Miller (1802 – 1856), a Scottish geologist, lay theologian, editor of a newspaper called *The Witness*, and an opponent of the theory of evolution, believes that Christ's redemptive work applies to inhabitants of other worlds, denying multiple incarnations of the Logos, asserting that "though only one planet and one race may have furnished the point of union between the Divine and the created nature, the effects of that junction may extend to *all* created nature....If it was necessary that the point of junction be somewhere, why not here" (cited in Crowe 322). Miller appears to desire to maintain the integrity of both pluralism and Christianity by defending both revelation and natural theology (ibid.). Rev. Josiah Crampton (1809 – 1883), alumnus of Trinity College, Dublin, and "rector of Killesher in Ireland" (Crowe 334) publishes in 1857 *Testimony of the Heavens* in which he claims that other worlds are inhabited and also shows how the science of astronomy defends Christianity, which is consistent with pluralism, writing that Christ's ascension into the heavens, to where he vowed to his disciples he would bring them, demonstrates the truth that "the material heavens [are] places of habitation" (cited in Crowe 335).

Rev. Charles Louis Hequembourg in 1859 publishes *Plan of the Creation; or, Other Worlds, and Who Inhabit Them* (Boston) in which he argues against pluralism in the sense that other worlds are not now inhabited because the universe is still in its infancy but will be inhabited by resurrected people from Earth (cited in Crowe 344 – 345). Camille Flammarion (1842 – 1925), a Frenchman who first studies theology but eventually becomes an astronomer of note, also expresses belief in the non-Christian metempsychosis (the transmigration of souls, which usually means transmigration to other bodies whether human or animal on Earth but in this case means transmigration of souls to other planets) while maintaining support for Brewster's contention that Christ's redemptive work affects inhabitants of other worlds.

Abbe Francois Moigno (1804 – 1884) of Paris, a cleric and scientist, says that he received permission from "the Commission of the Roman Index to declare formally to [Flammarion] that the creation and the redemption are by no means an obstacle to the existence of other worlds, of other suns, of other planets, etc., etc." (cited in Crowe 414).

Theophile Ortolan (b. 1861), a priest and theologian, in *Astronomie et theologie*, cites Scripture passages such as the shepherd searching for the one lost lamb while leaving the others behind and the one in which Christ says "In my Father's house are many mansions" (John 14:2) to support his pluralist interpretations (Crowe 417). Ortolan suggests that either extending the benefits of Christ to inhabitants of other worlds or claiming that they have not fallen are equally supportable by Scripture and Christian theology.

Johann Ebrard (1818 –1888), a German Reformed church theologian who teaches at Erlangen University (Crowe 428) and whose anti-pluralism is influenced by Whewell, writes *Der Glaube an die heilige Schrift und die Ergebnisse der Naturforschung* (1861) and *Apologetik* (1874 – 1875) in which he argues against multiple incarnations in response to pluralist authors discussing the problem of the atonement with respect to inhabitants of other worlds, citing Scripture to support his views, while simultaneously maintaining that applying Christ's redemptive work to inhabitants of other worlds does not contradict Christian theology (Crowe 428).

Aubrey Thomas Hunt de Vere (1814 – 1902), an Irish Catholic poet, critic, and essayist, who was influenced by his friendship with the astronomer Sir William Rowan Hamilton, writes "The Death of Copernicus" in which the fictional Copernicus reflects:

> 'Tis Faith and Hope that spread delighted hands
> To such belief; no formal proof attests it.
> Concede them peopled; can the sophist prove
> Their habitants are fallen? That too admitted,
> Who told him that redeeming foot divine
> Ne'er trode those spheres?

He goes on:

> Judaea was one country, one alone:
> Not less Who died there died for all. The Cross
> Brought help to vanished nations: Time opposed
> No bar to Love: why then should Space oppose one?
> (cited in Crowe 444)

Rev. Edwin T. Winkler (1823 – 1883), a Baptist minister, writes in the *Baptist Quarterly* (1871) that the Incarnation, while occurring only on the Earth, has universal effects:

> As a battle may be fought at some grey pass of
> Marathon…that shall change the fortunes of a world for a
> thousand years, so here, on this small world, a triumph may
> have been achieved by the Son of God, that distributes its
> spoils to all systems, through all times; and for the temptation

and anguish of Jesus of Nazareth, the sweet influences of the Pleiades may be fuller of vernal promise…and seasons of salvation may have befallen all the signs of the zodiac…(cited in Crowe 450)

Rev. George Mary Searle (1839 – 1918), a Catholic member of the Paulist order, astronomer, graduate of Harvard University, and professor at the U.S. Naval Academy, as well as observatory director at the founding of the Catholic University of America, early in his career is an opponent of pluralism but later warms to the subject, arguing that other worlds may be inhabited by human-like beings but denying multiple incarnations (Crowe 454), questioning why the Logos decided to become incarnate on the Earth.

All of the above authors in Category 5 aver in one way or another that the work of Christ is salvific for the souls of both inhabitants of the Earth and inhabitants of other worlds.

In summary, Category 5 authors generally tend to view the universe as inhabited by a variety of beings all of whom are created by God and nurtured by God while steadfastly maintaining that God became incarnate exclusively upon the Earth to save all intelligent beings of whatever race and planet of origin. Although the specifics of the process vary, the authors of this category are consistent in their belief in Christ as redeemer of all who sin and repent. In Chapter 3, I will examine the arguments of modern thinkers who fall into the various categories to see where the ideas of earlier authors discussed in this chapter lead. Modern authors and theologians are sometimes hampered by an anti-pluralist bias common in the twentieth and twenty-first centuries, but many give sober thought to the very important religious issues being discussed in this book.

Chapter 3

Modern Thinkers

The true light, which enlightens everyone, was coming into the *kosmos*.
   – John 1:9

The world is hot and cruel,
We are weary of heart and hand,
But the world is more fully of glory
Than you can understand.
   -- G.K. Chesterton, "The Mortal Answers"

Now, my suspicion is that the universe is not only queerer than we
suppose, but queerer than we *can* suppose....I suspect that there are more
things in heaven and earth than are dreamed of, in any philosophy. That is
the reason why I have no philosophy myself, and must be my excuse for
dreaming.
   -- J.B.S. Haldane, *Possible Worlds* (1927)

Many Catholic and Protestant authors, past and present, are
divided on this issue of the Incarnation, maintaining that we really do
not know how it will apply to inhabitants of other worlds yet and will
not know until we encounter extraterrestrials in the flesh (Crowe and
Dick et al.). Nevertheless, new theologies being developed in
response to pluralist issues will have to grapple with the basic
Christian message and commandment of the founder of Christianity to
spread the Gospel throughout the universe (cf. Matthew 28:19-20;
Mark 16:15).

Modern thinkers of the twentieth and twenty-first centuries
hold a broad range of ideas about the nature of the Incarnation, its
effects on both humans and inhabitants of other worlds, and why
humanity was chosen as a vehicle of God's grace. For example, E.A.
Milne (1896 – 1950), a British astronomer and Fellow of Trinity
College, Cambridge, suggests that, because the Incarnation is unique
to the Earth, humans can engage in radio contact with inhabitants of
other worlds to spread the message of the Gospel. Milne, in an
attempt to break out of the Ptolemaic[27] focus on the Earth alone, asks:

---

[27] Relating to the beliefs of Ptolemy, a second century A.D. Greek
astronomer in Alexandria who contended in his *Almagest* that the sun,
moon, planets, and stars orbited a stationary Earth, which geocentric theory

"Is it irreverent to suggest that an infinite God could scarcely find the opportunities to enjoy Himself, to exercise His godhead, if a single planet were the sole seat of His activities?" (Davies 45). Arthur Peacocke, a D.Phil. in physical biochemistry, ordained priest in the Church of England, and author of nine books on science and religion, writes:

> Christians have to ask themselves (and skeptics will certainly ask *them*), What can the cosmic significance possibly be of the localized, terrestrial event of the existence of the historical Jesus? Does not the mere possibility of extraterrestrial life render nonsensical all the superlative claims made by the Christian church about his significance? Would ET, Alpha-Arcturians, Martials, et al., need an incarnation and all it is supposed to accomplish, as much as *homo sapiens* on planet Earth? Only a contemporary theology that can cope convincingly with such questions can hope to be credible today. ("The Challenge and Stimulus of the Epic of Evolution to Theology" in Dick's *Many Worlds* 103)

If God created all things for the benefit of humans alone, then I think Milne would agree that the universe is an awfully big waste of space. As God permeates all of space and time, it seems logical to conclude that God exercises his power throughout spacetime by giving life to other worlds and granting redemption to their inhabitants.

In a vein similar to the view that God ubiquitously permeates and transcends the universe for the benefit of everything and everyone in it, Miguel de Unamuno, a Spanish philosopher, educator, and author, who lived from 1864 -- 1936, writes in his *Tragic Sense of Life*:

> "Why!" the reader will exclaim again, "we are coming back to what the Catechism says: 'Q. For whom did God create the world? A. For man.'" Well, why not? – so ought the man who is a man to reply. The ant, if it took account of these matters and were a person, would reply "For the ant," and it

---

was accepted by scientists generally until Copernicus and later Kepler developed the heliocentric theory that the Earth revolves around the sun.

would reply rightly. The world is made for consciousness, for each consciousness.

…

If the sun possessed consciousness it would think, no doubt, that it lived in order to give light to the worlds; but it would also and above all think that the worlds existed in order that it might give them light and enjoy itself in giving them light and so live. And it would think well.

…

If consciousness is, as some inhuman thinker has said, nothing more than a flash of light between two eternities of darkness, then there is nothing more execrable than existence.
(Unamuno 12 – 13)

Although Unamuno is not speaking of inhabitants of other worlds, one may interpret his words to apply to inhabitants of other worlds. In other words, while Christian inhabitants of Earth may believe that God created the universe for human beings, it may equally be supposed that extraterrestrials may believe that God created the universe for inhabitants of their worlds, while Christians on Earth may suggest that they believe rightly. In the view of philosophers like Unamuno, everything that experiences consciousness desires to know God on some level or another, whether superconscious or subconscious. To desire to know the universe is to desire to know not only what God creates but *why* God creates. It is the desire to know the mind of God. The human desire to know the mind of Christ permeates our quest for life on other worlds, for what is it to know the mind of Christ if not to know the conscious desires of the beings God creates? The desire to understand the mystery of the Incarnation translates to an implacable and insatiable quest for the meaning of life in the universe that is God's creation. The two quests, for God and for intelligent life in the universe, are the twin themes of this book. For many Christians, the quest for God culminates in the Incarnation, expands their conscious will to experience the cross, and explodes their minds to rise within the resurrection of Christ. It is possible that encounters with inhabitants of other worlds will expand the consciousness of everyone of whatever species because we may learn from one another what it means to desire God.

While Unamuno may be interpreted as favoring the notion that God creates and sustains every creation and creature in the universe, Charles Davis, a widely respected Catholic scholar in Britain who later left the Church, writes an essay, "The Place of Christ," in 1960 in which he argues that the events surrounding the experiences of Jesus Christ are the center of all of space and time. Christ is the center of the universe because Jesus is God and the God-man permeates the cosmos, filling everything with his presence and infusing everyone on all inhabited planets with his grace and love which all creatures can accept or reject as they choose. Humanity's place in the universe as only one species among many does not conflict with Christocentrism (Charles Davis 711). What is the relationship of inhabitants of other worlds to Christ? Davis writes:

> The entire material creation is understood as involved in His work and destined to be transformed by the glory of His resurrection. This is an anthropocentric view of the universe, based on the primacy of Christ, and Catholic theology has long accepted its application to creatures naturally superior to man, the angels. Must it be extended to embrace other possible rational creatures, so that man would remain, whatever the physicists might say, the centre of the cosmos? He would not be the centre in a physical sense nor according to the natural order, but according to that higher plan or pattern which God has decreed for this universe and which is known to us only by faith. The fact of the incarnation and the exaltation of human nature in Christ would give man this central position…all the movements and forces of the universe and history are taken up into a higher integration, which is supernatural and centred on Christ. (712 – 713)

Davis's argument implies that, if there are multiple incarnations, then Christ's work on Earth loses "its universal significance" (713 – 715). If Christ became incarnate a multiplicity of times on a multiplicity of worlds, then our understanding of the Second Coming would be adversely affected. If Christ comes millions of times, what is the significance of his coming again to Earth? (715) If Christians have no Christocentric view of the universe, then we cease to believe that Christianity has a unique message affecting the whole of creation, and if we cease to believe that the message of Christ, the Gospel, the Good News of God in Christ, is unique, then we cease to practice Christianity because we have reduced the Incarnation of God to a mere local event with only local implications. Davis cites Colossians 1:15-19, Ephesians 1, Hebrews 1, and 1 Corinthians 15:27-28 to support his contention that Christ's atoning work is universal in scope (716). Jesus demands that Christians submit to him as a Person and experience him in a deeply personal relationship in a way that is central to the Catholic faith, and for this reason Christ's Person, the Being of God the Son, is the center of all of space and time, so that Christ is the God of all inhabitants of all inhabited worlds including Earth (717). In other words, Christ is not a local god with only local powers but the cosmic God with cosmic powers who became mortal on what some astronomers consider to be an insignificant world in the spiral arm of an ordinary galaxy, but God is described in the Bible as often raising up insignificant people through whom to show his great power. Christ, the God-man, is unique, and Christians accept no substitutions. In the Creed, Christians aver, "We believe in *one* God...etc." Thus, it seems consistent with Christian theology to believe that Christ is the unique God of the universe who rules all inhabitants on all inhabited worlds.

On the other hand, E.L. Mascall, an Anglo-Catholic, in *Christian Theology and Natural Science* (1956), disagrees with Milne, claiming that no sound theological reasons exist to deny multiple incarnations and atonements (J.J. Davis 27). J.J. Davis writes:

> If the Incarnation involved no diminution in deity, why could not the Son of God, in principle, assume other created natures? For Mascall, there would seem to be no compelling reason why "other finite rational natures should not be united to that person too." This raises the somewhat bizarre image not of the historical "God-man," but of a "bionic Redeemer" who unites to his divine nature not only the nature of *Homo Sapiens* but the natures of many other sentient, embodied creatures as well. (27)

Mascall acknowledges that other races of intelligent creatures may have so different a civilization that incarnations of Christ on such worlds are unnecessary (J.J. Davis 27). However, the meaning of "unnecessary" is debatable. Does "unnecessary" mean that such extraterrestrials are sinless or that they need no local Incarnation of the Logos because God chooses not to redeem them? By contrast, Rev. Billy Graham, a Baptist and author of many popular books, writes, "I firmly believe there are intelligent beings like us far away in space who worship God, but we would have nothing to fear from these people. Like us, they are God's creation" (Graham, cited in Peters, "Contemporary Theology" 2). I agree with Graham that extraterrestrials may well believe in God, but to believe humans have nothing to fear from them is a belief based on paltry evidence.

In another vein, Father Andrew Greeley, a popular Catholic writer of both nonfiction and science fiction, and a professor of sociology both at the University of Chicago and the University of Arizona, has written stories in which angels like Gabriel are portrayed as extraterrestrials with unusually long lifespans who serve God as messengers. Father Greeley wrote in 1996, "I think your idea of a survey of what Catholics believe about other life in other places is great. My own feeling is that the Church should be very modest about what it says on the subject and about evangelizing what might be other economies of salvation. We should not mess up as we did in India and Japan when the Jesuit attempt to adjust to those cultures was slapped down by Rome" (personal email to author, 24 September 1996, 1). Greeley seems to imply that "other economies of salvation" may mean multiple visitations by Christ and not necessarily multiple incarnations, though his position is not clear.

In support of the multiplicity of Incarnations for the redemption of extraterrestrials, Paul Tillich (1886 – 1965), a German-born American theologian and philosopher, writes:

> A question arises which has been carefully avoided by many traditional theologians, even though it is consciously or unconsciously alive for most contemporary people. It is the problem of how to understand the meaning of the symbol "Christ" in the light of the immensity of the universe, the heliocentric system of planets, the infinitely small part of the universe which man and history constitute, and the possibility of other worlds in which divine self-manifestations may appear and be received…our basic answer leaves the universe

open for possible divine manifestations in other areas or periods of being. Such possibilities cannot be denied. But they cannot be proved or disproved. Incarnation is unique for the special group in which it happens, but it is not unique in the sense that other singular incarnations for other unique worlds are excluded…Man cannot claim to occupy the only possible place for incarnation. (cited in Peters, "Contemporary Theology" 2 – 3)

So, Tillich falls into Category 2, apparently, because he argues in a slightly different way that multiple incarnations are possible though each incarnation is unique to individual worlds. In other words, other economies of salvation do not denigrate the uniqueness of the Incarnation on planet Earth nor its universal effects.

In this chapter, we have seen that the dispute within Christianity over the Incarnation of the Logos and the redemption of the people of the Earth with respect to the possibility of the Incarnation on other worlds and the redemption of their inhabitants permeates religious writings of both Catholics and Protestants well into the twentieth and twenty-first centuries. Tension between pluralism and Christianity contributed to many notable figures abandoning Christianity (Paine, Shelley, Emerson, Flammarion, Harrison, Twain, and others). Indeed, Maunder and Whewell oppose pluralism precisely because for them it conflicts with their Christian faith (Crowe 557). The writings of other authors, like Tillich and Greeley, indicate that humans should broaden their understanding of what it means to be a creation of God saved by the Logos. Such authors seem to agree that the Logos saves intelligent creatures with the only question being how.

Crucial distinctions between Christians and non-Christians disappear in the debate over extraterrestrials, with many Christians favoring pluralism for the sake of Christianity, and with many non-Christians favoring pluralism at the expense of Christianity, many Christians opposing pluralism on religious grounds, and many non-Christians opposing pluralism for non-religious reasons. Central to the Christian debate, of course, are the teachings of the Bible. Therefore, it is logical to examine the various texts of Scripture speaking to the topic of the meaning of the Incarnation not only to humans but also to possible inhabitants of other worlds. Inasmuch as

Christians regard the Bible as the Word of God, it should be possible to determine whether the notion that all of God's creations, including inhabitants of other worlds, are saved or can be saved is either found in Scripture or is at least consistent with Scripture (see Chapter 1).

Chapter 4

Inhabitants of Other Worlds and the Church

Moreover, we have seen and testify that the Father sent his Son as savior of the *kosmos.*
      — 1 John 4:14

The whole visible world is only an imperceptible speck in nature's ample bosom, no idea comes near it. We have puffed up our conceptions beyond imaginable space, we have only given birth to atoms compared with the reality of things. It is an infinite sphere whose center is everywhere, whose circumference nowhere. In the end, the greatest palpable sign of the omnipotence of God is that our imagination loses itself in thinking about it. What is a man, within the infinite?
      -- Blaise Pascal, *Pensees*[28]

Some people today believe that the very existence of inhabitants on other worlds makes the story of the Incarnation of the Logos as a human being an anthropocentric myth, threatening Christianity and the authority of the Church. Others maintain that the discovery of inhabitants of other worlds will simply expand our horizons without causing the disintegration of the Church. Who is right? Arthur C. Clarke writes in his 1951 *The Exploration of Space* (191) that some people "are afraid that the crossing of space, and above all contact with intelligent but nonhuman races, may destroy the foundations of their religious faith. They may be right, but in any event their attitude is one which does not bear logical examination – for a faith which cannot survive collision with the truth is not worth many regrets" (cited in Dick, *Cosmotheology* 2 and *The Biological Universe* 517 and *Life on Other Worlds* 247). If and when Christianity comes into contact with the discovery of inhabitants of other worlds, the result will probably not be an annihilation of the Church but an expansion of the Church's understanding of God's creation. Will some people abandon the Church upon the discovery of intelligent life elsewhere in the universe? Undoubtedly, but, then, untold numbers of people have left the Church for lesser reasons. The discovery of inhabitants of other worlds may ring alarm bells in the

---

[28] *Pensees* (1657-58), Fragment 230, "Disproportion of man"

Church, but if the Catholic Church fails to demonstrate resiliency and rise to the occasion, then its demise will not be worth many regrets.

One of the challenges that will face the Church upon the discovery of inhabitants of other worlds is interpretation of Scripture and tradition; some will argue that Scripture's failure to mention inhabitants of other worlds indicates Scripture's unreliability while the silence of Church tradition/teachings on the matter will echo this conclusion. Fortunately, Catholicism is not a religion solely of the Bible but also of tradition which clarifies Scripture, and the Church certainly has the authority to interpret Scripture in new ways to accommodate revelations of new life in the *kosmos* of which we were previously unaware. According to Catholic teachings, God inspired Scripture to teach Christians about salvation and not about the nature of the universe. Therefore, it seems safe to say that knowledge of extraterrestrials is not strictly necessary to save souls. For this reason, the topic of this book is currently a matter of speculation, albeit one that I believe it is likely we will have to face one day.

The great authors and theologians of our planet, many of whom I have discussed in this book so far, prove that speculations about inhabitants of other worlds provoke discussions on themes of sin and repentance, virtue and liberation, infinite diversity in infinite combinations (with compliments to *Star Trek*), and the dependence of creatures throughout the universe on the common God who, Giuseppe Tanzella-Nitti claims, created all of us (3). The idiosyncratic nature of the subject cries for a meeting of minds among scientists and theologians, anthropologists and philosophers, to satisfy both our curiosity and religious desires. When and if the opportunity arises, thinking Christians will want to question inhabitants of other worlds about their ideas of the meaning of life and consciousness, about their knowledge of the creator and his work in their societies, about their mythologies telling of the great battle between good and evil, and about God's intervention to effect a sense of morality and common decency and respect for one another, which are the meeting points between barbarism and civilization. Tanzella-Nitti writes:

> The search for alien beings can thus be seen as part of a long-standing religious quest as well as a scientific project. This should not surprise us. Science began as an outgrowth of theology, and all scientists, whether atheists or theists, and

whether or not they believe in the existence of alien beings, accept an essentially theological world view. (Davies 137 – 138)

So, really the religious resonance just highlighted reveals a last important interdisciplinary dimension of the debate: that of the relationship with theology. Christian theology, in a particular way, would be largely involved in such a debate. In fact, it usually reasons in terms of a "register of uniqueness" which seems to regulate the relationship between God and man, an apex reached in the mystery of the Incarnation of the Son of God made man. (cited in *Interdisciplinary Encyclopaedia of Religion and Science: Extraterrestrial life* 4)

Finally, Tanzella-Nitti writes:

If the mystery of the Incarnation refers to a Christocentric and not geocentric cardinality, then it can be explored and expressed with cosmic and universal categories, not anthropological. The third fixed point should therefore be, for our attention, the revealed and salvific universal value, and not only local, of the Incarnation. The cardinality of Christ, God-man, for the angel creatures (cf. Heb 1,3-14 and 2,5-18) would be interpreted as revealing his cardinality for all possible creatures (cf. Eph 1,10; Col 1,20). The somehow infinite greatness of the hypostatic union gives also the vicar sacrifice of Christ an infinite and meritorious value. The way in which this is applicable to the whole universe would remain a mystery for Christian theology, but the efficacy of this sacrifice does not increase even if you multiply it. The celebration of the Holy Mass, for example, applies in different times and places the fruits of that same historical event, without multiplying it. I believe, contrarily to that which is suggested by other authors, that the very participation of such salvation and efficaciousness on a cosmic plane – where it could be necessary for other intelligent and free beings – cannot depend on an interplanetary and missionary impetus, nor on an indirect communication (although these factors can and perhaps must operate). It could only depend on an economy guided by the Holy Spirit, who also works in a way which is mostly unknown for us, but certainly the only one able to secure the universality and interiorization of salvation. As it happens in the Earth's salvific economy, the Spirit would again lead to the Son and would render him in some way present. And all that having the logical conviction that the Creator has in each place his own inimitable ways to make himself recognizable, and perhaps also to make himself present within his creatures. (Tanzella-Nitti 13)

The Incarnation of the Logos, the crucifixion of Jesus of Nazareth, and his death, resurrection, and ascension are the crux of the theological universe brimming with intelligent life seeking meaning in the quest for knowledge of the creator. For Christians, Jesus is the center of all of space and time and will be an essential component of the exchange of knowledge with creatures the nature of whose minds and consciousness are known at present only to God but may become known to human beings who seek out new thoughts and ideas in the vast reaches of interstellar space. Indeed, it may be regarded by Christians as Christian duty to accelerate research into space travel in order to facilitate the mission of interstellar missionaries.

In this book so far, I have argued that it is consistent with Catholic teachings including Scripture that the Incarnation of Jesus Christ is a unique universal event affecting the whole of creation, and Jesus Christ came to redeem and save inhabitants of other worlds (if they exist) as well as human beings by his grace via his life, death, and resurrection. These beliefs are consistent with the Christian thought and theology of many prominent authors, both Catholic and Protestant, as well as compatible with the concepts of universal redemption, justification, sanctification, and salvation as historically put forth by the Catholic Church in both its oral tradition and Bible.

Chapter 5

Nature of the Logos and *Kosmos*

There are more things in heaven and earth, Horatio, than are dreamt of in your philosophy.
-- William Shakespeare, *Hamlet* Act I Scene V 166-167

In this fateful hour
I place all Heaven with its power
And the sun with its brightness,
And the snow with its whiteness,
And the fire with all the strength it hath,
And the lightning with its rapid wrath,
And the winds with their swiftness along their path,
And the sea with its deepness,
And the rocks with their steepness,
And the earth with its starkness,
All these I place
By God's almighty help and grace
Between myself and the powers of darkness!
-- Madeleine L'Engle, *A Swiftly Tilting Planet*

The stars, like dust, encircle me
In swirling mists of light,
And all of space I seem to see
In one vast burst of sight.
-- Isaac Asimov, *The Stars, Like Dust* (1951)

A reasonable question to ask is why did the Logos become incarnate on the Earth out of all the billions of planets in the *kosmos*? The answer to that question brings with it a whole host of new questions about Christ and the Incarnation and whether his redemptive work on Earth applies to all planets in the universe. Some writers, like C.S. Lewis, ponder the question and come up with the solution that other worlds need not necessarily have fallen in the same way that Adam and Eve fell from grace in the Garden of Eden, and that subsequent incarnations are therefore unnecessary. Some scholars contend that inhabitants of other worlds are not the descendents of Adam and Eve and therefore are not held to the same covenants or subject to the same inherited disease of original sin. Perhaps extraterrestrial people fell just as Adam and Eve fell, and so all extraterrestrial races are fallen in the same way that the human race is fallen. It's possible that falling from grace is an inevitable consequence of free will. I will argue that it is consistent with Christian theology to maintain that inhabitants of other worlds have fallen into sin as an inevitable consequence of free will and that the unique Incarnation on Earth as well as the unique crucifixion and resurrection purchase the benefits of salvation to sinful humans and sinful extraterrestrial intelligent beings alike.

Camille Flammarion (1842 – 1925), author of "L'humanité dans l'univers," according to Crowe, lists "four solutions to these problems…:

> (1) God simultaneously became incarnate and died on all planets where sin had occurred. (2) God became incarnate on various planets at different times. (3) God came only to the earth, because only there did sin arise. (4) Christ's earthly actions brought redemption to all the planets. The third is described as Chalmers's solution, the fourth as Brewsters's, with Flammarion favoring the latter." (Crowe 383)

The Reverend Thomas Chalmers suggests that Scripture passages may have meanings beyond the original intent of the authors, because the meaning of the term *kosmos* can be expanded to include the entire universe even though the original author's understanding of the extent of the universe was quite limited at the time of original composition.

> But tell me, O tell me, would it not throw the softening of a most exquisite tenderness over the character of God, should we see him putting forth his every expedient to reclaim to himself those children who had wandered away from him; and few as they were when compared with the host of his obedient worshippers, would it not just impart to his attribute of compassion the infinity of the Godhead, that rather than lose the single world which had turned to its own way, he should send the messengers of peace to woo and to welcome it back again; and if justice demanded so mighty a sacrifice, and the law behooved to be so magnified and made honorable, tell me whether it would not throw a moral sublime over the goodness of the Deity, should he lay upon his own Son the burden of its

atonement, that he might again smile upon the world, and hold out the scepter of invitation to all its families? (Chalmers 94)

Whewell writes in contrast:

> The earth, thus selected as the theatre of such a scheme of Teaching and of Redemption, cannot, in the eyes of any one who accepts this Christian faith, be regarded as being on a level with any other domiciles. It is the Stage of the great Drama of God's Mercy and Man's Salvation; the Sanctuary of the Universe; the Holy Land of Creation; the Royal Abode, for a time at last, of the Eternal King. This being the character which has thus been conferred upon it, how can we assent to the assertions of Astronomers, when they tell us that it is only one among millions of similar habitations, not distinguishable from them, except that it is smaller than most of them that we can measure; confused and rude in its materials like them? Or if we believe the Astronomers, will not such a belief lead us to doubt the truth of the great scheme of Christianity, which thus makes the earth the scene of a special dispensation? (64)

Some Christian scholars maintain that the prospect of inhabitants of other worlds has no deleterious effects on Christian theology but indeed expands and leavens theological thought with ebullience, an idea rejected by such Christian scholars as William Whewell who expresses opposition to the notion of inhabitants of other worlds on the grounds that their very existence challenges the validity of Christian faith.

We will see in the course of the discussion on the Incarnation of the Logos that the development of the idea of the nature of the *kosmos* influenced many of the authors and theologians explored in this book. Scientific advancements in our understanding of the *kosmos* caused certain theologians to expand their thoughts to include the notion that the Incarnation was not simply a local event on earth but a cosmological event with universal implications. Subsequent to the Copernican revolution and Kepler's discovery of the laws of planetary motion, many people, educated and lay alike, developed a greater appreciation not only for the nature of the universe but the extent of the *kosmos*. These scientific discoveries expanded

Christological thought to include the idea that the Logos rules a vast expanse of space that has not yet been measured and that Christ's domain of power includes both humans and inhabitants of other worlds alike.

In many cultures, science, religion, and philosophy are not necessarily distinct areas of study but like different shades of the same color. In the Bible, statements or implications about the nature of the sky and the nature of things reflect ancient Biblical Jewish science rather than ancient Biblical Jewish theology, though the ancient Israelites themselves may have regarded this modern distinction as no different than trying to distinguish or separate soul and spirit and body. Aristotle and Plato and other Greeks began the process of distinguishing among religion, philosophy, and science in a way that profoundly influenced Christianity and the later views of Christian theologians and philosophers and scientists. By failing to see these disciplines in a unified whole, modern Christians often think of religion as being believed on Sundays and science as being believed the rest of the week. In some ways, the ancients, whose beliefs made no such distinctions, knew what we have forgotten, even while we speculate on what they never knew. For the early mystical Christians, the Logos is the creator and designer who became incarnate to show the people of this planet how to experience eternal life, while the nature of the *kosmos* he designed and created was conceptualized as the place where humans experience the process of coming to know God. Romans 1:20 tells us: "Ever since the creation of the *kosmos*, his invisible attributes of eternal power and divinity have been able to be understood and perceived in what he has made." For Thomas Aquinas, Paul's assertion predicates the existence of God as an eternal truth (*Summa Contra Gentiles, Book I, Section 12*). As their understanding of the nature of the creation grew, so did their appreciation for the design and the designer. Soon, many began speculating on the design of other worlds as well as the design of their inhabitants, always with a keen eye on the designer.

Many cultures for many years made little if any distinction among the disciplines of science, philosophy, and theology (Davis and Poe 24). However, with Plato and Aristotle, these disciplines came to be thought of as separate in the West, a feature of Western culture that many other cultures find puzzling at best and simply strange at worst. For better or worse, this breaking up of the scholastic disciplines led to the unfortunate attitude that science, philosophy, and theology have nothing to say to one other (Davis and Poe 24). However, I will argue that these disciplines have much to say to each other and their confluence[29] has much to say to us. The notion that the universe is designed is a feature common to many (if not most) religions (Davis and Poe 24). Modern thinkers have begun discussing not simply the design of the universe but the intelligent design of the universe (Davis and Poe 24 – 25) and are now are revisiting the notion that the Logos is the organizing force through which the universe was intelligently designed with innumerable intelligent creatures, *hnau*, made in the spiritual image of their creator.

Certainly, in my view, the vast reaches of interstellar space are no obstacle to the God who is everywhere. The notion that the Incarnation occurred in a place-where (that is, on Earth, in Israel) does not alter my conviction that the resurrection results in justification for inhabitants throughout the universe. When one gazes upon the Mona Lisa from the south, the east, and the west, it appears as though the eyes gaze upon each person in each position simultaneously. Similarly, Jesus appears to be everywhere, gazing upon each person individually, whether an inhabitant of the earth or an inhabitant of another star system, because his flesh is glorified.

Jesus is regarded by Christians as their redeemer and liberator from slavery to their sins. Just so, Christianity is a religion capable of embracing the notion that Jesus liberates all intelligent beings from slavery to their sins. Thus, it seems to be consistent with Christian theology that the commission of sins is, for all practical purposes, an inevitable consequence of free will (the exception, of course, is God whether spirit or incarnate) so that all intelligent beings of whatever origin are sinners in need of redemption. In this view, Jesus redeems all sinners who repent and grants them eternal salvation in heaven. As an aside, I would argue that, while "heaven" in Scripture and tradition sometimes means the sky or space, it can also mean not so much a place-where as a relationship with God. In this view, hell is not a place-where either but a lack of a relationship with God. Heaven is a condition of the soul such that God allows the citizens of

---

[29] Confluence is used here to apply to the flowing together of concepts which were initially distinct from one another.

heaven to interact via prayers or visions with people still living in the mortal sphere of existence, that is, on a variety of worlds in the universe or anywhere betwixt and between.

The Incarnation can be construed as a problem for those who believe intelligent life exists elsewhere in the universe in terms of ubiquity. That is, the notion Christ or his body are everywhere in the universe at the same time is regarded as an attribute of God. Since Christ is ubiquitous, it follows that he is present amidst inhabitants of other worlds in ways that perhaps neither humans nor they fully comprehend. It is possible that inhabitants of other worlds see the risen Christ in different forms in the same way that the disciples saw the risen Christ in different ways. Some people say that people create God in their own image. I would say that people have different images of God that change as they grow older, but this is not "creating" God in different images but imagining God in different images. God is Spirit, and spirits can take many forms. While the incarnate Logos has taken the physical form of a human being, the eyes of faith may see Christ in whatever way the cultural and religious beliefs of the individual so guide a person. Different people see Christ in different ways on their individual faith journeys, and the faith journeys of inhabitants of other worlds can surely be no stranger than the wide varieties of religious experiences people have on earth (cf. William James's *Varieties of Religious Experience*). So, whether humans bring the Gospel to inhabitants of other worlds, or, as Lewis suggests, human encounters with extraterrestrials result in our being instructed by them, "Jesus Christ is the same yesterday, today, and forever" (Hebrews 13:8). Extraterrestrial interpretations of the risen Christ may be just as profound if not more so than the interpretations of the greatest of terrestrial sages and theologians. As Scripture attests, "For [Wisdom] is the refulgence of eternal light, the spotless mirror of the power of God, the image of his goodness" (Wisdom 7:26). Certainly, the incarnate Wisdom can be regarded by all, human and extraterrestrial alike, as the true image of God, the creator of all things.

The Bible contains not only fable but fact, myth as well as history, legend as well as logical treatises on theology because what is unknown is inestimably greater than what is known and in the demesne of the mysteries of God the imagination and intuition are sometimes better guides than raw intellect and logic. Scripture tells us that we are "servants of Christ and stewards of the mysteries of God" (1 Corinthians 4:1), and this is no light task for disciples of any era. In the sometimes dim ancient past, before the days of written records, the curious were often beset with disturbing questions the answers to which evolved into waves of theories without proof along with a multitude of treasures of tradition that is every Christian's heritage in an effort to understand the mysterious lore that gave rise to both the Old Testament and the New Testament. These books of this tradition attempt to explain our most elemental innate fears and inherent indwelling hopes and to express humanity's continuous quest for the meaning of life, the purpose of death, and the desire to know the answers to the mysteries of eternal life. The Scriptures, for many Christians, have the purpose of bringing faith in the presence of doubt, hope in the presence of despair, light into "this present darkness," joy in the midst of sadness, purpose in the midst of the vicissitudes of life, and order (i.e., *kosmos*) in the midst of chaos. In the midst of the creation of the *kosmos*, the Logos gave order to the chaotic eruptions of the Deep, and much later, according to Christology, became flesh to show people the way to heaven. Earlier, it was pertinent to examine the meaning of *kosmos*, *Logos*, soul, and other terms in an effort to appreciate the profundity of the Scripture passages that imply that human beings are not alone in experiencing the salvation of Christ.

On the other hand, all human beings are God's creations and yet humans often fear other humans, as individuals and as nations, because history is replete with wars and individuals harming other individuals for the sake of sordid gains. Simply because extraterrestrials are God's creations is no reason to believe that we automatically have nothing to fear from them. If we pray for extraterrestrials to be good Christians, the extraterrestrials may pray, "God, we thank thee for the booty we are about to receive from the humans we are about to conquer." After all, the Promised Land was conquered. We can only hope that prayers for peaceful relations will be heard and granted.

According to Crowe, the following scholars cite Scripture to support extraterrestrial life: Beattie (102), Brewster (303), Burr (451), T. Dick (197, 200-201), Ilive (37), E. King (104), R. Knight (336), Lord (343), Montignez (412-413), and Sturmy (35). According to Crowe, the following scholars cite Scripture in opposition to ET life: Catcott (92), Kurtz (262), Leavitt (342), A. Maxwell (195), Thomas Aquinas (4), J. Wesley (94).

While John Calvin (1509 – 1564), a French theologian and a foundational Protestant Reformer, argues that the designed universe is evidence for the existence of God (Poe and Davis 41), René Descartes, a French philosopher, mathematician, scientist, metaphysical rationalist, and father of modern philosophy as well as the father of epistemology, takes the opposite tack in his process of Cartesian doubt[30] to conclude that the universe exists based on his faith in God (Poe and Davis 45). Sir Isaac Newton (1642 [1643 New Style] – 1727), the famous English scientist, physicist, and mathematician who spearhead the scientific revolution of the 17th century, also dabbled extensively in theology, although he was not a Trinitarian but a theist who believed that God created, organized, and sustains the universe. Newton's views were embraced by members of the Deist movement who argue that God set the universe in motion but does not interfere with the clockwork in any way and certainly does not interfere in the affairs of human beings (or extraterrestrials, for that matter) (Poe and Davis 130). Blaise Pascal (1623 – 1662), a French physicist, mathematician, and philosopher of religion, and defender of rational Christianity, argues similarly that the nature and structure of the universe do not prove the existence of God, but rather faith in God gives people the ability to comprehend the nature and structure of the universe (Poe and Davis 49 – 50). Pascal is also famous for what has come to be known as Pascal's Wager, which is essentially a bet one makes about whether one should have faith in God: If there is no God, an agnostic or an atheist gains nothing by

---

[30] Cartesian Doubt refers to Descartes's effort to doubt that everything in the universe exists by doubting his senses and supposing that an evil demon is pouring into his mind a kind of hallucination to make him believe that the universe does exist. Descartes comes to the conclusion that he exists based on his famous dictum "I think therefore I am" (in Latin, "Cogito ergo sum" and in the original French "Je pense, donc je suis"), which is not a syllogism but an axiom. From his rational determination that God exists and that God, because he is good, would not deceive him about the existence of the universe, Descartes concludes that the universe really exists. Interestingly, this is the opposite approach of most rationalists who conclude that the universe is evidence for the existence of God, whereas for Descartes the universe is real because God is real, that is, God's reality is evidence for the reality of the universe.

believing in him; on the other hand, if the Christian God does exist, the agnostic or the atheist by changing to a faithful Christian gains eternal life. Thus, faith is the way to bet. William James disapproved of Pascal's Wager on the theory that it is not a rational belief since one may use the argument to embrace any religion and any god or gods. William Paley (1743 – 1805), a British Anglican priest, Utilitarian, and author of numerous books on science and religion, Christianity and morality, argues famously that, if one finds a watch, even if one knows nothing about watches, one may deduce from observing its construction and design that it must have had a constructor and designer (Poe and Davis 65-67). Perhaps the Father is the designer, the Logos is the constructor, and the Holy Spirit is the sustainer.

F.R. Tennant (1866 – 1957), a British philosopher and theologian who advocated harmony between science and religion while embracing the theological sciences empirically, argues in favor of design theory but with a twist: he argues that, because the soul exists as a necessary cause of consciousness, then God must exist, and without a soul it is irrelevant whether God exists, theologically (Poe and Davis 76 – 77). Tennant believes that Jesus Christ ultimately showed people the path to God and the divine intention for the universe better than anyone else and so is due appropriate reverence (Poe and Davis 76). Tennant's "cosmic teleology" implies that the *kosmos* has a goal in the mind of its designer, and that this goal is the development of life (Poe and Davis 77). Tennant argues that the emergence of life is extremely improbable, leading to the inescapable conclusion that the emergence of life must have had a divine impetus (Poe and Davis 77). The nature and interaction of subatomic particles leads to the conclusion that the universe is fine-tuned for life (Poe and Davis 91 – 92). The fine-tuning of the universe for life leads to the conclusion that a fine-tuner is necessary for the fine-tuning to occur.

Perhaps it is because God is immanent in the *kosmos* that the author of the Book of Wisdom says to us:

> Wisdom 16:17 *For against all expectation, in water which quenches anything, the fire grew more active; For the* kosmos *fights on behalf of the just.*

How can the *kosmos* fight on behalf of the just unless God is panentheistically in the *kosmos* battling the forces of evil on behalf of *hnau*?

Immanuel Kant (1724 – 1804), a very influential German philosopher of ethics, aesthetics, and epistemology, writes *Universal Natural History and Theory of the Heavens* in 1755 in which he questions whether inhabitants of the large planets in our solar system may be "too noble and wise" to commit sins and also questions whether the inhabitants of the smaller systems "are grafted too fast to matter…to carry to the responsibility of their actions before the judgment seat of justice." He also speculates that Martians may be just as sinful as the inhabitants of the Earth (Crowe 53).

Edward Young (baptized 3 July 1683 – d. 5 April 1765), an English poet, dramatist, and literary critic, composes *The Complaint* or *Night Thoughts* (1742 – 1745) in which he writes not only "An undevout astronomer is mad" (Night IX line 773) but also:

> …How various are the works of god?
> But say, what thought?
> Is Reason here enthroned?
> And absolute? Or Sense in arms against her?
> Have you two lights? Or need you no
> reveal'd?…
> And had your Eden an abstemious Eve?…
> Or, if your mother fell, are you
> redeem'd?…
> Is this your final residence? If not,
> Change you your scene, translated? Or by death?
> And if by death; what death? – Know you disease?
> (IX, 1773 – 1781)

Moreover, Young writes in praise of God the Son:

> And Thou the next! Yet equal! Thou, by whom
> That blessing was convey'd; far more! Was bought;
> Ineffable the price! By whom all worlds
> Were made; and one redeem'd!…
> Thou God and mortal! Thence more God to man!…
> Who disembosom'd from the Father, bows

The heaven of heavens, to kiss the distant earth!
Breathes out in agonies a sinless soul!
Against the cross, Death's iron scepter breaks!
(IX, 2262 – 2265, 2348, 2352 – 2355)

Famous writers as divergent as Napoleon, John Wesley, and William Blake cherished this poem and encouraged its wide dispersion, keeping it alongside their Bibles and John Bunyan (Crowe 86). Yet Young's vision of a fallen Earth amidst a wide variety of fallen inhabited planets inspires Thomas Chalmers and, in the 20th century, the great C.S. Lewis, proving that the ideal of a plurality of worlds populated with redeemable inhabitants is within the realm of traditional piety and its Christian practitioners (Crowe 86).

Barthold Heinrich Brockes (1680 -- 1747) (Note: Crowe says 1680 -- 1740), an influential Hamburg poet of the early German Enlightenment, writes:

Should Christ have died
Solely for a single world
Or how have the first Adams
Fallen on all of them also?
Have a thousand Eves also been deceived
By a thousand snakes through a thousand apples?
(cited in Crowe 141)

Crowe notes that, of the published Christians examined in America and Europe between 1860 and 1900, fourteen Catholics and nineteen Protestants support pluralism while ten Catholics and four Protestants oppose pluralism (457).

Chapter 6

Intelligent Design and the Logos

Know this my Prakriti[31]
United with me:
The womb of all beings.
I am the birth of this cosmos:
Its dissolution also.
I am He who causes:
No other beside me.
Upon me, these worlds are held
Like pearls strung on a thread.
          -- *Bhagavad Gita* VII: Knowledge and Experience[32]

Where were you when I founded the earth?
Tell me, if you have understanding.
Who determined its size; do you know?
Who stretched out the measuring line for it?
Into what were its pedestals sunk,
And who laid the cornerstone,
While the morning stars sang in chorus
And all the sons of God shouted for joy?
          -- Job 38:4-7

But if a man would be alone, let him look at the stars. The rays that come
from those heavenly worlds, will separate between him and what he
touches. One might think the atmosphere was made transparent with this
design, to give man, in the heavenly bodies, the perpetual presence of the
sublime. Seen in the streets of cities, how great they are! If the stars
should appear one night in a thousand years, how would men believe and
adore; and preserve for many generations the remembrance of the city of
 God which had been shown! But every night come out these envoys of
beauty, and light the universe with their admonishing smile.
          -- Ralph Waldo Emerson, *Nature* (Chapter 1)

Saint Augustine changed his religion from Manichaeism to
Christianity partially as a result of his inability to reconcile the

---

[31] "Prakriti" is the power of Brahman who causes all mind and matter to
exist in Hinduism (*The Song of God: Bhagavad-Gita,* translated by Swami
Prabhavananda and Christopher Isherwood, in Appendix I, *The Cosmology
of the Gita* 133).
[32] Translated by Swami Prabhavananda and Christopher Isherwood. New
York: Penguin Books, 1972. Pages 70 – 71.

science of his day with Manichaen dualism. Augustine developed his belief that God transcends all of space and time in response to his reception of the Christian faith (Davis and Poe 32 – 33). In attempting to reconcile the apparent incompatibility of a good God with evil in creation, Augustine came to the conclusion that God needed to become incarnate to mingle with his creation so that good might be brought out of evil (cf. Davis and Poe 34 – 35).

Saint Thomas Aquinas gave five traditional proofs for the existence of God, and the fifth proof is *the argument from governance*, which is an important argument for design theory. Thomas argues that nonsentient things move towards a best goal or end, and that therefore a sentient being must be directing their efforts. Thomas concludes that the sentient being doing the directing is God: "Therefore some intelligent being exists by whom all natural things are ordered to their end; and this being we call God" (*Summa Theologica*, Question 2, Article III, Whether God Exists?;[33] cited in Poe and Davis 37). Thomas believes the traditional and Scriptural view that the universe had a beginning, although he denies that the beginning of the universal is necessarily temporal, so that one may say the universe is eternally created by God even though it has a beginning and an ending (Poe and Davis 39). One may argue that the ending of the universe, in Christian apocalyptic terminology, will simply be a restructuring of the universe atemporally. This discussion on design theory is important because the Logos, while not part of the original design because it is eternal with God and is God (according to Christian theology), becomes part of the design when it becomes incarnate and subject to the constraints of time and space, i.e., the *kosmos*. The *kosmos* is not simply space but, according to modern relativity theory, the spacetime continuum that has a beginning and an ending. That the Logos is part of the spacetime continuum and yet is eternal is a paradox, a puzzle without resolution, that causes many theologians and authors as well as scientists to reexamine and contemplate their theories on nature and metaphysics. The Incarnation of the Logos, for many, challenges the randomness theory of quantum mechanics, while, for others, the Incarnation is proof of design theory.

---

[33] Cf. Note 9 above and Appendix B.

How do these ideas about intelligent design relate to the Incarnation of the Logos and its effect on inhabitants of other worlds? When we look at patterns in nature, particularly the interrelatedness of living things and their relationship to the *kosmos*, what we are experiencing is similar to the poetry of the Bible – full of imagery and the sense of wonder. Living things, particularly human beings, long for their creator the way, according to the psalmist, the parched land thirsts for water (Psalm 63:2-3) or "My soul looks for the Lord more than sentinels for daybreak. More than sentinels for daybreak" (Psalm 130:6). It seems to be a natural thing for intelligent beings to yearn for the creator and to yearn, in the winter of our discontent, for the Eden where spring comes. The desire to know where we come from is just as intense as the desire to know where we are going, and the search for inhabitants of other worlds reflects the human desire to reach out beyond the stretch of our arms to other creations of other worlds. Human beings cannot see where they are going without remembering whence they came, and this is why the Bible is so important in our quest not only to know ourselves but to learn about other creations of God. The Bible may guide Christians to simultaneously remember the past and look towards the future, which may include relations with inhabitants of other worlds. To see the *kosmos* as an intelligently designed system yields speculation on the other things, particularly living things, that the designer has designed. For those who believe the pre-incarnate Logos is the designer, this is both a scientific and a poetic enterprise, particularly for those who believe that the designer Logos became part of the designed.

Poe and Davis remark:

Belief in an Intelligent Designer forms the foundational article of faith for Islam, Judaism, and Christianity. Within these faiths design does not function as a proof but as a "self-evident truth." (211)

Later, Poe and Davis ask, "Is the universe more like a machine as the Deists suggested, or a body as Plato suggested, or a work of art as the Bible suggested? Is God an engineer or an artist?" (226). I ask, what's the difference? To engineer things, whether inanimate things or living things, is a work of art. The universe is like a machine that has been artfully designed. The engineer is the artist. Faith in God is not the same as faith in anything else, including "faith" in the existence of inhabitants of other worlds or "faith" in the science or scientific enterprises that may one day result in the discovery of inhabitants of other worlds. Faith in God and the belief that the Bible is the Word of God lead us to recognize that the Scriptures can help us to see the "self-evident truth" that the design of the *kosmos* is an indication that creation is more vast and amazing than any human being has yet thought, or, as Shakespeare put it, "There are more things in heaven and earth, Horatio, than are dreamt of in your philosophy" (*Hamlet*). So, now, Christians may turn to the Bible to help make sense of this theory that the Logos not only creates but cares about all of his creations on both earth and elsewhere in the *kosmos*. The purpose of the discussion leading up to interpreting Scripture verses in terms of their relationship to inhabitants of other worlds is to suggest that design theory implies more about salvation than meets the eye. That is, salvation is a broad term encompassing inhabitants of Earth and inhabitants of other worlds, and humans cannot understand extraterrestrial salvation without understanding human salvation.

While Darwinism tells how life evolves, the theory of evolution says nothing about how life *began*. The creation of life is a process independent of the realm of natural laws (Whewell 252). Similarly, the Incarnation of the Logos in the womb of the Virgin Mary is a process independent of the realm of natural laws inasmuch as it is nothing less than miraculous. That said, Clarke's Law famously states, "Any sufficiently developed technology is indistinguishable from magic." In the technical sense, "magic" is any effect attributed to a supernatural cause. Thus, any miracle is by the technical definition a kind of magic. Hence, one might argue that the creation of original life on Earth is a miraculous event, just as is the begetting of life in the womb of the Virgin Mary by the Holy Spirit. Certainly, one is not more miraculous than the other. A miracle is a miracle. C.S. Lewis calls the Incarnation, crucifixion, and resurrection of Christ "deep magic." It would not surprise me that God causes the miracle of life on innumerable worlds, but I still maintain that the Incarnation is unique to the Earth because the resurrected flesh of Jesus is a glorious eternal body, and this would not be true if the Logos had to become spiritual again in order to become Incarnate on world after world throughout the universe. Once flesh, always flesh, even in glorification.

I would like to conclude this chapter on intelligent design theory and the logos with the observation that many Fundamentalist Christians as well as some mainstream Christians want science teachers to teach intelligent design theory in the classroom. This is a sticky problem. Intelligent design theory says very little about who the intelligent designer is or even whether there are multiple designers. One high school science teacher petitioned, as a result of a law, to teach that the Flying Spaghetti Monster may have created the universe. His point is that the intelligent designer could have been the Christian God's Logos or the FSM or invisible unicorns or the gods of ancient Greece and Rome. The scientist simply does not know. As a mainstream Christian, I am not averse to teaching intelligent design theory in an English classroom or a history class, social studies class, or political science class, but I have my doubts about the wisdom of teaching the theory in a science class because perhaps inevitably questions arise about who the intelligent designer is -- and this is a question which the science teacher should not be expected to answer. That said, many of the more active proponents of intelligent design theory appear to be anti-science, but there is a different group of ID proponents, such as John Polkinghorne or even Alvin Plantinga, who seem to conform to accepting existing scientific theories on the origin of the universe while adding that it must have been God who started the process. Plantinga makes this point clear in an otherwise muddled review of Dawkins' *The God Delusion* in which he avers agreement with the theory of evolution but not unguided evolution. The problem with the atheist/theist controversy is that the two camps are both convinced they are right, and, in any public debate, both sides tend to claim victory. I've seen this over and over again in public debates among philosophers and religious apologists with scientists. While all sides are capable of putting together very polished arguments, most critics and news reporters don't delve below the surface of the argument in order to determine which speakers were making logical arguments and which weren't. My opinion is that the intelligent design theory is both a scientific argument and a religious argument, depending on which way you look at it. While both science classes and English/history/social studies/political science classes can discuss the scientific side of the ID debate as well as the religious side, science teachers should not be expected to comment on the theistic side of the debate because science teachers are untrained in theology and theistic arguments are outside their area of expertise. Finally, I believe firmly that English teachers should be allowed to teach authors who write on ID theory, history teachers should be allowed to teach the history of the debate, social studies teachers should be allowed to teach the social dimensions of the debate, and political science teachers should be allowed to teach the political ramifications of the debate, while science teachers can teach that ID theory is a theory of the origin of the universe like any other without commenting on who or what the intelligent designer is or intelligent designers are. A science teacher can comment on the intelligent design of a watch without commenting on whether the watch was made by Timex, Seiko, Rolex, or any other intelligent designers of watches.

Chapter 7

Catholics, Protestants, Fundamentalists, and Unbelievers

[4] As I looked, a stormwind came from the North, a huge cloud with flashing fire (enveloped in brightness), from the midst of which (the midst of the fire) something gleamed like electrum.[5] Within it were figures resembling four living creatures that looked like this: their form was human, [6] but each had four faces and four wings, [7]and their legs went straight down; the soles of their feet were round. They sparkled with a gleam like burnished bronze. [8] Human hands were under their wings, and the wings of one touched those of another. [9] Their faces (and their wings) looked out on all their four sides; they did not turn when they moved, but each went straight forward. [10] Their faces were like this: each of the four had the face of a man, but on the right side was the face of a lion, and on the left side the face of an ox, and finally each had the face of an eagle. [11] Each had two wings spread out above so that they touched one another's, while the other two wings of each covered his body. [12] (Each went straight forward; wherever the spirit wished to go, there they went; they did not turn when they moved.) [13] In among the living creatures something like burning coals of fire could be seen; they seemed like torches, moving to and fro among the living creatures. The fire gleamed, and from it came forth flashes of lightning. [14] [15] As I looked at the living creatures, I saw wheels on the ground, one beside each of the four living creatures. [16] The wheels had the sparkling appearance of chrysolite, and all four of them looked the same: they were constructed as though one wheel were within another. [17]They could move in any of the four directions they faced, without veering as they moved. [18] The four of them had rims, and I saw that their rims were full of eyes all around. [19]When the living creatures moved, the wheels moved with them; and when the living creatures were raised from the ground, the wheels also were raised. [20] Wherever the spirit wished to go, there the wheels went, and they were raised together with the living creatures; for the spirit of the living creatures was in the wheels.
(Ezekiel 1:4-20 NAB)

The views of mainstream Catholics and Protestants differ from those of Protestant Fundamentalists in that the former generally accept the idea that extraterrestrials exist and can be saved, whereas the latter tend to reject those beliefs. Even those Fundamentalist authors who accept the existence of inhabitants of other worlds often portray them as evil demons who spiritually attack people. For example, Frank Allnut claims that UFOs are demons out to destroy the souls of Christians by encouraging them to believe that "ET theology" can save us rather than Christ. Hal Lindsey is another who

believes that UFO's are satanic, eschatological manifestations.
Lindsey writes: "I believe these beings are not only extraterrestrial
but supernatural in origin. To be blunt, I think they are demons. The
Bible tells us that demons are spiritual beings at war with God. We
are told that demons will be allowed to use their tremendous powers
of deception in a grand way in the last days" (cited in Wojcik 203).
Other Fundamentalists with similar ideas include David Allen Lewis
and Randall Baer (ibid.). The position asserted by the Vatican is that
UFO's, whatever they are, are not demons (Coyne). Again, this book
is not primarily about these ideas, interesting as they are. I am simply
trying to emphasize that many Catholics and mainstream Protestants
tend to think in general that extraterrestrials are part of the natural
order of the universe, whereas many Fundamentalists tend to think in
general that inhabitants of other worlds are evil and must be defeated.
As a result, many Fundamentalist Christians believe that the
Incarnation is unique to the Earth and applies only to human beings
on Earth while many other Christians believe that the effects of the
Incarnation and redemptive work of Christ apply to extraterrestrials
also. Still other Christians believe that the Incarnation takes place on
other worlds as well in order to effect the salvation of other beings. In
this book, we are exploring these questions through an examination of
several contemporary and historical theological positions. What do
each of these authors contribute to our understanding of the
theological status of inhabitants of other worlds? What are the
strengths and weaknesses of each position? Then, in the conclusion, I
will argue that the mainstream Christians are theologically sound to
believe that inhabitants of other worlds can be saved and that it is
consistent with Christian theology to believe that evangelism is
imperative for Christians to propagate the Gospel throughout the
cosmos.

Not all fundamentalists believe UFO's are evil. Some UFO
enthusiasts reinterpret Biblical texts to suggest that visions of
prophets were UFOs as in Ezekiel 1:4-28 and the Star of Bethlehem
in Matthew 2:1-11 as well as the light blinding the Apostle Paul on
the road to Damascus in Acts of the Apostles 9:3. Other
interpretations include the notion that Gabriel was an extraterrestrial
who artificially inseminated the Blessed Virgin Mary with the seed of
an extraterrestrial so that her Son might bring the message from space
and that God is an extraterrestrial who parted the Red Sea for the

Israelites and gave them the Ark of the Covenant that was actually a communications device for Moses to receive instructions from the particular ET sent to Earth (Wojcik 184 – 185). Most mainstream theologians and authors reject these ideas as farfetched or lunatic fringe. For myself, I take the Bible at face value – I believe that Scripture is an accurate portrayal of events in the Israelite and later Christian communities, and I do not believe that God is an extraterrestrial per se but the Creator of the universe.

The debate in Protestant churches of previous centuries revolved around whether human life existed on other planets. Protestants were vexed that extraterrestrials were not mentioned in Scripture, so any proof of inhabitants of other worlds would lie in secular science, making an important fact about our universe determined by reason rather than faith. Since Protestants like Luther[34] and Calvin reject the Thomistic position that humans can use reason to make discoveries about the universe (although they do not reject reason entirely), it might follow that many Protestants should, if they follow the Sola Scriptura arguments of their churches, reject the possibility of inhabitants of other worlds on the grounds that Scripture does not mention extraterrestrials. Critics assert that such logic is akin to arguing that the Atlanta Braves do not exist because Scripture does not mention them. Responding to such criticism, many Protestants do not in fact so reject the possibility of extraterrestrials because theology among some Protestants is shifting towards allowing reason to tell us many important facts about our universe, leaving Scripture to teach about redemption and salvation rather than the nature of the universe. As Galileo once said, "It is clear from a churchman[35] who has been elevated to a very eminent position that the Holy Spirit's intention is to teach us how to go to Heaven, and not how the heavens go" (*Letter to Madame Christine of Lorraine, Grand Duchess of Tuscany* in 1615). Thomas F. O'Meara of Notre Dame writes: "Where Christian faith is centered solely in Jesus of Nazareth,

---

[34] Martin Luther wrote: "Reason is the greatest enemy that faith has: it never comes to the aid of spiritual things, but -- more frequently than not -- struggles against the divine Word, treating with contempt all that emanates from God" (*Table Talk*, 353).
[35] Many scholars believe that Galileo's "churchman" is Cesare Baronio (1538 -- 1607), an Italian church historian and Catholic apologist as well as a member of the Oratory in Rome.

where a few Pauline passages linking Christ to the creation are taken to refer to the man Jesus without qualification, and where Christian revelation is one single light in an extensively fallen race and world, theology has difficulty with the existence of extraterrestrials because their mode of religious life would not be centered on Jesus Christ" (2). O'Meara indicates that the possible frequent deaths and resurrections of the Logos would do a disservice to the uniqueness of the work of the Incarnate Logos on Earth (3), placing him in one of the latter three categories of Chapter 1.

In this book, I am arguing that, prior to the 20th century, the vast majority of intellectuals in the West believed that a plurality of worlds populated with inhabitants existed, and many Christians attempted to reconcile Christianity with pluralism. Strangely, in the 20th century and into the 21st century, pluralism lost some of its respectability. I speculate that this loss of respectability may be the result of science fiction books and films depicting a variety of extraterrestrials, some hostile and some friendly, in a way that many of the intelligentsia interpreted as cheesy. Crowe writes that Henry Draper (1837 – 1882) writes in 1866 "Are There Other Inhabited Worlds?" in which Draper suggests that the famous Moon Hoax of 1835 by journalist R. A. Lock who inaccurately reported in his newspaper that life had been discovered on the Moon, only to have the story proven completely false, "left behind an unfortunate skepticism" (Crowe 364). While true that others have perpetuated hoaxes including UFO sightings and alien abductions, it is also true that scarecrows do not prove that cornfields are uninhabited. O'Meara says that "…after World War I, with the discovery of multiple galaxies through the fashioning of more advanced telescopes, the possibility of other intelligent life reasserted itself" (3). In this book, I am attempting to make the subject respectable again by pointing out that the debate has been going on for centuries among reputable scholars and theologians and authors.

As a contrast to the theological debate, one must note that some authors favor a plurality of worlds while disbelieving Christianity. An example is Thomas Paine (1737 -- 1809), an English-American political writer of inflammatory pamphlets (such as "Common Sense," published 10 January 1776, and "Rights of Man," published 13 March 1791, and "Rights of Man, Part II," published 17 February 1792) fanning the flames of American discontent with

British rule and powerfully influencing American revolutionaries, who in "The Age of Reason" (published 1794, followed by "The Age of Reason, Part II," published 1796) argues that there must be a plurality of worlds (McMullin 164) while ridiculing the idea of a multiplicity of Christs who lived and died and rose again on a multiplicity of worlds (165). Paine argues that one cannot be both a Christian and a pluralist at the same time (Crowe 117). Paine is not a Christian but apparently a Deist who questions Christianity and opposes organized religion in general. Nevertheless, many of Paine's critics called him an atheist, despite his stated belief in a Supreme Being, and even Theodore Roosevelt referred to him as "that filthy little atheist." James Anthony Froude (1818 -- 1894), an English historian, novelist, biographer, and essayist, writes about pluralism in 1849 in his autobiographical novel *Nemesis of Faith* by suggesting it is preposterous that the great Creator of the universe became a mortal human on a world of paltry importance in the grand universe to save souls (Crowe 333). He seems to imply that human beings are arrogant to suppose that God would deign to become incarnate on our miserable world of little value. Unsurprisingly, Froude was forced to resign his Oxford fellowship (ibid.). Gottfried Wilhelm Leibniz (1646 – 1716), a German philosopher, mathematician, metaphysician, and logician who independently invented the calculus, favors the plurality of worlds theory along with a belief that inhabitants populate planets around other suns and asks pertinent questions as to whether those inhabitants can be Baptized and serve as priests:

> If someone…came from the moon…, like Gonsales [Godwin's cosmic voyager]…, we would take him to be a lunarian; and yet we might grant him…the title *man*…; but if he asked to be baptized, and to be regarded as a convert to our faith, I believe that we would see great disputes arising among the theologians. And if relations were opened up between ourselves and these planetary men – whom M. Huygens says are not much different from men here – the problem would warrant calling an Ecumenical Council to determine whether we should undertake the propagation of the faith in regions beyond our globe. No doubt some would maintain that rational animals from those lands, not being descended from Adam, do not partake of redemption by Jesus

Christ....Perhaps there would be a majority decision in favour of the safest course, which would be to baptize these suspect humans conditionally....But I doubt they would ever be found acceptable as priests of the Roman Church, because until there was some revelation their consecrations would always be suspect....Fortunately we are spared these perplexities by the nature of things; but still these bizarre fictions have their uses in abstract studies as aids to a better grasp of the nature of our ideas. (cited in Crowe 29)

Jewish and Christian theologians of yesteryear adopted the pagan Greek concept of the Logos, the organizing force through which the universe was created, to develop the idea that human beings are rational because we are made in the image of the ultimate Rational Being, the Logos. Many theologians of later centuries write that inhabitants of other worlds are also rational because they are also made in the image of the Rational/Logos. Hence, the rationality of God becomes, after a fashion, somewhat comprehensible in the light of the rationality of the ordered universe which produced rational beings in the image of the Rational Creator Logos. If life, especially intelligent life, has developed on other worlds, then rational creatures throughout the universe must yearn for knowledge of not only where we come from but also where we are going, and both searches ultimately wind up in God.

Saint Thomas Aquinas (A.D. 1225 – 1274), an Italian Dominican philosopher and theologian known as Doctor Angelicus (the Angelic Doctor), suggests that the other Persons of the Trinity other than the Logos could become incarnate. Thomas F. O'Meara of Notre Dame writes, "Incarnation is only one divine activity, involving one creature as the object of that one special divine relationship: it hardly presents all that God can do and is doing" (5). Thomas Aquinas appears to believe that the Logos became Incarnate only once as Jesus Christ.

Guillaume de Vaurouillon (c. 1392 – 1463), avers that intelligent beings on other worlds have not sinned after the manner of Adam. He writes: "As to the question whether Christ by dying on this earth could redeem the inhabitants of another world, I answer that he was able to do this not only for our world but for infinite worlds.

But it would not be fitting for him to go to another world to die again" (O'Meara 6).

O'Meara writes that Melanchthon warns against multiple incarnations and redemptions on the grounds of the Protestant conviction that salvation comes from the God-man Jesus Christ and the Bible (O'Meara 2). Melanchthon wrote in *Initia doctrinae physicae* (Wittenberg, 1550), fol. 43:

> We know God is a citizen of this world with us, custodian and server of this world, ruling the motion of the heavens, guiding the constellations, making this earth fruitful, and indeed watching over us; we do not contrive to have him in another world, and to watch over other men also…the Son of God is One; our master Jesus Christ was born, died, and resurrected in this world. Nor does He manifest Himself elsewhere, nor elsewhere has He died or resurrected. Therefore it must not be imagined that there are many worlds, because it must not be imagined that Christ died and was resurrected more often, nor must it be thought that in any other world without the knowledge of the Son of God, that men would be restored to eternal life. (cited in Dick, *Plurality of Worlds* 89)

Timothy Dwight (1752 – 1817), American theologian, poet, and Yale president/minister, writes a series of sermons collected as *Theology Explained and Defended* in which he argues that Christ's Incarnation and Redemption are not only unique to Earth but that Redemption applies only to human beings: "in this world there exists a singular and astonishing system of Providence; a system of mediation between God and his revolted creatures.…This system, never found elsewhere, is accomplished here.…" (cited in Crowe 177). Dwight also argues, among other things, in favor of pluralism and inhabited worlds, claiming that the Lord made

> …the countless multitude of Worlds, with all their various furniture. With his own hand he lighted up at once innumerable suns, and rolled around them innumerable worlds. All these…he stored, and adorned, with a rich and unceasing variety of beauty and magnificence; and with the most suitable means of virtue and happiness. Throughout his

vast empire, he surrounded his throne with Intelligent creatures, to fill the immense and perfect scheme of being.... (cited in Crowe 175)

Dwight argues that the Lord can understand a cosmos "inhabited by beings...emphatically surpassing number" yet whose minds he knows intimately (cited in Crowe 175 – 176). He argues forcefully the traditional view that Christ created the universe and continues to maintain it:

> Throughout immensity, [Christ] quickens into life, action, and enjoyment, the innumerable multitudes of Intelligent beings. The universe, which he made, he also governs. The worlds, of which it is composed, he rolls through the infinite expanse with an Almighty and unwearied hand....From the vast store-house of his bounty he feeds, and clothes, the endless millions...and from the riches of his own unchangeable Mind informs the innumerable host of Intelligent creatures with ever-improving virtue, dignity, and glory. (cited in Crowe 177)

Dwight's position is that Christ's Incarnation and Redemption are not only unique to Earth but that Redemption applies only to human beings. Rev. William Leitch (1818 – 1864), a Presbyterian minister, believes the Incarnation of Christ is unique to the Earth and also rejects the idea that the merits of Christ's atoning sacrifice applies to extraterrestrials (Crowe 452). Leitch believes that extending the atonement to inhabitants of other worlds is unscriptural with the implication that only inhabitants of the Earth require redemption (cited in J.J. Davis 26).

Friedrich Gottlieb Klopstock (1724 – 1803), a German poet, wrote enthusiastically about a universe created by God with Christ at the center. He portrays the angel Gabriel traveling from planet to planet, all with Fallen creatures, including the Earth, but describes the Earth as

> ...Queen amongst the earths,
> Focal point of creation, most intimate friend of heaven,
> Second home of the splendor of God, immortal witness
> Of those secret sublime deeds of the great Messiah!
> (cited in Crowe 145)

For Klopstock, the universe is Christocentric, and his poetry reflects his belief that Christ is the redeemer of Fallen humanity while simultaneously portraying the life, death, and resurrection of Christ amidst a plurality of worlds populated with intelligent beings (Crowe 144). Nevertheless, Klopstock believes that "only the inhabitants of the earth have fallen into sin and they alone need salvation through a divine mediator" (cited in Crowe 145). Even so, Klopstock believes that Christ brought goodness that permeates the universe (ibid.).

The theological significance of intelligent beings who are not descendents of Adam and Noah is that such beings are not bound to the covenants God establishes with Adam and Noah (Rabbi Norman Lamm) and may have other economies of salvation (Greeley). Scripture attests that where there is no law, neither is there violation (Romans 4:15). Therefore, in order for inhabitants of other worlds to sin, they must violate a set of laws that are different from the ones given to inhabitants of the Earth of whom, if one takes Scripture literally, all are descendents of Adam and Noah. This raises questions such as whether morality is truly universal. The Divine Command Theorist asserts that God's laws are just and right and good because God commands them, but if God's commandments do not apply to inhabitants of other worlds, then extraterrestrials may have different economies of salvation (Greeley).

Another question this raises is the nature of sin: What is wrong for one species may not necessarily be wrong for another, unless one takes the view that the concept of sin is universal and that moral rules are also universal and must be universally applied. One may also take the view that some sins are universal while others are specific. For example, certain actions are sins for Jews but not for non-Jews. Since Christians are not antinomians,[36] it follows that

---

[36] Antinomian has two definitions: (1) one who rejects the idea that under the gospel dispensation of grace obedience to moral laws is unnecessary

some moral rules may be universal while others apply only to either Jews or inhabitants of the Earth and not necessarily to inhabitants of other worlds, while other rules are universal and do apply to extraterrestrials. Certainly, it is not currently possible to attempt to define what moral rules are universal in the absence of knowledge of the cultural and theological beliefs and ethics of beings from other worlds. William Whewell argues that "truth and falsehood, right and wrong, law and transgressions, happiness and misery, reward and punishment" stem from divine Government, claiming that "to transfer these to Jupiter or to Sirius, is merely to imagine those bodies to be a sort of island of Formosa, or new Atlantis, or Utopia, or Platonic Polity, or something of the like kind....there is no more wisdom or philosophy in believing such assemblages of beings to exist in Jupiter or Sirius, without evidence, than in believing them to exist in the island of Formosa, with the like absence of evidence" (61 – 62). I am arguing that God's divine Government is quite capable of extending to inhabitants of other worlds.

Some Jews also wonder whether or not there are Jews on other planets. A friend of mine, who prefers to remain anonymous, wrote me the following in an email message (26 September 2010):

> I do recall years ago talking to my sister about whether or not there were Jews on other planets. We were children, and we weren't being serious, but it seemed like an interesting idea.

---

and irrelevant to salvation because one is saved by faith alone so that the moral law is not binding on Christians; and (2) one who rejects a morality or moral system generally accepted by a society. Catholics generally believe that, while the ceremonial law of the Old Testament (i.e., circumcision and obedience to Jewish dietary regulations) no longer applies to Christians, nevertheless Christians are required to obey the moral law, and obedience or disobedience to the moral law can affect one's salvation. Many Protestants hold a similar position that Christians should obey the moral law (not the ceremonial law) but reject the view that obedience or disobedience to the moral law has any effect on salvation on the premise that one is justified by faith alone and saved by grace alone. Catholics typically respond that the theological theories sole fide (faith alone) and sola gratia (grace alone) violate James 2:24 while sola Scriptura violates 2 Thessalonians 2:15 and 3:6 (referring to Traditions) as well as 1 Timothy 3:15 (referring to the Church as "the pillar and foundation of truth").

> We came to the conclusion that if there were Jews, they
> wouldn't be called "Jews." Of course, we didn't go on to
> consider whether or not they would have the same prayers, an
> oral and written Torah[37], etc., but I wonder whether such a
> point was ever discussed in one of the Jewish academies and
> made its way into the Talmud somewhere. The Talmud would
> most likely wonder if such an alien could count as part of a
> minyan[38] or some other such practical matter. I happen to
> know that the problem of a minyan was considered for a
> "golem" which was a type of man-made robot or monster,
> most popularized in the legend of Rabbi Loew in Prague.

I find the question of whether a golem could be considered a Jew for
the purpose of a minyan interesting because it would say something
about whether an intelligent being from another world could be
considered Jewish enough to qualify as a Jew to make up an minyan.
Would it be possible for extraterrestrials to convert to Judaism just as
extraterrestrials could convert to Christianity? Orthodox Jews do not
consider a woman or women in the count of Jewish men to make up a
minyan. In other words, women may worship in a synagogue or
Jewish communal worship service, but it requires ten Jewish men to
make up a minyan, and, if there are nine men and one woman, there is
not a minyan. However, among Conservative Jews and Reform Jews,
a quorum of ten adults of either sex constitutes a minyan. For
Orthodox Jews, the question is what defines a Jewish "man"?
Suppose an extraterrestrial race of beings has three genders: Which
would be considered a "man" in order to qualify as a "Jewish man" to
make a minyan? According to Faye Levine, "Qualities of the

---

[37] For Jews, the Torah consists of the Pentateuch or the first five books of
the Bible (the Five Books of Moses), but the word Torah can also refer to
the rest of the Bible (the Prophets and the Writings) as well as the Oral
Torah (the Mishna and the Gemara collectively make up the works of
Jewish Oral Law and wisdom called the Talmud) including the teaching
and judicial decisions given by both the ancient Hebrew priests and later
rabbis. The word "torah" in Hebrew means "teaching" or "instruction" but
is often translated "law."

[38] A minyan is a quorum of Jewish males (Orthodox) or Jews of either sex
(Conservative and Reform) who are at least thirteen years of age required
for formal Jewish worship.

Golem," medieval Jewish rabbis actually discussed whether a golem can help make up a minyan. Faye Levine writes:

> Some medieval rabbis actually debated the hypothetical social situations which might arise if dealing with a golem: is it considered murder when you deactivate it? Does it count as a person when you need the *minyan* (ten people) required to have synagogue services? Should its corpse be handled as a Jewish corpse, and does nonstandard handling of its corpse cause impurity?

Rabbi Katz, citing Rabbi Loew, provides some answers:

o   A golem is exempt from performing the commandments in the Torah, but may. (Rabbi Loew ordered the golem to perform certain commandments to avoid suspicion in the community.)

o   A golem's body does not cause impurity after its "death" because it was made, not born.

o   A golem who rescues the Jewish people from catastrophes will have a share in the World to Come.

o   A golem should not be part of a *minyan*, because it has no legal status as a child of Israel (not having been born of children of Israel), and because it is not responsible for following any of the commands in the Torah.

The general consensus was that the golem is a non-human entity, because it does not possess a soul, nor was it born. It is also suggested that golem animals, like the three year-old calf mentioned in the Talmud, need not be slaughtered according to kosher laws and may be eaten with milk/cheese/etc., because it was not born of a mother. (This in reference to the prohibition of eating dairy products and meat together.)

It is unclear to me, based on the third bullet above, how a golem can have a share in the world to come if it lacks a soul. It was apparently Rabbi Tzvi Ashkenazi (The Chacham Tzvi) about 250 years ago who discusses whether a golem may be counted in order to make up a minyan, and the rabbi shows from the Talmud that it cannot ("Ask the Rabbi": http://ohr.edu/ask_db/ask_main.php/12/Q1/). What is the Jewish view towards whether inhabitants of other worlds who are not descended from the children of Adam and Eve can have souls? Even if extraterrestrials do not have souls, if they save Jews or humanity from catastrophe, may inhabitants of other worlds have a share in the world to come? Do the bodies of extraterrestrials cause impurity after their deaths, even though they are not "made" and may have hatched rather than have been born in a live birth as homo sapiens are? Do extraterrestrials definitionally have no legal status as children of Israel because they are not born of the children of Israel? Thus, because they are not born of a Jewish mother or even a homo sapiens mother, are extraterrestrials therefore not responsible for following any of the commands in the Torah? We know that Christians and people of other religions may convert to Judaism, so can extraterrestrials convert to Judaism, too? If extraterrestrials convert to Judaism, are they bound by the kosher laws even if they eat no earthly foods on their home planets? If extraterrestrials are capable of eating earthly foods, are extraterrestrials who convert to Judaism bound to keep the kosher laws on Earth? Since kosher laws often involve the humane slaughter of animals, would kosher laws apply to the humane slaughter of animals on other worlds? By the same token, if human beings travel to other worlds and are required to eat the food there to survive, do kosher laws apply to extraterrestrial animals for Jewish homo sapiens (i.e., no animals with cloven foots unless they chew the cud, etc.)? Can Jews, whether human or converted extraterrestrials, eat dairy products made from the milk of extraterrestrial animals and meat on the same day? In the Talmud are several discussions about whether it is kosher to eat cheese on chicken, with some rabbis saying no and some saying yes, because chickens lack mammary glands so there is no danger of violating the commandment against boiling a kid in its mother's milk (Exodus 23:19; 34:26: and Deuteronomy 14:21). If certain extraterrestrial animals have no mammary glands, is it kosher to eat them along with the dairy products of either Earth or extraterrestrial animals?

Back to Christianity, William Whewell writes Carl Friedrich Gauss (1777 – 1855) on 4 March 1854 that the only inhabited planet in the universe is the Earth since "all intelligent beings are by their nature sinful and the redemption (crucifixion) can not be repeated on the many millions of nebulae observed by Rosse" (cited in Crowe 208). Gauss replies on 5 May 1854 that the notion of extraterrestrials does not contradict even the most fervent defender of the Christian faith (ibid.).

In his *Plurality of Worlds* Whewell responds to Dr. Chalmers by suggesting that the very reason why humans are the only hnau in the universe is because God is mindful of them (17 – 18). Humans cannot be insignificant creatures on an insignificant planet because God was so mindful of us that he became Incarnate on our planet to redeem us.

William Haye (1694 – 1755) wrote *Religion Philosophi: or, The Principles of Morality and Christianity Illustrated from a View of the Universe, and Man's Situation in it* (London) that, like Copernicus, "with the greatest Probability (almost Certainty) imagine each Fixed Star to be a sun with Planets…surrounding it…; and all such Planets to be inhabited as well as the Earth…." In addition, he claims that "…Praise and Thanksgiving are continually ascending to [God's] Throne…from every Quarter of the Universe," making as a result "a general Religion, a joint Communion, a Universal Church" implying that we as human beings of Earth should love extraterrestrials "not as our own Species, but as our Fellow-creatures, and as Members of the same Church and Communion…." (cited in Crowe 86). Haye speculates that inhabitants of other worlds have fallen just as we have and God acts on those worlds either as "Judge" or as "indulgent Parent…. exalting the Rational Creatures of each Globe from a Material to a Spiritual, and from a Mortal to an Immortal State; transforming them into Angels; and from those Seminaries perpetually increasing the Host of Heaven (cited in Crowe 86-87). Nevertheless, Haye diverges from traditional Christianity by asserting that Jesus saves only human beings while extraterrestrials need the salvation of other extraterrestrials who were the Incarnations of the Logos with respect to their individual planets (Crowe 87), making him a Category 2 author.

Karl Rahner (1904 -- 1984), a modern German Catholic theologian and Jesuit priest and widely recognized as one of the foremost Christian scholars of the twentieth century, suggests that inhabitants of other worlds do not live their lives apart from sin and grace, implying that the grace of Jesus Christ applies to extraterrestrials as well as humans (O'Meara 7). Rahner regards the notion of the Incarnation of the Logos on our world as a problem for the intellect inasmuch as our world is but a tiny mote in a vast universe (ibid.). That said, Rahner does not dismiss the possibility of a multiplicity of incarnations (O'Meara 8).

Abbe Jean Terrasson (1670 – 1750), French priest and author best remembered for his fantasy novel *Life of Sethos, Taken from Private Memoirs of the Ancient Egyptians*, published in 1731, argues in favor of plurality and intelligent inhabitants, claiming that the teachings of the Church including the Bible do not unequivocally deny the pluralist position (Crowe 135). He also suggests that God became incarnate even on worlds which had not Fallen, claiming such inhabitants would deserve the honor even more than sinful beings (ibid.), making him a Category 1 author. He concludes, "We infer from all this not only that the Word has incarnated himself on all the planets, but in those where sin has not entered, he is born as other men" (cited in Crowe 135).

Crowe writes, "At another point he [Terrasson] counters the claim that Scripture explicitly states that there is but one Lord by interpreting it as applying only to the divine part of Christ's nature. Admitting that Christ's terrestrial incarnation and redemption have sufficient merit for the entire universe, he nonetheless suggests that, because Christ has a role both as savior and as teacher, his incarnation as teacher on sinless planets is fully appropriate (pp. 89 – 90)" (ibid.). Terrasson claims there is an infinite number of men on an infinite number of planets "chanting the praises of the Lord...." (cited in Crowe 135 – 136). He goes on, "What an admirable spectacle is also presented by the advance of the infinite number of men-God, who in the last day of the planet present to the eternal Father this infinite number of bands of the elect" (cited in Crowe 136). Terrasson further claims that angels are the resurrected souls of destroyed planets while demons are the resurrected evil souls (ibid.). The vast majority of authors in this era who expressed religious ideas, whether Catholic or Protestant, favor the idea of a plurality of worlds populated with inhabitants yet disagree on the issue of whether there are different economies of salvation, particularly with respect to multiple incarnations.

Scripture tells us that "all have sinned and fall short of the glory of God" (Romans 3:23). Therefore, it seems reasonable to conclude that inhabitants of other worlds fall under the category of "all" and have sinned, resulting in a fall from grace, just like Adam and Eve and all human beings (except Jesus and, according to Catholic teachings, the Virgin Mary who was preserved from the stain of original sin by the grace of Jesus Christ imputed to her at the very instant of her conception in the womb of Good Saint Anne). Again, I assert that it is possible that the grace of Jesus is imputed to sinful inhabitants of other worlds.

The Reverend Professor David Cairns in "Chalmers' Astronomical Discourses" suggests that, for Chalmers, Earth is a battleground between light and darkness that is going on to this day, although Jesus defeated Satan "in single combat" (419). The effects of Christ's defeat of Satan permeates the universe and its many inhabitants with God's grace, but the war goes on.

An anonymous author in 1858 wrote *The Stars and the Angels* which claims that Jesus redeems only human beings of Earth yet supports pluralism by saying that the inhabitants of other worlds are also made in the image of God (Crowe 340). The author speculates that humans from earth may resurrect to become inhabitants of other worlds (ibid.). Rev. Charles Louis Hequembourg in 1859 agrees with the theory that humans resurrect to become inhabitants of other worlds (Crowe 344 – 345). An anonymous reviewer of Whewell writes in favor of pluralism while maintaining that the Incarnation occurred only on the Earth while the benefits extend to inhabitants of other worlds (Crowe 349).

Sir David Brewster, as mentioned above, favors the notion that Christ's Redemptive work extends to inhabitants of other worlds. He writes, "the same constellations, Arcturus, Orion, and the Pleiades had sung together when the foundations of the world were laid and they rolled in darkness over Calvary, when the Prince of Life was slain" (19). He also writes:

> If we reject, then, the idea that the inhabitants of the planets do not require a Saviour, and maintain the more rational opinion, that they stand in the same moral relation to their Maker as the inhabitants of the Earth, we must seek for another solution of the difficulty which has embarrassed both the infidel and the Christian. How can we believe, says the timid Christian, that there can be inhabitants in the planets, when God had but one Son whom He could send to save them? If we can give a

satisfactory answer to this question, it may destroy the objections of the infidel, while it relieves the Christian from his anxieties.

When, at the commencement of our era, the great sacrifice was made at Jerusalem, it was by the crucifixion of a man, or an angel, or a God. If our faith be that of the Arian or the Socinian, the skeptical and the religious difficulty is at once removed: a man or an angel may be again provided as a ransom for the inhabitants of the planets. But if we believe, with the Christian Church, that the Son of God was required for the expiation of sin, the difficulty presents itself in its most formidable shape.

When our Saviour died, the influence of His death extended backwards, in the past, to millions who never heard His name, and forwards, in the future, to millions who will never hear it. Though it radiated but from the Holy City, it reached to the remotest lands, and affected every living race in the old and the new world. Distance in time and distance in place did not diminish its healing virtue." (148 – 149)

Brewster seems to believe that the benefits of the Incarnation, Crucifixion, and Resurrection of Christ extend to the inhabitants of other worlds throughout the universe in the same way that they extend to the inhabitants of lands on the Earth outside Jerusalem (149 – 150).

O'Meara notes, "When some Protestant theologies identify salvation, sanctification, and redemption with Calvary's atonement, they conflate quite different enterprises. Incarnation precedes and follows (in the Resurrection) the sufferings of Jesus. The Cross is not the only theology of redemption, nor is it doctrinally the necessary or full purpose of Incarnation" (11). Indeed, the position of the Catholic Church is that everything Jesus said and did is redemptive including his creation of the *kosmos*, his giving the Commandments, the utterances of his prophets, his Incarnation, birth, teachings, healings, miracles, passion, suffering, crucifixion, death, Resurrection, and ascension, as well as everything he has been doing on our world and in the *kosmos* since then. I maintain that the Incarnation is unique to the Earth, although Jesus may have visited and may continue to visit other worlds throughout the cosmos. O'Meara suggests that divine messengers on other worlds may bring important theological messages of truth, but they would not be incarnations (11). In the same paragraph, O'Meara seems to suggest that other incarnations are possible; I'm a little confused about what his position is.

Mainstream Protestants, like mainstream Catholics, are more sympathetic to the view that extraterrestrials are not demons but are probably ordinary people just like we are. Billy Graham also writes in a book on angels, "Some...have speculated that UFOs could very well be part of God's angelic host who preside over the physical affairs of universal creation. While we cannot assert such a view with certainty...nothing can hide the fact that these unexplained events are occurring with greater frequency around the entire world...UFOs are astonishingly angel-like in some of their reported appearances" (ibid.).

E.A. Milne in *Modern Cosmology and the Christian Idea of God* writes that many people have trouble with the concept of the Incarnation in a universe teeming with intelligent life (J.J. Davis 26 – 27). In response to the suggestion of multiple incarnations, Milne writes that a disciple of Jesus would "...recoil in horror from such a conclusion" and avers that Christians cannot believe in their wildest dreams the notion of "...the Son of God suffering vicariously on each of a myriad of planets" (ibid. 27). Milne defends the uniqueness of the Incarnation and Atonement by appealing to the uniqueness of the Earth. He suggests that the necessity of multiple incarnations can be avoided with the evangelization of ET's by radio (ibid.).

Krister Stendahl, former Bishop of Stockholm and former Dean of Harvard Divinity School, writes at a symposium sponsored by NASA in 1972, when asked about contact with inhabitants of other worlds, "That's great. It seems always great to me, when God's world gets a little bigger and I get a somewhat more true view of my place and my smallness in that universe" (ibid.).

A. Durwood Foster asks, "is faith in any way threatened by the possibilities here in view? Why should it be?" (ibid.). Foster suggests that the abiding mystery of God means that we should be open to the prospects of the unanticipated, including, one must assume, encounters with extraterrestrials (ibid.).

Lewis Ford, one of the disciples of the philosophy of Alfred North Whitehead known as process theologians, says, "salvation is not just limited to men but applies to all intelligent beings wherever they may dwell" (ibid.). Ford asserts that God causes evolution to occur throughout the universe so that God causes in a good way a universe that is more integrated and precious in his eyes and includes both terrestrial and extraterrestrial complex beings for whom he sets in motion processes so that they evolve and develop.

Some Fundamentalist Protestants who are literalists seem to hold the view that inhabitants of other worlds cannot exist because the Bible says nothing about them. Therefore, belief in extraterrestrials is anti-Biblical and de facto anti-Christian. These Fundamentalists seem to hold the view that Jesus died for the sins of human beings only and not inhabitants of other worlds because the Bible says only that Jesus died for human beings and does not say he died for extraterrestrials. The argument is unfounded because it claims that anything the Bible doesn't mention is untrue or unreal. This goes against John 21:25, "There are also many other things that Jesus did, but if these were to be described individually, I do not think the whole world would contain the books that would be written." The Bible also does not mention automobiles, computers, and the Internet, but that doesn't mean these things don't exist.

Some Fundamentalists seem to hold the view that belief in inhabitants of other worlds supports the theory of evolution since the extraterrestrials must have evolved separately on different worlds, and the theory of evolution they regard as a direct threat to their Christian faith because they believe God created the Earth and humanity alone in all the universe. Frank Allnut avers that UFOs are demons threatening to steal salvation from otherwise God-fearing Christians by causing them to believe the extraterrestrials may teach us a better way of life and religion when nothing is better than faith in Jesus Christ since in Christ alone can humans find redemption.

What is the Catholic response? These Fundamentalist views give rise to the need for a Catholic response; Catholics and mainstream Protestants have often been more open to broader interpretations of the Bible with respect to extraterrestrials than conservative Fundamentalist authors. Historically, Catholics are more open to the topic than others. Increasingly, Fundamentalists are loosening their stridency against evolution theory in the past 15 or so years. The notion that perhaps 7 days of creation are metaphorical and not necessarily 24 hour days is an increasingly acceptable idea among Fundamentalists recently. They believe we must redo interpretations while keeping Scripture infallible. Nevertheless, the main assessment is that Fundamentalists are historically opposed to evolution. What is at risk when someone says that extraterrestrials can be saved? For some Fundamentalists, what is at risk is demoting humanity to a lesser position in the eyes of God. As a Catholic, I believe that the salvation of extraterrestrials promotes humanity to an even greater position in the eyes of God: that of witnesses to Christ whose purpose is to spread the Good News throughout the cosmos.

I have argued that Scripture supports the idea that the redemptive work of Christ extends to extraterrestrials throughout the cosmos. I argue that the Scriptural usage of the term *kosmos* implies that the message of Christ, the Gospel, applies to all intelligent beings throughout the universe. If the Incarnation is an event unique to the Earth yet with universal effects, then it follows that Scripture should support this view, and I have argued that it does. Brewster writes:

> Neither in the Old nor in the New Testament is there a single expression incompatible with the great truth, that there are other worlds than our own which are the seats of life and intelligence. Many passages of Scripture, on the contrary, are favourable to the doctrine, and there are some, we think, which are inexplicable, without admitting it to be true. The beautiful text, for example, in which the Psalmist [Psalm 8:3-4 – cms] expresses his surprise that the Being who fashioned the heavens and ordained the moon and the stars, should be mindful of so insignificant a being as man, is, we think, a positive argument for a plurality of worlds (9 – 10)....He whom God made a little lower than the angels, whom He crowned with glory and with honour, and for whose redemption He sent His only Son to suffer and to die, could not, in the Psalmist's estimation, be an object of insignificance, and measured, therefore, by his high estimation of man, his idea of the heavens, the moon, and the stars must have been of the most transcendent kind (10 – 11)....The Psalmist must, therefore, have written under the impression either that the planets and stars were worlds without life, or worlds inhabited by rational and immortal beings (11).

Thomas O'Meara writes:

> Our species on earth is the subject of the biblical narratives.
> At no point in the Hebrew or Christian Scriptures do we learn
> that there is another race elsewhere in the universe, or that
> there is not. Nor is there any reason to think that the
> "economy of salvation," a phrase of Greek theologians, is
> anything other than a divine enterprise for our terrestrial race,
> the people in and for which it is enacted. It is superficial and
> arrogant to assert that the Christian or Jewish revelation of a
> wisdom plan for salvation history on earth is about other
> creatures. Faith affirms that the Logos has been incarnate on a
> planet located, in past Ptolemaic astronomy, in a small, closed
> system. The Logos, the second person of the divine Trinity,
> indeed has a universal domination, but Jesus, Messiah and
> Savior, has a relationship to terrestrials existing within one
> history of sin and grace (8).

O'Meara suggests that Christ as begotten Son (not created) makes
Jesus greater than celestial beings, arguing that the Resurrection is the
means of comprehending Christ's relationship to the Church and is
meant to be understood eschatologically (8 – 9). The story of Jesus is
the story of Creation, especially in the sense that every newborn
Christian is a new creation in Christ. Christ's Resurrection causes
believers to die in Baptism and be born again as new creations in
Christ. In my opinion, extraterrestrials can also experience this
spiritual rebirth in the waters and Spirit of Baptism. The message of
Christ is truly universal, in the eyes of the faithful, and so should
apply to inhabitants of other worlds. I believe that the universality of
the Incarnation and Resurrection is consistent with Scripture and
Christian theology. For O'Meara, Christ is the crux of terrestrial
theology, but I think Christian theology should expand to include
exotheology[39] if Christianity is to survive in a post-discovery-of-

---

[39] Exotheology is a term developed in the 1960s or early 1970s, perhaps
coined by Norman Lamm in his title "A Jewish Exotheology" in *Faith and
Doubt Studies in Traditional Jewish Thought*, Ktav Publication House,
1971, page 107 (see Bibliography); the word typically means the kind of
theology involved in explanations of how extraterrestrials fit into the
religious schema of the Jewish and Christian traditions.

extraterrestrials universe. O'Meara also notes, "Roch Kereszty reflects on the probability of other worlds and their relationships to the Son through incarnation, redemption, or another stance. He notes that without qualifying God's freedom the divine plan, as we experience it, suggests the offer of divine personal communion to intelligent creatures, and in this hypothetical theology Kereszty grounds a view of the cosmos as populated by creatures who are – in graced nature – our relatives" (10). In my opinion, it is consistent with Scripture and Christian theology to say that the Incarnation, Crucifixion, and Resurrection of Christ make humans and extraterrestrial intelligent beings brothers and sisters. It is consistent to say that all intelligent creatures, regardless of the color of their skin or the shape of their form, are made in the spiritual image of God and can be reborn in the spiritual image of Christ.

Brewster supports my interpretation of certain Scripture passages as evidence for the plurality of worlds theory. He writes:

> It is evident, from the text we have been considering [Psalm 8:3-4 above – cms], and from other passages of Scripture, that the word *Heavens*, so distinctly separated from the moon and the stars, represents a material creation, the work of God's fingers, and not a celestial space in which spiritual beings may be supposed to dwell; and hence we are entitled to attach the same meaning to the term wherever it occurs, unless the context forbids such an application of it. The writers, both in the Old and New Testament, speak of the heavens as a separate material creation from the earth, and there are passages which seem very clearly to indicate that they were regarded as the seat of life. When Isaiah [14:22] speaks of the heavens being *spread out as a tent to dwell in*, when Job [9:8-9] tells us that God, who *spread out the heavens, made Arcturus, Orion and Pleiades,* and the *chambers* of the south, and when Amos [9:6] speaks of Him who buildeth His stories in the heavens, (His house of *many mansions,)* they use terms which clearly indicate that the celestial spheres are the seat of life. In the book of Genesis [2:1], too, God is said to have finished the heavens and the earth, and *all the host of them.* Nehemiah [9:6] declares that God made the *heaven, the heaven of heavens, and all their host*, the earth and all things

that are therein, and that *the host of heaven worship Him.* The Psalmist [33:6] speaks of *all the host of the heavens as made by the breath of God's mouth,* (the process by which He gave life to Adam;) and Isaiah [14:12] furnishes us with a striking passage, in which the occupants of the earth and of the heavens are separately described. "I have made the earth, and created man upon it: I, even my hands, have stretched out the heavens, and all *their host have I commanded.*" But in addition to these obvious references to life and things pertaining to life, we find in Isaiah [14:18] the following remarkable passage, "For thus saith the Lord, that created the heavens, God himself that formed the earth and made it; he hath established it, *he created it NOT IN VAIN, he formed it TO BE INHABITED.*" Here we have a distinct declaration from the inspired prophet, that the *earth would have been created IN VAIN if it had not been formed to be inhabited;* and hence we draw the conclusion, that as the Creator cannot be supposed to have made the worlds of our system, all those in the sidereal universe in vain, they must have been formed *to be inhabited.*

In the New Testament we find passages not only in perfect harmony with the doctrine of a plurality of worlds, but which cannot be well explained without admitting it to be true. When St. John [1:3] tells us that the *Worlds* were made by the word of God, and St. Paul [Hebrews 1:3], that by our Saviour, the heir of all things, were made the *worlds*, we cannot suppose that they mean Globes of matter revolving without inhabitants, or without any preparation for receiving them. Our Saviour is described [Ephesians 1:9-10] as having made *All things*, and God is spoke of as purposing to "gather together in one *all things* in Christ *which are in the Heavens, and which are on the Earth.*" The creations thus described, under the name of *all things*, are clearly *creations in the heavens, or above them*, for Paul tells us [Ephesians 4:10] that Christ "ascended up *far above all heavens, that he might fill all things.*" In another place the Apostle speaks [Ephesians 3:9-11] of the "mystery hid in God, who created *all things* by Jesus Christ; to the intent that now, unto the principalities and powers in heavenly places, might be known by the church the manifold wisdom of God." When our Saviour speaks of the sheepfold of which He is the door, and of the sheep who follow Him and know His voice, and for whom He was to lay down His life, He adds, "and *other sheep I have which are not of this fold:* them also I must bring, and they shall hear my voice; and there shall be *one fold*, and one Shepherd" [John 10:16]. (12 – 14).

Brewster, then, clearly demonstrates my position that Scripture supports the plurality of worlds theory including the notion that Christ not only came for humans but also for inhabitants of other worlds.

Lewis suggests that Romans 8:19-23 implies that Paul, looking forward to the redemption of the cosmos, believes the benefits of the Atonement may extend to inhabitants of other worlds (J.J. Davis 28). J.J. Davis discusses Colossians 1:15-20 as providing Scriptural evidence that fallen beings throughout the universe may be redeemed by the Incarnation and atoning work of Christ on Earth without the necessity of multiple incarnations and atonements (28). Davis writes:

It is evident that in the Christological hymn of Colossians 1:15-20 redemption is cosmic in scope. The fact that in the space of six verses there are seven occurrences of the words "all," "all things," or "everything" is a clear indication that the redemptive effects of the atoning death of Christ are not limited to humanity, but extend in some way to the entire created universe. The apostle stresses in the most emphatic way the absolute supremacy of Christ in every realm of space, time, and human experience. This supremacy of Christ is asserted in creation (vv. 15, 16), providence (v. 17), incarnation (v. 19), reconciliation (v. 20), resurrection (v.l 18b), and in the church (v. 18a). (31)

Davis goes on to assert, essentially, that Christ is Lord of all Creation, the entire cosmos, who established order in the universe (31). Christ is the cause, the goal, and the end of the orderly universe (cf. John 1:3 and 1 Corinthians 8:6) (31). Both the pre-existent and existent Christ permeate Creation in a way that provides a stabilizing force in the structure of the universe (32). Christ's atoning death on the cross fills all of space and time and is the crux of the space-time continuum, the center of the universe and the center of time (32 – 33). Obviously, then, the benefits of the work of Christ extend to inhabitants of other worlds throughout the universe (33). Davis speaks of Reformation theology, specifically the Westminster Confession of Faith (1647), which asserts that "Christ the Mediator….fully satisfied the justice of his Father, and purchased…reconciliation…for all those whom the Father hath given him" and that the benefits of the Redemption permeate all of time, and if the Redemption is not limited by time, then it is not limited by space either, so that Christ's work on Earth redeems intelligent beings throughout God's created and divinely sustained universe (33 – 34). Thus, inhabitants of other worlds may be members of the elect just as people on Earth are members of the elect because all intelligent beings are redeemed people (cf. Romans 5:12 – 21 and 1 Corinthians 15:45 – 49) (34). Davis maintains that his "conclusion is consistent with the earlier opinions of Aquinas, Vorilong, Chalmers, and Milne, but is based on a more developed exegetical argument from biblical theology" (34).

The website www.out.org/torah/ti/5760/vayeitzei60.htm discusses the Jewish four levels of interpreting Scripture. The first level is *pshat* or the literal or the plain meaning, that is, the simple reading of the text in the context of the rest of the text. The second level is *remez* or allusionary or the implied meaning (for example, the Torah codes). The third level is *drush* or exegesis or metaphorical or a non-literal reading that gives a scholarly meaning. The fourth level is *sod* or the hidden meaning or mystical which is synonymous with Kabbalah/Nistar. Translating the Greek word *kosmos* as "universe" or "known sphere of existence" is perhaps the mystical fourth level of interpretation.

The Encylopedia Britannica cites "four major types of hermeneutics….the literal, moral, allegorical, and anagogical" (*Hermeneutics: Bib. Crit.*):

> Literal interpretation asserts that a biblical text is to be interpreted according to the "plain meaning" conveyed by its grammatical construction and historical context. The literal meaning is held to correspond to the intention of the authors. This type of hermeneutics is often, but not necessarily,

associated with belief in the verbal inspiration of the Bible, according to which the individual words of the divine message were divinely chosen. Extreme forms of this view are criticized on the ground that they do not account adequately for the evident individuality of style and vocabulary found in the various biblical authors. Jerome, an influential 4th-century biblical scholar, championed the literal interpretation of the Bible in opposition to what he regarded as the excesses of allegorical interpretation. The primacy of the literal sense was later advocated by such diverse figures as Thomas Aquinas, Nicholas of Lyra, John Colet, Martin Luther, and John Calvin.

A second type of biblical hermeneutics is moral interpretation, which seeks to establish exegetical principles by which ethical lessons may be drawn from the various parts of the Bible. Allegorization was often employed in this endeavour. The Letter of Barnabas (c. 100 AD), for example, interprets the dietary laws prescribed in the Book of Leviticus as forbidding not the flesh of certain animals but rather the vices imaginatively associated with those animals.

Allegorical interpretation, a third type of hermeneutics, interprets the biblical narratives as having a second level of reference beyond those persons, things, and events explicitly mentioned in the text. A particular form of allegorical interpretation is the typological, according to which the key figures, main events, and principal institutions of the Old Testament are seen as "types" or foreshadowings of persons, events, and objects in the New Testament. According to this theory, interpretations such as that of Noah's ark as a "type" of the Christian church have been intended by God from the beginning.

Philo, a Jewish philosopher and contemporary of Jesus, employed Platonic and Stoic categories to interpret the Jewish scriptures. His general practices were adopted by the Christian Clement of Alexandria, who sought the allegorical sense of biblical texts. Clement discovered deep philosophical truths in the plain-sounding narratives and precepts of the Bible. His successor, Origen, systematized these hermeneutical principles. Origen distinguished the literal, moral, and spiritual senses but acknowledged the spiritual (i.e., allegorical) to be the highest. In the Middle Ages, Origen's threefold sense of scripture was expanded into a fourfold sense by a subdivision of the spiritual sense into the allegorical and the anagogical.

The fourth major type of biblical hermeneutics is the anagogical, or mystical, interpretation. This mode of interpretation seeks to explain biblical events as they relate to or prefigure the life to come. Such an approach to the Bible is exemplified by the Jewish Kabbala, which sought to disclose the mystical significance of the numerical values of Hebrew letters and words. A chief example of such mystical interpretation in Judaism is the medieval Zohar. In Christianity, many of the interpretations associated with Mariology fall into the anagogical category.

Scripture also indicates that Yahweh is the God of the sky or the heavens. For example, Jesus teaches his disciples to pray "Our Father who art in heaven." Another example is the descent of the Holy Spirit on Jesus at his Baptism and also his ascent into heaven as described in Acts of the Apostles (Lewis xii). Since God lives in the sky, it follows that God is an extraterrestrial, in a sense, although not per se an inhabitant of another world but perhaps an honorary inhabitant of all worlds since God is the creator of all worlds. The very existence of all the worlds in the universe is evidence for the existence of God, leading us to the idea of a divine Designer.

Chapter 8

Impact on Christianity in the Twentieth and Twenty-first Centuries and Beyond

No matter how far out belief in extraterrestrials may seem to some people, the fact is that belief in their existence has become both widespread and en vogue.   In an issue of *Popular Mechanics*, Kenneth Nealson, a scientist on the National Academy of Sciences Subcommittee for Solar System Exploration, said, "The search of life is no longer a fringe type of thing." Politicians, scientists, astronauts, and various celebrities (America's unofficial worldview spokespersons) concur that intelligent extraterrestrial life must exist within the universe and that it is "arrogant" to presume that humanity is the only intelligent life form. A survey by *USA Today* revealed that "61 percent of Americans say they believe humans are not the only life form in the galaxy."
> -- Bobby Brewer: "Seven Things You Should Know about UFO's" in the *Christian Research Journal, Vol. 25, Number 2 (2002)*

Reason is our soul's left hand, Faith her right.
> -- John Donne on Faith

Faith is reason grown courageous.
> -- Sherwood Eddy on Faith

Intelligence must follow faith, never precede it, and never destroy it.
> -- Thomas a Kempis on Faith

Empirical knowledge cannot be certain, but the Catholic Church teaches that religious knowledge imparted to us via the medium of the Catholic Church is indeed certain because it is revealed by God. The position of the Catholic Church is that the Tradition of the Catholic Church is the Word of God, and the Bible is the revealed Word of God that is true because the Bible is part of the Tradition of the Catholic Church. The Bible contains stories and ideas that lend support to the argument that extraterrestrials exist in the universe. The Bible, in citations given above, support the idea that God has destined Christians to spread the Gospel of Jesus Christ to inhabitants of other worlds in the far flung reaches of the universe.

The Catholic Youth Bible (New American Bible) comments on the Gospel of John 1 on page 1354:

"The 'Cosmic Christ': Science fiction or fantasy movies and books often include important eternal beings or powers. The *Star Wars* series has 'the Force.' The Chronicles of Narnia, a fantasy series by C.S. Lewis, has Aslan, the noble lion who is the creator and savior of Narnia. The poem that begins the Gospel of John reads like something from a great science fiction classic. Only, in this case, the story is not fiction but God's revelation! The poem presents Jesus as the Word, who has existed from all time, the one through whom all things came into being. The Scriptures tell us a great mystery here: the man named Jesus, who lived in Nazareth some two thousand years ago, is the eternal God, who 'became flesh and made his dwelling among us' (Jn 1, 14). No one has ever seen God. But Jesus, the perfect image of God, 'has revealed him' (verse 18) in flesh and blood."

George V. Coyne, S.J., priest, astronomer, and former director of the Vatican Observatory, writes, "To use the concepts coined by Galileo, both the Book of Nature and the Book of Sacred Scripture can be sources of coming to know God's love incarnate in the universe" ("Extraterrestrial Life" 185). Coyne also writes, "There is deeply embedded in Christian theology, throughout the Old and New Testament but especially in St. Paul and in St. John the Evangelist, the notion of the universality of God's redemption and even the notion that all creation, even the inanimate, participates in some way in his redemption" ("Extraterrestrial Life" 187). Michael Crowe writes, "[Reverend Robert] Knight next argues that passages in the New Testament, especially in the Pauline epistles, refer to a plurality of worlds (pp. 39-48)" (336). [Knight is an Anglican vicar in Polesworth in central England.] The divine universe-creating act is miraculous. The miracle of creation may be a breakdown in an already existing system. Genesis 1:1 seems to support such an idea by beginning its tale in medias res ("in the middle of things").

In the Modern Catholic Church, the idea of extraterrestrials and their salvation is not new but is frequently accepted by Catholic scholars who have given the idea a reasonable amount of thought. George Coyne of the Vatican Observatory writes positively about extraterrestrials and their salvation. Earnest Barnes, Bishop of

Birmingham, addressed the question about extraterrestrials in his Gifford Lectures in 1927 and 1929. E. A. Milne, an Oxford cosmologist, writes:

> Is it irreverent to suggest that an infinite God could scarcely find the opportunities to enjoy Himself, to exercise His godhead, if a single planet were the sole seat of His activities? (Davies 45)

Milne also wrote in his book *Modern Cosmology and the Christian Idea of God* :

> It is not outside the bounds of possibility that these are genuine signals from intelligent beings on other "planets," and that in principle, in the unending future vistas of time, communication may be set up with these distant beings (Davies 45)

All Christians are "creationists" in the sense that all believe that God is our Creator, but not all creationists embrace so-called "creation science" propagated by certain Protestant evangelical groups. Certainly, the Catholic Church does not necessarily embrace so-called "creation science," as many Catholics embrace the Augustinian idea that God may have engineered the universe to produce life in the same way that engineers engineer their products to function in particular ways such as heaters being engineered to produce heat or air conditioners being engineered to produce cold air. It's possible that the creation of the first cell may have needed a divine impetus (McMullin 157). So, the development of extraterrestrials may have occurred by similar evolutionary procedures because God wants creatures to develop intelligence, indicating a guiding divine hand in the development of intelligence in God's creatures.

Carl Sagan wrote: "Space exploration leads directly to religious and philosophical questions" (Peters, "Introduction" 1). Many people seem to think that Christianity will disintegrate when extraterrestrials are encountered, but I think that, while it will have a profound effect on religious beliefs, Christianity will survive. Christianity will be strengthened by the discovery of extraterrestrials. Many Christian theologians have greeted the issue positively.

L.C. McHugh, SJ, says that inhabitants of other worlds "would fall under the universal dominion of Christ the King, just as we and even the angels do." J. Edgar Bruns, a New Testament scholar and president of Notre Dame Seminary in New Orleans, says, "...the significance of Jesus Christ extends beyond our global limits. He is the foundation stone and apex of the universe and not merely the Savior of Adam's progeny" (cited in Peters, "Contemporary Theology" 3). In this view, it would seem that the Catholic Church should evangelize inhabitants on other worlds just as the early explorers of the New World evangelized the Indians. Karl Rahner, an important Catholic scholar, appears to have some agreement with Tillich, saying that the existence of extraterrestrials "can today no longer be excluded" (cited in Peters, "Contemporary Theology" 3). Rahner continues, "In view of the immutability of God in himself and the identity of the Logos with God, it cannot be proved that a multiple incarnation in different histories of salvation is absolutely unthinkable" with the result that human theologians "will not be able to say anything further on this question" on the grounds that God's revelation to humanity has not yet provided any information on the matter since Christian Revelation has the task of providing information on "the salvation of humankind, not to provide an answer to questions which really have no important bearing on the realization of this salvation in freedom" (ibid.).

Grace Wolf-Chase, Ph.D., writes "One Scientist's Thoughts on the Theological Implications of the Existence of Extraterrestrial Life." In it, she cites Colossians 1:15-20: "(Jesus) is the image of the invisible God, the firstborn of all creation, for in him all things in heaven and on earth were created, things visible and invisible...all things have been created through him and for him...for in him the fullness of God was pleased to dwell and through him God was pleased to reconcile to himself all things, whether on earth or in heaven by making peace through the blood of his cross." She claims that the Incarnation and the Cross profoundly change everything in the universe (2). Even though we have not yet encountered extraterrestrials, it is not simply academic to explore the theological and Christological implications of the Incarnation, Crucifixion, Death, and Resurrection of Jesus of Nazareth for the entire created universe. Are all beings in the created universe separated from God as the result of the Fall of Adam and Eve? (2). She asks: "Are the 'memes'[40] (to use Dawkins' term) of civilization as universal as the laws of nature are? Are all civilizations in the cosmos 'fallen' and in need of a savior? If so, it is not just an intellectual exercise to ask who will be their savior, or how we will relate to them as children of God" (ibid.). She also writes, "What effects might such a discovery have on our Christian understanding of God?" (4). I believe the answer to the first question is "yes" in terms of Romans 3:23 ("all have sinned and are deprived of the glory of God"); to the second question "yes" because, whatever our differences with extraterrestrials, mentally and spiritually we should be alike enough to communicate and exchange ideas and cultures and memes; to the third question is "yes" not only in terms of Romans 3:23 but also in terms of 1 John 2:2 ("He is expiation for our sins, and not for our sins only but for those of the whole *kosmos*"); and to the fourth and last question the answer is that discovery of extraterrestrials will have a tremendous impact that will enhance and expand our understanding of God as well as what it means to be made in the image of God. We will no longer see God as restricted or limited to the creation of human beings exclusively but as the greater Creator of a wide variety of intelligent beings scattered throughout the cosmos. The more complex our understanding of the universe becomes, the more we realize how much more complex is the God who created that universe.

If extraterrestrials exist, did Christ come to save them? Did inhabitants of other worlds sin and need redemption? George Coyne says "yes" to both questions (*The Many Worlds and Religion*). What are the theological implications for our understanding of God? Did God choose a different way to redeem inhabitants of other worlds? Saint Paul and Saint John both speak vigorously of universal redemption and salvation, and all Creation participates in Christ's redemptive work (Coyne, *Many Worlds and Religion*). God sent his Son to redeem ETs (Coyne, ibid.). Can Jesus Christ the God-Human exist simultaneously on other planets? This question is difficult to answer because we lack proper knowledge of other worlds, at least at

---

[40] Richard Dawkins is a British scientist who coined the word "meme" in *The Selfish Gene* (1976), meaning an evolutionary principle which explains how ideas and cultural phenomena spread throughout societies. Examples of memes include not only religious beliefs but also music, lyrics, and technology.

this time (Coyne, ibid.). Thomas Aquinas, while disagreeing with pluralism, nevertheless argues that all rational creatures have souls, so, if extraterrestrials are discovered to have rational minds, it follows that they have souls in need of redemption.

Some Christians are uncomfortable with the concept of extraterrestrials because it puts humans in a non-unique place in the universe. Michaud writes: "Many scientists believe that more advanced intelligences, if they ever have organized religions, will abandon them. [Jill C.] Tarter argued that the monotheistic religions typical of Earth would be inconsistent with very long-lived civilizations; if such civilizations had any religion, it would be devoid of factions and disputes. For old technologies to exist, such a universal religion must be compatible with scientific inquiry" (206). Philosophers and theologians have debated for centuries whether or not an infinite number of Sons of God will be required among inhabitants of other worlds including an infinite number of resurrections (Tarter 144). Discovery of extraterrestrials will affect most human religions, and Christianity is no exception, but will the Catholic Church react with aplomb, outrage, reconciliation, or rejection? (cf. Tarter 144). Tarter suggests that any civilizations we detect with our radio telescopes will necessarily be longer-lived than we are precisely because it took so long for the signal to arrive on Earth, and so, being technologically superior, they will probably have outgrown religious beliefs, if they ever had religions to begin with (Tarter 145). I completely disagree. Tarter also claims that the very existence of technologically-advanced civilizations means that they either had no religion to begin with or they will have a solitary religion without disputes over its technical points (Tarter 146). I think this is nonsense. As a scientist, Tarter seems to be creating extraterrestrials in her own image. That's a big mistake. Tarter says that human history shows that more technologically primitive cultures tend to adopt the religion of technologically superior cultures they encounter, so we will probably adopt the religion of extraterrestrials, if they have one. I think Tarter is ignoring the very common occurrence of syncretism in which religions tend to influence one another, and I think our encounter with extraterrestrials will no doubt result in similar syncretistic trade of religious beliefs.

Tarter creates a dichotomy between science and religion that, in my opinion, does not exist, at least in the thinking of the Catholic

Church which has produced some of the greatest scientists the world has ever known. Tarter assumes that encounters with extraterrestrials will cause human religions to disintegrate under the weight of their own disproven mythologies. I think human religions will adapt the way they always do. Tarter writes, "In contrast, those religions with the most catholic of doctrines will begin to adopt a more cosmic perspective" (148). I think the Catholic Church has already adopted a more cosmic perspective and will not go quietly into the night, bowing to the altar of science. Science is not by definition atheistic, and it is wrong for both scientists and the laity to think so. Catholics in general embrace both science and religion as compatible theories of the nature of things.

Covenant Theology suggests that extraterrestrials who are not the descendents of Adam and Eve may not be bound by the covenants God made with Adam and Eve, Noah, Abraham, Moses, and Jesus. If God made other covenants with extraterrestrials, will humans respect them? McMullin says, "Baptism is open, however, to people of any race who choose to be followers of Christ" (McMullin 161). McMullin doesn't address whether Baptism is necessary for an unFallen race. Baptism may be construed as conferring grace to extraterrestrials who have sinned. I speculate that extraterrestrials are probably Fallen just like humans are on the grounds that the Bible says that no one is perfect because "all have sinned and fall short of the glory of God," assuming that "all" includes humans and inhabitants of other worlds.

McMullin asks, "Is salvation possible outside the chosen group?" (161). If extraterrestrials can be saved, then what is the purpose of the Bible which tells of the salvation history of God's chosen people, Jews and Christians? Will every extraterrestrial race have its own "Eve" who commits Original Sin and infects the extraterrestrials with a genetic predisposition to sin? Walter Miller in "Canticle for Leibowitz" and C.S. Lewis in "Perelandra" address the question of an Eve preserving the sacred innocence of her descendants (McMullin 168). McMullin writes, "There is nothing, it would seem, about the doctrine of original sin that would make it more or less likely that there should be ETI out there in the first place" (169).

The question arises as to whether extraterrestrials have souls. It would seem that inhabitants of other worlds must have souls given them by God in order for them to develop into a rational society. If inhabitants of other worlds do not have souls, then, as rational creatures ourselves, we might conclude that humans have no souls, which is clearly unacceptable theology. McMullin asks, "How can we limit the ways in which the Creator of a galactic universe might relate to agents like ourselves on other distant planets?" (172). A second or multitude of incarnations on different planets is unnecessary because the grace of Jesus Christ overflows to the whole universe. The universe is fine-tuned towards life (Leslie and Coyne), so God may have established a pattern resulting in many forms of intelligent life in the universe. The anthropic principle[41] may be invoked to assert that God deliberately fine-tuned the universe with a disposition towards the development of life, including intelligent life. God is more than a chef who put together the right ingredients to produce a miraculous universe teeming with intelligent life. Fred Hoyle suggests that the anthropic principle is evidence for the intelligent design theory (Davies 137).

What will the discovery of inhabitants of other worlds mean for our Christian worldview and our place in the universe? The atoning sacrifice of Christ was a onetime event which saves humans and inhabitants of other worlds alike. C.S. Lewis in *Perelandra* discusses the view that some extraterrestrials may not have experienced a Fall and so may not need the atoning sacrifice of Christ. God, some think, has become incarnate in a variety of extraterrestrial forms to save everyone. Rock singer Sydney Carter sang the following:

> Who can tell what other cradle,
> High above the Milky Way,
> Still may rock the King of Heaven
> On another Christmas Day?

God may appear in an infinite variety of forms on an infinite variety of worlds without diminishing his power anymore than the Cross

---

[41] The anthropic principle (1974) in cosmology is divided in two: The weak anthropic principle is that the observed conditions of the universe are geared (or designed) so that the observer must exist; the strong anthropic principle is that the universe is geared (or designed) so that the existence of intelligent life is necessary and inevitable.

diminished his power. The Logos who is Jesus embodies and is "the power of God and the wisdom of God" (1 Corinthians 1:24). Wisdom in the Old Testament is feminine (the Hebrew concept for the organizing force through which the universe was created, the Greek counterpart being the masculine Logos), so God is both male and female, both Father and Mother, so we can assume that, since God creates intelligent beings in God's own image, extraterrestrials are also male and female. Norman Lamm suggests that, while human beings are not necessarily the only apple of God's eye, our lack of uniqueness does not mean that humans are insignificant or inconsequential (133). God, according to Lamm, is concerned with all creatures throughout his vast universe (ibid.). Lamm adds:

> For Maimonides, and this is certainly a viable and reasonable position for contemporary theists, man may not *be* the purpose *of* the universe, yet he may *have* a purpose *in* the universe. Every species in creation, according to Maimonides, has as its immanent purpose the will of God. Mechanistic origin and teleological end are identical: all existence comes from God and exists for God. Mankind, like every other kind, fulfills the will of God by its very existence. Whatever detracts from man's existence frustrates the purpose and will of the Creator.
>
> For the believing Jew, therefore, man can accept a far humbler place in the universe than previously assigned to him without surrendering his intrinsic worth and meaningfulness before God. The religious person does not consider mankind, even if it is not the "axle of the world," as nothing but a swarm of two-legged vermin emerging accidentally from a primitive scum to disfigure the face of the earth; even as he does not take seriously Hegel's brash statement that the stars are nothing but "a rash on the sky." All that exists is endowed by the Maker with the dignity of purpose. The purpose of man's life, therefore, is profoundly religious and very real – and unaffected by the fact that he is not the sole *telos* for which all else was called into being. (138)

One may conclude, therefore, that every intelligent creature is precious in the eyes of God, male or female, human or extraterrestrial.

The purpose of hnau is to glorify God not ourselves. The Incarnation of the Logos does not change God; it changes us. Lamm also writes: "The discovery of fellow intelligent creatures elsewhere in the universe, if indeed they do exist, will deepen and broaden our appreciation of the mysteries of the Creator and His creations. Man will be humble, but not humiliated. With renewed fervor he will be able to turn to God, whose infinite goodness and Providence are not limited to, but certainly include, one small planet on the fringes of the Milky Way" (157). Humans may be only one species of creatures among many, but we are still unique. Indeed, every individual, human or extraterrestrial, is unique in the eyes of God the creator and sacred in the sense of being part of a sacred universe.

Indeed, the natural universe is sacramental in character. Catholics believe the universe contains infinite sacramentals, whereas the Greek Orthodox say all is sacrament. This is a very panentheistic view. Jesus is the God become Man who ascended to heaven to sit at the right hand of God the Father because Jesus is God the Son, so all of us can become like Jesus, including inhabitants of other worlds, assuming we evangelize them (or find ourselves being evangelized by them). Jesus's transformation was a prelude to the transformation all Christians experience as born-again-in-Baptism children of God. It is significant that water is an essential component in both the development of life and rebirth in Baptism. Will inhabitants of other worlds hold the same reverence for water? Peacocke says, "But because it is (albeit unique for Christians) a manifestation of this eternal and perennial mode of God's interaction in, with, and under the created order, what was revealed in Jesus the Christ could also, in principle, be manifest both in other human beings and indeed also on other planets, in any sentient, self-conscious, nonhuman persons (whatever their physical form) inhabiting them that are capable of relating to God." This vision of a universe permeated by the ever-acting, ever-working, and potentially explicit self-expression of the divine Word/Logos was never better expressed than in the poem of Alice Meynell cited above.

Human life is either a fluke, a cosmological imperative, or a miracle (Paul Davies who concludes that human life is a cosmological imperative). Ernan McMullin and George Coyne discuss the view that our ideas about Christ, including his life, teachings, healings, miracles, crucifixion, death, resurrection, and ascension might need to be modified to reflect the new cosmological order. What is Redemption for us and for inhabitants of other worlds? Is Redemption the same for us and inhabitants of other worlds or different? Did extraterrestrials have their own Christ and should we worship at the altar of these other "Christs"? The current Catholic view seems to be that Christ became mortal only once, died only once, and rose again only once to effect the salvation of all, including, by my theory, inhabitants of other worlds. Some Catholics like Andrew Greeley suggest that it is presumptuous of us to think we know everything about what God has done on other worlds throughout the cosmos (personal email exchange with Fr. Greeley). Coyne suggests that Scripture and Tradition depict God as loving us without explaining himself or his creation to us (see the Book of Job in which God asks Job why he questions the justice of God in the face of the reality of the divine creation) (Dick, *Many Worlds* xi). Thomas Chalmers admonishes us, "Think it not enough that you carry in your bosom an expanding sense of the magnificence of creation, but pray for a subduing sense of the authority of the Creator" (*Discourse VII* 240).

If we accept that God became human in the person of Jesus of Nazareth, then the question arises as to why God chose the Earth out of all the planets in all the galaxies in all the vast universe upon which to become Incarnate. Is the Earth special or unique in some way? Some astronomers claim that the Earth is orbiting an ordinary star in the spiral arm of an ordinary galaxy of the vast universe, but what is the definition of ordinary in the context of planets? Earth may not be ordinary at all, but we currently lack the knowledge to say one way or the other with any kind of accuracy.

What is the cosmic significance of the historical Jesus who was born on an ordinary planet in an ordinary galaxy in the vast universe? Do extraterrestrials damage our theology of Christ as God Incarnate? Peacocke says, "Only a contemporary theology that can cope convincingly with such questions can hope to be credible today" (103). If the universe were governed strictly and exclusively by natural laws, then everything would be completely uniform without diversity, whereas if chaos were the norm, then no patterns would develop capable of producing life, so the only possible explanation for our orderly universe with diversity of planets and living things is that laws and chance cooperate to produce what we know as reality

(Peacocke 104). Only God could have produced such an ingenious system. God is the ultimate basis and source of both law and chance (Peacocke 104).

Some science fiction authors like James Blish suggest that our Fallen nature is part of the divine order of things by depicting in his novel a planet of completely rational snakes with no war or crime that has no room for religious faith such that the planet is an object of temptation for humanity and must be destroyed/exorcised for the sake of maintaining the divine order. Do the snakes have preternatural innocence or prelapsarian innocence? Is preternatural innocence a threat to faith? Greg Bear comments in his introduction to Blish's novel that Lithia is "[a] *planet without original sin -- and without God.* Yet in Catholic theology, Satan can create only illusion, not real works. Lithia is solid, real...Unless it is the most extravagant deception in the long and tormented history of the Fall! The tale proceeds with all due speed through politics and theology, villains and heroes, to a stunning and brilliantly ambiguous conclusion. And the questions remain: Is God cruel, and Satan creative? Is it best to live on a virtually perfect world, oblivious to the truth, like a glowing brick surround by the fulgurous evil of Satan's furnace?" (vi -- vii). Walter Miller found Blish's ideas "theologically insane." Is preternatural innocence indeed a threat to the Catholic faith? C.S. Lewis maintains that humanity's Fall from Grace was neither desired nor part of the divine order of things by depicting a race on another planet whose inhabitants are not Fallen and experience thriving societies with great faith in their Creator. Some critics denounce Lewis as "anti-sf" on the theory that "real" science fiction not only does not allow for the existence of God but also is actively hostile to organized religion in general. For some authors, God is indeed persona non grata, but not so for many great science fiction writers and their stories. For many, God is just as real as the text you are reading and just as impossible to ignore.

E. A. Milne writes in his book *Modern Cosmology and the Christian Idea of God* :

> [It is] of the essence of Christianity that God intervenes in History....God's most notable intervention in the actual historical process, according to the Christian outlook, was the Incarnation. Was this a unique event, or has it been reenacted

on each of a countless number of planets? The Christian
would recoil in horror from such a conclusion. We cannot
imagine the Son of God suffering vicariously on each of a
myriad of planets. The Christian would avoid this conclusion
by the definite supposition that our planet is in fact unique.
What then of the possible denizens of other planets, if the
Incarnation occurred only on our own? We are in deep waters
here, in a sea of great mysteries. (Davies 45-46)

Milne suggests that we humans may convey the idea of the
Incarnation to inhabitants of other worlds by means of radio
technology. E. L. Mascall is a philosopher priest who completely
rejects Milne's ideas in his Hampton Lectures of 1956. Mascall
writes: "It is in sharp contrast with the attitude of the great classical
tradition of Christian thought" with respect to the Passion of Jesus to
believe that "the necessary and sufficient condition for it to be
effective for the salvation of God's creatures is that they should know
about it" (Davies 46). Mascall is of the opinion that Christ died and
rose again only for human beings of Earth and not for extraterrestrials
elsewhere in the universe. George Coyne suggests that the
Incarnation of God into the forms of extraterrestrials is not necessary
for inhabitants of other worlds to be saved, claiming that God is
powerful enough to save such inhabitants who have sinned in ways
other than literal incarnations (Davies 47). So, multiple incarnations
of God are not only not necessary but not even likely in terms of
Catholic theology. Davies writes: "The difficulty this presents to the
Christian religion is that if God works through the historical process,
and if mankind is not unique to his attentions, then God's progress and
purposes will be far more advanced on some other planets than they
are here on Earth. As Barnes pointed out long ago: 'If God only
realizes Himself within an evolutionary progress, then elsewhere He
has reached a splendour and fullness of existence to which Earth's
evolutionary advance can add nothing'" (Davies 50). Davies believes
that ETs may be more spiritually advanced than human beings, and,
while some humans would regard this as an opportunity to learn more
and become more spiritually advanced themselves, other humans
would regard this as a threat to our species and religious convictions
(Davies 50-51). Davies speculates that other intelligent beings may
be right in our own backyard in the form of intelligent computers, and

what does that mean for our theology? (Davies 51-53). Davies also suggests that humans will either reject religion as inhabitants of other worlds have done, or, in the face of spiritually advanced extraterrestrials, humans will adopt their religion (Davies 54-55). I do not agree with this at all. I agree with Coyne that God chooses whatever means is best to save all people, humans and extraterrestrials alike, but, if inhabitants of other worlds are more spiritually advanced than humans, then the result will be two-way syncretism of one another's religions.

In science fiction stories, extraterrestrials are either portrayed as conquering warriors out to destroy the Earth or space brothers here to bring peace and prosperity to all humanity. In reality, I think our encounter with extraterrestrials will be somewhere in between: Extraterrestrials will have their own cultures whose people want to preserve their way of life even while exploring new worlds and developing new relationships with new races of beings such as humans who to them are inhabitants of another world. Just as encounters of some human cultures with other human cultures have often been both beneficial and harmful, especially to less technologically advanced cultures, so our encounters with extraterrestrials may bring beneficent cultural exchanges as well as cultural conflicts. Cultures of inhabitants of other worlds may be just as varied as human cultures, and we should not expect beginning encounters to be anything other than complex. Beginnings are always delicate times. If extraterrestrials are friendly, we may feel comfortable evangelizing them, but if they are unfriendly, we may be more cautious. Although this is a sociological issue, it has bearing on this book because Jesus told us not only to love one another but also to love our enemies, so how we will react to and interact religiously with friendly or unfriendly extraterrestrials is relevant. Spreading Christianity by the sword was popular in Christian history but is Christologically unacceptable because the Catholic Church teaches that conversion must be voluntary or it means nothing. Again, although in Christian history this teaching has been honored primarily in the breach, it is important that we treat extraterrestrials with the same respect with which we would like to be treated. As C.S. Lewis notes in *Out of the Silent Planet*, we may find ET's evangelizing us.

I believe it is consistent with Catholic theology to say that the Redemption purchased for us by the blood of Christ must apply to all people, Protestants and Catholics, Jews and Gentiles, men and women, blacks and whites, humans and ET's alike, or it means nothing. To believe that Christ died and rose again exclusively for humans of Earth is to trivialize the Gospel and mock the Cross. To preach salvation to humans alone and not also to extraterrestrials is arrogant and unbecoming of Christians. Whether extraterrestrials are more powerful than we are or less powerful than we are, many Christians believe we must preach the Gospel because that is our destiny. To preach to those more powerful than we are as well as less powerful than we are is to teach ourselves what true power is and what true glory is. Docendo discimus: We learn by teaching. To preach the power of the Resurrection without the scandal of the Cross is to preach healing without cleansing the wound and forgiveness without conversion. Easter without Calvary is meaningless. Believing that humans alone are the only hnau in the universe is like Easter without Calvary. For all practical purposes, it denies the magnificence of God and the glory of God's universe.

Chapter 9

Science and Faith

Some see in this religious belief the foundations of modern science. A rigorous attempt to observe the universe in a systematic way and analyze those observations by rational processes, principally using mathematics, will be rewarded with understanding because the rational structure is there in the universe to be discovered by human ingenuity. Since God has come among human beings in his Son, humans can discover the meaning of the universe, or at least it is worth the struggle to do so, by living intelligently in the universe. Religious experience thus provides the inspiration for scientific investigation.

-- http://www.enotes.com/science- religion- Encyclopedia/christianity- roman-catholic-issues-science

The present life of man, O king, seems to me, in comparison of that time which is unknown to us, like to the swift flight of a sparrow through the room wherein you sit at supper in winter, with your commanders and ministers, and a good fire in the midst, whilst the storms of rain and snow prevail abroad; the sparrow, I say, flying in at one door, and immediate out at another, whilst he is within, is safe from the wintry storm; but after a short space of fair weather, he immediately vanishes out of your sight, into the dark winter from which he had emerged. So this life of man appears for a short space, but of what went before, or what is to follow, we are utterly ignorant.

-- Saint Bede the Venerable, *Ecclesiastical History of the English People*, II, 13

Science has sometimes been said to be opposed to faith, and inconsistent with it. But all science, in fact, rests on a basis of faith, for it assumes the permanence and uniformity of natural laws -- a thing which can never be demonstrated.

-- Tyron Edwards on Faith

Question with boldness even the existence of God; because, if there is one, he must more approve of the homage of reason than that of blindfolded faith.

-- Thomas Jefferson on Faith

Science and Faith are compatible: The Catholic Church has no fear of science or scientific discovery. The Catholic Church teaches that faith and science complement one another and, when understood properly, do not conflict, so the discovery of extraterrestrial intelligent life should not adversely affect Catholic theology but rather living Tradition will develop an evolved understanding of the nature of humanity in the vast universe. The Catholic Church teaches that the theory of evolution does not conflict with Catholic teachings. Thus, God could have initiated life to evolve on Earth as well as on other planets, and God could have created extraterrestrials in God's own image as well since God creates intelligent beings in God's spiritual image and not physical image. By exploring space and searching for extraterrestrials, humanity may one day find that what we know now is miniscule compared to what we have the power of learning.

Is the Logos the organizing force through which God created the universe peopled with humans and inhabitants of other worlds? Does the intelligent design of the universe imply an Intelligent Designer who is the Logos? These questions may be construed as scientific questions about the origin of the universe as well as the evolution of life throughout the cosmos. It is important to note that Darwinism tells us how life evolves but says nothing about how life began. How life began is just as mysterious to the scientist as it is to the theologian. Pope John Paul II said:

> ....it is necessary for [the] relationship between faith and science to be constantly strengthened and for any past historical incidents which may be justly interpreted as being harmful to that relationship, to be reviewed by all parties as an opportunity for reform and for pursuing more harmonious communication. In brief, it must be the sincere desire of all to learn from history so as to gain insight into the positive direction that we must take together in the future (Dick, "Extraterrestrial Life and Our World View." (207)

This clarity is what Pope John Paul II had in mind when he wrote, "both religion and science must preserve their autonomy and distinctiveness" (John Paul II 1988, M8). The Holy Father adds that in order for the separate disciplines of science and religion to edify, both must maintain their separate senses of integrity by being "radically open to the discoveries and insights of the other" (John Paul II 1988, M9).

Genesis 1-11 tells us more about God than about the way God created the universe. Sir Isaac Newton comments in his "Opticks":

> blind fate could never make all the planets move one and the same way in orbits concentrick....Such a wonderful uniformity in the planetary system, must be the effect of providence. This coplanarity has only now been understood -- it's a natural outcome of the Solar System's origin as a spinning protostellar disc. (Rees 71)

Why did the universe expand uniformly except by the guidance of the divine? Newton argues that God imposes order in the form of laws of nature on the universe. Newton also disagrees with the nebular hypothesis, arguing that it leads to atheism. In a letter to Dr. Bentley, Newton writes:

> The growth of new systems out of old ones [averred by Whewell – cms], without the mediation of a Divine power, seems to me apparently absurd. The diurnal rotation of the planets could not be derived from gravity, *but required a Divine* arm to impress them. The same power, whether natural or supernatural, which placed the sun in the center of the six primary planets, placed *Saturn* in the centre of the orbs of his five secondary planets; and *Jupiter* in the centre of his four secondary planets; and the *Earth* in the centre of the moon's orbit; and therefore had this cause been a blind one, *without contrivance or design*, the sun would have been a body of the same kind with *Saturn, Jupiter*, and the *Earth*; that is, *without* light or heat. Why there is one body in our system qualified to give light and heat to all the rest, I know no reason, but because the Author of the system thought it convenient: and why there is but one body of this kind, I know no reason, but because one was sufficient to warm and enlighten all the rest (Newtoni Opera, tom, iv.p. 430). (cited in Brewster 224)

There is a rational structure to the universe in which we live and breathe. The Greeks believed that the Logos (Reason) is the organizing force through which the universe was created. Jesus is the incarnation of the Logos. The Creator became part of his Creation. Humans and extraterrestrials are both part of God's creation. Coyne writes, "Religious experience thus provides the inspiration for scientific investigation" ("Extraterrestrial Life" 184). Brewster writes: "Science ever has been, and ever must be the handmaid of religion. The grandeur of her truths may transcend our failing reason, but those who cherish and lean upon truths equally grand, but certainly more incomprehensible, ought to see in the marvels of the material world the best defence and illustration of the mysteries of their faith" (139). I myself, as a matter of personal philosophy, do not put *blind faith* into the Almighty God. Like Saint Thomas Aquinas and many others, I use reason to understand God along with revelation. Reason and revelation must be compatible or neither is valid. Earlier, Brewster remarks, "It is as injurious to the interests of religion, as it is degrading to those of science, when the votaries of either place them in a state of mutual antagonism....In freely discussing the subject of a plurality of worlds, there can be no collision between Reason and Revelation" (138). My only disagreement with Brewster is with his assertion that nothing in Scripture or reason leads us to believe that the Earth is impermanent (208 – 209) because most scientists acknowledge that our Sun, Sol, is a second generation star that one day, albeit millions of years hence, will burn out, leaving the Earth a lifeless hulk. We may hope that before entropy causes the death of our Sun human beings will be scattered in colonies throughout the universe, but the fact remains that Earth must one day be left behind or humanity will cease to exist. If, one day, all the stars burn out so that not even cinders remain, then our only hope is that the spiritual realm is eternal. Personally, I like to think that the stars will replenish themselves for eternity, that entropy can be reversed, as it says in the doxology, "Glory be to the Father, and to the Son, and to the Holy Spirit; as it was in the beginning, is now, and ever shall be; world without end." Perhaps we should say "Cosmos without end."

Genesis 1-11 does not tell us about the origins of creation but about God's declaration that God's creation is good/beautiful (Coyne, *Evolution*). Creation is good/beautiful because God created it, and God is good/beautiful. Scientific search for beauty in the universe leads us to conclude that God designed the universe to be observed and investigated and enjoyed as beautiful. Since God designed the universe to be observed, it follows that the universe is teeming with observers, that is, with inhabitants of a variety of worlds. Polkinghorne suggests that the universe is fine-tuned to produce life because God fine-tuned the universe to produce life (Rees 74). The anthropic principle may be employed to explain our universe and its properties, so that we develop the gist of a theory for the nature of the universe even without knowing exactly what it implies in minute detail (Rees 76). Searching for clues to the origin of the universe may be an unending task for which we may not ever obtain a satisfactory answer, but the quest itself is fruitful (Rees 77). Neither relativity nor quantum theory gives us any reason to suppose that time originated with the Big Bang (Smolin 82). Our experiences as Christians lead us to become scientists who are concerned with the nature of our experiences in God's universe. Brewster writes:

> From the time when the Earth was without form and void to the present hour, Astronomy has been the study of the shepherd and the sage, and in the bosom of sidereal space the genius of man has explored the most gigantic works of the Almighty, and studied the most mysterious of his arrangements. But while the astronomer ponders over the wonderful structures of the spheres, and investigates the laws of their motions, the Christian contemplates them with a warmer and more affectionate interest. From their past and present history his eager eye turns to the future of the sidereal systems, and he looks to them as the hallowed spots in which his immortal existence is to run. Scripture has not spoken with an articulate voice of the future locality of the blest, but Reason has combined the scattered utterances of Inspiration, and with a voice, almost oracular, has declared that He who made the worlds, will in the worlds which he has made, place the beings of His choice. In the spiritual character of their faith, the ambassadors of our Saviour have not referred to the materiality of His future kingdom; but Reason compels us to believe, that the material body, which is to be raised, must be subject to material laws, and reside in a material home – in a system of many planets – a house of many mansions, though not made with many hands.

Human beings are not simply a chance occurrence in a universe without purpose (de Duve 13). Since human beings have purpose, it follows that inhabitants of other worlds have purpose as well, but is their purpose the same as ours? Brewster suggests that future generations of philosophers will contemplate other worlds orbiting other stars with an eye towards the sublime while future generations of Christians will admire such planets and stars as altars upon which to offer their sacrifices of praise and thanksgiving (262).

The development from chaos to order and eventually to consciousness is part of the natural order of things, implying that God designed the laws of nature, so intelligent beings on both Earth and elsewhere in the universe are inevitable. The existence of ETs in the universe strengthens the notion that the universe was intelligently designed by a divine Designer (Davies, "Biological Determinism, Information Theory, and the Origin of Life," 15). The belief that inhabitants of other worlds exist is, after a long and arduous journey, the majority view of people from all walks of life from scientists to theologians to the person in the street (Davies, "Biological Determinism, Information Theory, and the Origin of Life" 15). Darwinism explains how life evolves but deals only with already existing life and does not explain in any way how life originated. If life is common in the universe, then it would seem that life is part of the cosmic order, an idea which leaves atheism in the dust and provides evidence of intelligent design by an intelligent Designer. Some cite a lack of evidence for inhabitants of other worlds as a reason why we should disbelieve that extraterrestrials exist, but I say that absence of evidence is not evidence of absence. The same could be said for the existence of God. George L. Murphy, Ph.D., writes:

> Johnson makes his belief more explicit by distinguishing between "theistic naturalism," which he rejects, and his own "theistic realism." The distinction is made clear in his oft-quoted statement:
>
>> God is our true Creator. I am not speaking of a God who is known only to faith and is invisible to reason, or who acted undetectably behind some naturalistic evolutionary process that was to all appearances mindless and purposeless. That kind of talk is about

the human imagination, not the reality of God. I speak of a God who acted openly and left his fingerprints all over the evidence. We have to ask, however, if such a God is the one revealed in the cross and resurrection of Christ.

Contrast Johnson's last sentence with a thought of Pascal:

What meets our eyes denotes neither a total absence nor a manifest presence of the divine, but the presence of a God who conceals Himself. Everything bears this stamp.

Pascal had Isaiah 45:15 in mind, and Luther refers to the same verse in arguments for the Heidelberg Book which set out his theology of the cross. (7-8)

Science, rather than contradicting Catholic theology, provides a stimulus to encompass and include ideas about the Creator God, including ideas about the nature of the Incarnate Logos. Christianity shines brightest when presented with challenges stemming from new areas of thought from the Greeks (the concept of the Logos) to the neo-Platonists and Aristotelianism supported by Saint Thomas (Peacocke 91). The current challenge to the Christian faith is the onslaught of science in the sense of naturalism, the idea that the universe evolved naturally without divine guidance, changing our understanding not only of human beings but also of God.

Darwinism had a more profound effect on science, our understanding of the universe around us, than any other discipline, leading Theodosius Dobzhansky, an Orthodox Christian, to remark, "Nothing in biology makes sense except in the light of evolution" (Peacocke 92). Any theology attempting to understand the universe is doomed to fail without taking into account recent developments in scientific thought. We may assume that God is a scientist or an engineer who scientifically designed and engineered the universe and devised its natural laws. Since we are participants in the natural universe, we are natural parts of the universe, yet God designed us to be natural parts of the universe, so understanding our place in the natural universe that was divinely created is essential to our progress as a species and as children of God (cf. Peacocke 92). The notion that all things can be broken down into basic constituent elementary particles supports the Biblical view that God made human beings from the dust, and that humans will eventually return to the dust from which we were made (Peacocke 93). Many people, because scientists have not been able to produce life from inanimate matter in the laboratory, conclude that divine intervention is necessary for life to originate (Peacocke 94). Peacocke seems to think that life develops naturally from inanimate matter, but he fails to acknowledge that God may have designed the universe to be predisposed to developing life from inanimate matter. Is the purpose of life and evolution to produce sentient beings like humans or do other living things, including inhabitants of other worlds, have value in and of themselves in the eyes of God? (Peacocke 95).

Genesis tells us, "God looked at everything he had created, and he found it very good" (1:30b). No doubt this means that God created not only humans but inhabitants of other worlds "very good." Not all scientists are convinced that evolution's natural selection as a process always accounts for the emergence of new species (Peacock 96). Biological death of individuals is essential to the survival of the species and is the means by which God chose to develop new species (Peacocke 97). Peacocke says, "Of course, the myths of Adam and Eve and of the Fall have long since been interpreted nonhistorically and existentially by modern theologians and scholars" (98). Father Leverdiere agrees that the first eleven chapters of Genesis are mythical in character, though he claims these myths are profoundly true on a metaphysical level. Since God has created humans through the process of evolution, it may be that God has created inhabitants of other worlds through the process of evolution, and the convergence theory tells us that such inhabitants may have sense organs like humans and may have developed intelligence in ways similar to human evolution. That we evolved rather than Fell does not mean that we no longer need to be redeemed by Christ; in fact, our need for redemption is even more acute, as is also true for extraterrestrials.

Panentheism, the idea that God permeates the universe so that everything in the universe exists in God and God exists everywhere in the universe, finds support in the Bible when Paul says to the Athenians, "In him we live and move and have our being" (Acts 17:28). Panentheism describes how God relates to his Created universe. So, we may conclude that God not only lives in the human heart but also lives in the heart of the extraterrestrial. The Wisdom of God permeates the universe and all intelligent beings. Mortal wisdom is but a pale reflection of divine Wisdom. Spinoza says that humans are comprised of divine thought, so extraterrestrials must also be comprised of divine thought as well.

The nature of God and our relationships to God are just as theologically significant as our relationships to one another and to inhabitants of other worlds since both humans and extraterrestrials are creations of God and have the potential to become children of God. For many scientists, God is not a person but an explanation of the cause of the universe (Coyne, *Many Worlds and Religion* and *Intelligent Life* 177-178). Christians must view God as not only the cause of the universe but also the cause of our salvation. God is also the cause of the creation of extraterrestrials and the cause of the salvation of extraterrestrials (Coyne, *Many Worlds and Religion*). God is more than just a Mind/Spirit/Creator but a Redeemer and a Sanctifier, so God's revelation is more than simply the communication of knowledge/gnosis but is the very essence of in what we live and move and have our being (Paul citing Greek philosophy). Alan Sandage, Edwin Hubble's protege, says, "We can't understand the universe in any clear way without the supernatural" (Heeren). Theology and science have always intermixed in the search for inhabitants of other worlds but only recently have become separated. Science began as a branch of theology (Davies 138). The separation between the search for religious truths and the search for inhabitants of other worlds breaks down in the modern context. Many people yearn for the religious truths which they hope extraterrestrials can provide them. While it is important for us to be sensitive the possibility of the possibly very different religious beliefs of extraterrestrials, we must also acknowledge and be sensitive to the religious experiences related to the mysteries of God (Coyne, *Many Worlds and Religion*). When we seek God, we should not seek God exclusively as scientists or exclusively as theologians but as Christians who embrace both science and Christian theology, a practice that will boost our efforts to come to terms with the existence of inhabitants of other worlds who may not share all of our beliefs about the universe and God.

Coyne says numerous times that God is not an Explanation but a loving Being who creates out of that love (*Evolution*). God is implicit in the universe because the Creator wills that intelligent life form and evolve not only on earth but on other worlds throughout the cosmos. God designed the universe with physical laws that allow matter to self-organize in such a way that conscious life emerges in the universe capable of discerning the laws of physics that led to the development of consciousness in the cosmos (Davies 127). The ability to develop and use mathematics is the most striking example of conscious thought, yet the rules of mathematics are largely a matter of popular vote (in the sense that math rules that work to solve problems are kept and math rules that do not work to solve problems are discarded by consensus), so we shouldn't assume that the mathematics of inhabitants of other worlds is necessarily the same as ours, though a convergence of thought, like a convergence of the development of biological organisms, may produce similar mathematical theories among extraterrestrials and humans. A physician may search the brain and not find the mind in the same way that a scientist can search the universe and not find God; that doesn't mean neither the mind nor God exists.

William Paley, an English clergyman, said in a famous analogy, that if we were to discover a watch, then, even if we did not know the purpose of the watch, we would realize that the watch was intelligently designed because of the way it was put together and functioned in a purposeful way, so he concludes that, because creatures on Earth seem intelligently designed to function in their respective environments, we realize that an Intelligent Designer made the creatures of the Earth (Davies 74). The theory of evolution contradicts the idea of the watchmaker, but it can be replaced with the idea of a Blind Watchmaker (Davies 74). Christian theologians have suggested that the progress of evolution on Earth implies a divine guiding hand with human beings as the culmination of a great divine experiment (Davies 74-75). Louis Agassiz says:

> The history of the Earth proclaims its Creator. It tells us that the object and term of creation is man. He is announced in nature from the first appearance of organized beings; and each important modification in the whole series of these beings is a

step toward the definitive term (man) in the development of organic life. (cited in Davies 75-76)

Some evolutionists reject the Design theory on the grounds that evolution is random and not purposeful. Thus, if there are inhabitants of other worlds, they are just as much a product of random evolution as human beings. Unamuno, as stated earlier, suggested that, if life is nothing more than a flash of light between two points of utter darkness, then we are the most pitiable people of all. The discovery of extraterrestrials may undermine traditional Darwinism on the grounds that, while traditional Darwinists maintain that the development of intelligence in humans is a random occurrence, Catholics may assert that the existence of intelligence in other beings on other worlds is evidence of a convergence of traits that may be the result of Design (Davies 86-87). The development of consciousness is a natural product of an orderly universe, so it shouldn't surprise us to discover other beings with consciousness throughout the cosmos (Davies 128-129). These conscious extraterrestrials are the product of a designed universe by a divine Designer. The Weak Anthropic Principle asserts that our region of space is one in which observers can exist. The Strong Anthropic Principle asserts that our universe is one in which observers can exist. Quantum Theory suggests that vast areas of the universe lack reality unless observed, and the only way vast areas of the universe can be observed is if there is a divine Observer who created the universe to be observed by intelligent beings. The universe exists because God observes it and created other observers. Observers are a necessary function of the universe. The very existence of the universe depends upon life, that is, living things that observe the universe. God has chosen to create the laws of physics of the universe so that observers could evolve in it.

The Teleological Principle demands that God create the universe for the sake of observers who evolve in it. The notion that God explains the universe's life-generating character very succinctly answers the problem of why intelligent life evolved on earth and perhaps elsewhere in the universe. God's explicit reasons for bringing into existence living beings who could observe the universe around them may be unfathomable, but the Bible gives us insight into the mind of God, implying that the nature of God as light and love explains why God created light for observers to see by and love for observers to experience in terms of their relationship to God and one another.

God made human beings in God's spiritual image, not physical image. We may exist for the purpose of not only observing the universe but also for the purpose of observing God in our own limited way. Divine selection may explain our existence better than any other theory. The universe seems tailor-made for observers because God indeed tailor-made the universe for us observers. Life demands a divine sustainer.

On the other hand, if life is abundant in the universe, then where are they? Perhaps life develops easily but intelligent life is a little harder to manage, except with divine assistance. For neoplatonists,[42] God is the word for the principle that the universe exists because of the ethical need for it. For Einstein, time couldn't have been created by a temporal being. Theorists like Hawking tend to treat the coming-into-being of the universe as a what rather than a why, while the Bible's story is more of a why than a what. We should be asking not whether God created extraterrestrials but why God created extraterrestrials, for the why may be the same for inhabitants of other worlds as for human beings. Sir Isaac Newton wrote: "And as Christ after some stay in or near the regions of this earth ascended into heaven, so after the resurrection of the dead it may be in their power to leave this earth at pleasure and accompany him into any part of the heavens, so that no region in the whole Universe may want its inhabitants" (Dyson 135).

Dyson suggests that the mystery of God stands the test of time because, even if we live long enough as a species to answer all the questions about the nature of the universe, God will remain mysterious and great. The Apostle Paul cites Isaiah 29:14 in 1 Corinthians 1:29: "I will destroy the wisdom of the wise, and the learning of the learned I will set aside." Greatness is found inside the

---

[42] Neoplatonism consists of the beliefs of such Neoplatonists as Plotinus (A.D. 205 -- A.D. 270), Porphyry (A.D. 234 -- A.D. 305), and Proclus (A.D. 419 -- A.D. 485) who combined Platonic ideas with Oriental mysticism. Platonists are followers of the Greek philosopher Plato (429 B.C. -- 347 B.C.) or those who hold to Platonic philosophy or doctrine or beliefs. The Neoplatonists considered themselves just Platonists, but later scholars have called them Neoplatonists to distinguish them from earlier philosophers.

mysteriousness that is God. The Incarnation of Christ on Earth will always remain a great mystery no matter how many extraterrestrials we discover. Encountering inhabitants of other worlds may affect not only our conception of God but also the doctrines of the Catholic Church. If in our study of the universe we encounter few if any intelligent inhabitants of other worlds, then some may embrace the empty outlook of atheism on the grounds that intelligent life is a mere accident of nature, while others may claim that the absence of extraterrestrials is an indication of the uniqueness of humanity as God's special creation. On the other hand, if we encounter numerous extraterrestrials, then some may embrace atheism on the grounds that humanity is neither unusual nor the unique creation of God, while others may claim that the pattern of intelligent life in the universe implies an intelligent Creator who designed the pattern. Since any of these views may be plausibly justified, what reason do we have for believing the truth of any one of them while rejecting the others? The Apostle Paul's response seems to be, "Faith is the realization of what is hoped for and evidence of things not seen" (Hebrews 11:1). Faith and reason and science go hand in hand. What is more important, theology or science? Theology is a science. "Theology without science is lame; science without theology is blind" (Einstein). We must be diligent in our quest for the truth if we wish for science and theology to engage in meaningful dialogue. With Anselm of Canterbury, scientists and theologians may say to each other that ours is a "fides quaerens intellectum" ("faith in search of understanding"). Both scientists and theologians share a common rational and noetic[43] heritage. Science and reason and theology need each other like faith, hope, and love.

Peacock suggests that the Creator creates Creation according to the natural order of things (Dick, *Many Worlds* x). John Leslie supports the idea that the universe is naturally compatible with the development of life, including intelligent life, because God has created it that way (ibid.). The Anthropic Principle according to Brandon Carter suggests that only universes that have been "fine-tuned" by God in life-generating procedures can produce observers who are necessary in Quantum Theory to the very existence of reality

---

[43] Noetic means that which originates or exists in the mind (Greek "nous"); pertaining to the act of thinking or perceiving in the mind or intellect.

(ibid.). Leslie supports this view by suggesting that life-generating qualities are the result of divine selection by design. Perhaps the ethics of God demands that God create the universe in the way that it has been created (ibid.).

Human reaction to the discovery of inhabitants of other worlds may vary from one extreme to another. If/when humans discover extraterrestrials, will we be ecstatic or unhappy? Amazed or nonchalant? Pleased or angry? Curious or fearful? Shocked or react by saying "It's about time"? Probably different human beings will experience all these different reactions in one way or another. Humans in general and Christians in particular are much more resilient than often given credit for. Christian theology will survive encountering extraterrestrials. If the extraterrestrials are friendly, no doubt we will greet them warmly. If they are unfriendly, warlike, or in any other way dangerous, then we will probably join together to meet the threat. If the extraterrestrials are much like us in the sense of very diverse, some friendly, some not so friendly, different people will react differently, some offering friendship, others mobilizing for war. Christian theologians will deal head on with extraterrestrials religions, if they exist, just as they have done with various religions on Earth, and the Catholic Church will encourage us to evangelize the extraterrestrials just as Catholics have evangelized various peoples of various cultures on Earth.

Will there be a government conspiracy/coverup? Doubtful. Example: When pulsars were discovered, scientists disseminated the information quickly around the world, even though some thought it could have been a signal from another world. The notion that members of government are somehow more enlightened than members of the general population and can therefore "handle" the existence of ETs with more aplomb is patently ridiculous.

The reaction of the Catholic Church will be, like most people's, one of curiosity and excitement. The Church will probably want, like scientists, to find out what extraterrestrials are like, how they think, what they know, and what they believe. After humans have gathered sufficient information about extraterrestrials, then the Church may consider evangelizing them. As Lewis suggests in his novel *Out of the Silent Planet*, we may discover ourselves being evangelized by extraterrestrials who understand who Christ is better than we do.

How would we react to the news that extraterrestrials believe God is on their side in a possible effort to conquer the Earth? How will we know whether extraterrestrials are friendly? The history of humanity has taught that warfare is common and may be just as common among inhabitants of other worlds. Is it possible that God might favor extraterrestrials in a battle of not only planets but ideas? With respect to evangelization of inhabitants of another world, Mary Doria Russell suggests in her novels that meetings between cultures are delicate matters and any number of mistakes can lead to catastrophic consequences for both the extraterrestrials and human beings alike. The meeting of human cultures on Earth has often resulted in catastrophic consequences for human cultures, particularly less technologically advanced cultures, and there is no reason to think things will be different when humans encounter extraterrestrial cultures. Inhabitants of other worlds who are less advanced may be destroyed by humans unless Earth people choose to maintain the equivalent of Star Trek's Prime Directive forbidding interference in developing cultures. Inhabitants of other worlds who are more advanced may accidentally destroy human cultures unless we are very careful.

The Catholic Church should be prepared to defend the Christian faith against the possible onslaught of extraterrestrial ideas and philosophies and religions that may be counter to Catholic teachings. Catholic teachings are just as valuable as the teachings of extraterrestrials, an idea that many New Age followers reject. We may want to ask ourselves why so many New Age ideas are embraced by so many people who hunger for spiritual fulfillment that they could find in their own backyard in the Catholic Church.

The discovery of extraterrestrials will have profound effects on human beings and the Catholic faith in particular, but the Catholic Church has made no "official" effort to respond to the possibilities that we are not alone in the universe, although some Catholic authors have addressed the issue directly. Many authors, Catholic and non-Catholics, have expressed concern that culture clashes between humans and inhabitants of other worlds may have the same catastrophic consequences as clashes among various human cultures throughout history. Thus, I believe it is incumbent upon us who embrace the Catholic faith to deal with the issue of contact with extraterrestrials so that we will be prepared when contact finally and actually occurs.

As a Girl Scout, I was taught the motto "Be prepared!" I am preparing for contact with inhabitants of other worlds by discussing my Catholic faith in terms of the cultural and religious impact such a discovery will entail. I hope this book will be a wake-up call to the Vatican to address the possible consequences of contact with inhabitants of other worlds before it occurs.

For the Catholic Church, the existence of inhabitants of other worlds poses no threat to the Catholic faith, but this is not necessarily true for members of the Fundamentalist Protestant denominations. The Catholic Church can provide a leadership role in explaining the truths of Christianity despite or perhaps because of contact with extraterrestrials, so that not only our separated brothers and sisters but also members of other religious faiths will find meaning in the event without destroying everything they believe and have always been taught. The Catholic Church in the person of the Pope should issue official statements from the Papal Bull explaining the Catholic position on inhabitants of other worlds so that Catholics and other human beings will have an anchor to hold onto when contact with extraterrestrials occurs.

God made human beings and extraterrestrials in God's own image. 1 Peter 3:15b tells us "Always be ready to give an explanation to anyone who asks you for a reason for your hope, but do it with gentleness and reverence, keeping your conscience clear, so that, when you are maligned, those who defame your good conduct in Christ may themselves be put to shame." All people, humans and inhabitants of other worlds alike, are creations of God, and we should make it our first priority to treat extraterrestrials as free persons who may also be or may also become children of God.

Chapter 10

History of the Many Worlds or Plurality of Worlds Theory and Religion

I bind unto myself today
The Strong Name of the Trinity,
By invocation of the same
The Three in One and One in Three.
By invocation of the same
I bind this day to me forever.
By pow'r of faith, Christ's Incarnation;
His baptism in Jordan river,
His death on Cross for my salvation;
His bursting from the spiced tomb;
His riding up the heav'nly way;
His coming at the day of doom;
I bind unto myself today.
The virtues of the star-lit heaven,
The glorious sun's life-giving ray,
The whiteness of the moon at even,
The virtues of the star-lit heaven,
The flashing of the lightning free,
The whirling wind's tempestuous shocks,
The stable earth, the deep salt sea,
Around the old eternal rocks.
Christ be with me, Christ within me,
Christ behind me, Christ before me,
Christ beside me, Christ to win me,
Christ to comfort and restore me,
Christ beneath me, Christ above me,
Christ in quiet, Christ in danger,
Christ in hearts of all that love me,
Christ in mouth of friend and stranger.
-- Saint Patrick's Breastplate[44]

---

[44] Versified from the Irish by C.F. Alexander, Poems (London, 1896) 59 – 62.

He shall take his zeal for armor
  and he shall arm creation to requite the enemy;
He shall don justice for a breastplate
  and shall wear sure judgment for a helmet;
He shall take invincible rectitude as a shield
  and whet his sudden anger for a sword,
And the universe shall war with him against the foolhardy.
  -- Book of Wisdom 5:17-20

He put on justice as his breastplate,
  salvation, as the helmet on his head;
He clothed himself with garments of vengeance,
  wrapped himself in a mantle of zeal.
  -- Isaiah 59:17

But since we are of the day, let us be sober, putting on the breastplate of
faith and love and the helmet that is hope for salvation.
  -- 1 Thessalonians 5:8

Finally, draw your strength from the Lord and from his mighty power. Put
on the armor of God so that you may be able to stand firm against the
tactics of the devil. For our struggle is not with flesh and blood but with
the principalities, with the powers, with the world rulers of this present
darkness, with the evil spirits in the heavens. Therefore, put on the armor
of God, that you may be able to resist on the evil day and, having done
everything, to hold your ground. So stand fast with your loins girded in
truth, clothed with righteousness as a breastplate, and your feet shod in
readiness for the gospel of peace. In all circumstances, hold faith as a
shield, to quench all [the] flaming arrows of the evil one. And take the
helmet of salvation and the sword of the Spirit, which is the word of God.
  -- Ephesians 6:10-17

God in the form of Christ is essential to the Catholic
understanding of the nature of the universe. We cannot speculate on
the theology of inhabitants of other worlds without first examining
great human theological ideas to think about. Therefore, I will begin
this chapter by delving into the history of the development of ideas
concerning the possibility of extraterrestrial intelligent life with
respect to the plurality of worlds theories and the theological
implications resulting therefrom.

Section 1:   The Ancient Greeks

The ancient Greeks regarded everything the eye could see, including the Earth, the Sun, the Moon, the stars, and the planets as part of a single *kosmos*, a Greek word meaning "world" or "universe" or "known sphere of existence" or "realm of existence." The Greeks questioned whether the *kosmos* is *pan* (the all) or *holon* (universe, all, entire) as well as whether there are innumerable *kosmoi* which each has its own planets and stars. We are indebted to the Greeks whose curiosity and strong desire for knowledge provided the impetus for the modern quest for extraterrestrial life.

Why did the Greeks seek extraterrestrial life or discuss its implications? Why do I in this book quest for the meaning of inhabitants of other worlds in terms of Catholic theology? I quest for this meaning because it helps us as Christians to understand ourselves better when we seek to understand others who are not like us or who perhaps may be more like us than we imagine.

Democritus (ca. 460 – 370 B.C.) was a Greek philosopher who was pivotal in the development of the atomic theory of the universe. Letter CXVII of the Letters of Saint Augustine paragraph 28 says:

> Democritus, however, is said to differ here also in his doctrine on physics from Epicurus; for he holds that there is in the concourse of atoms a certain vital and breathing power, by which power (I believe) he affirms that the images themselves (not all images of all things, but images of the gods) are endued with divine attributes, and that the first beginnings of the mind are in those universal elements to which he ascribed divinity, and that the images possess life, inasmuch as they are wont either to benefit or to hurt us. Epicurus, however, does not assume anything in the first beginnings of things but atoms, that is, certain corpuscles, so minute that they cannot be divided or perceived either by sight or by touch; and his doctrine is, that by the fortuitous concourse (clashing) of these atoms, existence is given both to innumerable worlds and to living things, and to the souls which animate them, and to the gods whom, in human form, he has located, not in any world, but outside of the worlds, and in the spaces which separate them; and he will not allow of any object of thought beyond

things material. But in order to these becoming an object of thought, he says that from those things which he represents as formed of atoms, images more subtle than those which come to our eyes flow down and enter into the mind. For according to him, the cause of our seeing is to be found in certain images so huge that they embrace the whole outer world. But I suppose that you already understand their opinions regarding these images.

For the record, Augustine goes on to disagree with this. While Democritus averred that other worlds existed which had no life, Epicurus (341 – 270 B.C.), a Greek philosopher who made contributions to physics, and Lucretius (flourished in the first century B.C.), a Roman poet and philosopher who wrote *De Rerum Natura* (On the Nature of Things), which is an affirmation of the physical theories of Epicurus, affirmed that other worlds existed which were teeming with life including animals and plants. Plato (427 – 347 B.C.), a Greek philosopher who was a student of Socrates and a teacher of Aristotle and founded the Academy, argued that the creator of the cosmos "distributed souls equal in number to the stars, inserting each in each" (cited in Wilkinson 13). Atomism asserts that the universe is formed by chance occurrences of atoms coalescing within the void of space (Peters, "Historical Theology" 1). Since the number of atoms is infinite, it follows that an infinite number of worlds *(aperoi kosmoi)* also exists (Peters, "Historical Theology" 1). Epicurus and Lucretius both believed that plants and other living creatures flourished on other worlds (Peters, "Historical Theology" 1). Augustine writes about Anaximander, a pupil of Thales, in *The City of God* Book VIII Chapter 2:

> "To him succeeded Anaximander, his pupil, who held a different opinion concerning the nature of things; for he did not hold that all things spring from one principle, as Thales did, who held that principle to be water, but thought that each thing springs from its own proper principle. These principles of things he believed to be infinite in number, and thought that they generated innumerable worlds, and all the things which arise in them. He thought, also, that these worlds are subject

to a perpetual process of alternate dissolution and
regeneration, each one continuing for a longer or
shorter period of time, according to the nature of the case; nor
did he, any more than Thales, attribute anything to a divine
mind in the production of all this activity of things."

Augustine also writes in Chapter 41 of *The City of God*: "Indeed, in
the conspicuous and well-known porch, in gymnasia, in gardens, in
places public and private, they openly strove in bands each for his
own opinion, some asserting there was one world, others innumerable
worlds; etc." Diogenes Laertius (3rd century A.D.) writes of
Leucippus in *Lives of Famous Philosophers*: "Leucippus holds that
the whole is infinite…part of it is full and part void…Hence arise
innumerable worlds, and are resolved again into these elements."
Diogenes also saved a letter Epicurus wrote to Herodotus that
atomism proves an infinite number of worlds exist (Dick, *Plurality of
Worlds* 10).

Pythagoreans such as Philolaus (5th century B.C.) opined that
the Moon was inhabited and pseudo-Plutarch writes that Pythagoreans
believed that the Moon had plants and animals superior to those of the
Earth. Plutarch[45] (ca. A.D. 45/46 – 120) himself wrote literary though
not scientific treatises on the subject of life on the Moon. Plutarch's
writings, particularly *De facie in orbe lunae*, influenced Johannes
Kepler who translated the works into Latin and who was instrumental
in the development and propagation of the Copernican theory that the
Earth revolves around the Sun. Pierre Gassendi (1592 – 1655), a
Catholic priest who revived atomism, claims that Plutarch's position
is consistent with the idea that the nature of God is amenable to a
plurality of worlds (Dick, *Plurality of Worlds* 56). Because God is
omnipotent, God has the power to create a finite universe. In other
words, nothing is infinite except God.

Plato (427 – 347 B.C.): In the Timaeus, the Pilot produced
order out of chaos. Plato may have influenced Aristotle when he
wrote in the *Timaeus:* "To the end that this world may be like the
complete and living Creature in respect of its uniqueness, for that
reason its maker did not make two worlds nor yet an indefinite

---

[45] This Plutarch is not to be confused with Plutarch of Athens (d. 431/432
CE).

number, but the Heaven has come to be and is and shall be hereafter one and unique" (Dick, *Plurality of Worlds* 14). For Plato, the Demiurge took pre-existent formless matter and created order in the universe, a view that is consistent with the in medias res[46] beginning of Genesis and an idea that continues to have adherents today.

Aristotle (384 -- 322 B.C.): Aristotle had a profound effect on medieval Christian theology, especially his belief that the earth is the only world, thus denying the plurality of worlds theory. For this reason, Davies and others sometimes assume that Christianity automatically places human beings at the center of the universe, when historically this is not necessarily the case (Peters, "Historical Theology" 2). Aristotle presented three arguments detailing his reasons why a plurality of worlds is impossible. The third argument, largely ignored by medieval philosophers and theologians, was that a plurality of worlds implied a plurality of first movers, which he regarded as clearly impossible. The first two arguments centered around the concept of natural place.

The Romans freely admitted that they derived many of their ideas from the Greeks. Indeed, Percy Bysshe Shelley (1792 -- 1822), an English poet and husband of Mary Shelley, wrote: "We are all Greeks. Our laws, our literature, our religion, our arts, have their root in Greece. But for Greece -- Rome, the instructor, the conqueror, or the metropolis of our ancestors, would have spread no illumination with her arms, and we might still have been savages and idolaters; or, what is worse, might have arrived at such a stagnant and miserable state of social institution as China and Japan possess" (Preface (written by Shelley himself) to his poem, "Hellas").

Section 2: The Ancient Romans

According to Michael Crowe, more than 170 books from the ancient Greeks to the modern world have been published discussing the possibility of intelligent life elsewhere in the universe (Davies xii).

---

[46] The literary expression "in medias res" means "in the middle of things" and originated with Horace, a Latin poet; the term refers to the literary technique of beginning a story in the middle of the action and then, as the story progresses, providing information about the past in the form of flashbacks or other devices.

Lucretius (98 -- 54 B.C.): In *On the Nature of Things*, Lucretius, a follower of Epicurus, writes: "Since there is illimitable space in every direction, and since seeds innumerable in number and unfathomable in sum are flying about in many ways driven in everlasting movement," it makes sense that a plurality of worlds exists, "especially since this world was made by nature" (Peters, "Historical Theology" 1). Through Lucretius the idea of the plurality of worlds and atomism spread throughout Europe. Dick writes in *Plurality of Worlds*: "Cosmos and chaos were polar opposites; even given the role of chance in Epicurean cosmogony, the formation of our cosmos could not have been an accident unrepeated throughout the universe" (11). Lucretius encouraged disbelief in the gods, an idea not warmly received by Christian Europe. However, if not an accident, then our universe must have been created according to someone's plan, in my opinion. The concept of an infinity of worlds was problematic for Christians because it implied that the creation of the universe was a random act that was not divine. The solution was to say that God had created a plurality of worlds.

Ephraim the Syrus wrote *Fifteen Hymns for the Feast of the Epiphany* Chapter XIV line 45: "The shout of the Watchers has come to my ears, -- lo! I hear from the Father's house – the hosts that sound forth the cry, -- 'In Thy Epiphany, O Bridegroom the worlds have life.'"

An unknown Critic of Whewell once wrote, "We deduce from this language of Scripture, ('When I consider the heavens....what is man?') a positive argument for the plurality of worlds; for *that* view makes the Hebrew poet's wonder intelligible" (Whewell 355). The Critic also says "that the provision made for the redemption of man by what took place upon earth eighteen hundred years ago, may have extended its influence to other worlds" (358).

Section 3: The Early and Medieval Catholic Church

There is in the universe neither center nor circumference.
-- Giordano Bruno, *On the Infinite Universe and Worlds, fifth dialogue*

Early Christian authors faced the momentous task of developing a reasonable theology in response to the views of the pagan Greek and Roman authors. In the beginning, the early Christian theologians rejected the concepts of a plurality of worlds and extraterrestrial life. Those who rejected these ideas included Hippolytus in the third century, Bishop Eusebius of Caesarea in the fourth century, Bishop Theodoret of Cyprus in the fifth century, and Saint Augustine of Hippo (A.D. 354 – 430).

Saint Augustine notes that "days" in Genesis are not to be taken literally, since what a "day" is before the creation of the Sun and stars on the fourth "day" is unclear. Time was created along with the material universe in a way that did not limit the power of the Creator (McMullin 155). Augustine argues that the Creation story in Genesis is best understood metaphorically (McMullin 155). If we discover life (not necessarily intelligent life) in our solar system, it would support Augustine's contention that the "seeds" of life are endemically present in the very fabric of the created universe (McMullin 157). Augustine also writes in *On the Merits and Forgiveness of Sins, and on the Baptism of Infants* Chapter 50: "In its [the Eastern Churches?] exordium one reads: 'God, who at sundry times, and in divers manners, spake in time past unto the fathers by the prophets, hath in these last days spoken to us by His Son, whom He hath appointed heir of all things, by whom also He made the worlds; etc.'" Nevertheless, Dick says that Augustine rejected the plurality of worlds idea because it implies that God must be active throughout the entire universe (*Plurality of Worlds* 56). Moreover, Augustine rejects the idea that people of the antipodes even exist, writing in *The City of God*:

Chapter 9.—Whether We are to Believe in the Antipodes.

But as to the fable that there are Antipodes, that is to say, men on the opposite side of the earth, where the sun rises when it sets to us, men who walk with their feet opposite ours, that is on no ground credible. And, indeed, it is not affirmed that this has been learned by historical knowledge, but by scientific conjecture, on the ground that the earth is suspended within the concavity of the sky, and that it has as much room on the one side of it as on the other: hence they say that the part which is beneath must also be inhabited. But they do not remark that, although it be supposed or scientifically demonstrated that the world is of a round and spherical form, yet it does not follow that the other side of the earth is bare of water; nor even, though it be bare, does it immediately follow that it is peopled. For Scripture, which proves the truth of its historical statements by the accomplishment of its prophecies, gives no false information; and it is too absurd to say, that some men might have taken ship and traversed the whole wide ocean, and crossed from this side of the world to the other, and that thus even the inhabitants of that distant region are descended from that one first man. Wherefore let us seek if we can find the city of God that sojourns on earth among those human races who are catalogued as having been divided into seventy-two nations and as many languages. For it continued down to the deluge and the ark, and is proved to have existed still among the sons of Noah by their blessings, and chiefly in the eldest son Shem; for Japheth received this blessing, that he should dwell in the tents of Shem. (47)

In the middle ages, Biblical disputes arose over the existence of people of the antipodes. Augustine argues that the descendants of Noah could not have reached the antipodes because, according to the Bible, it was not accessible. Rudolf Simek writes in 1992:

> Even if, for some reason, people did live in the hypothetical southern continent, this continent could not be reached because it was impossible to cross the equator. Therefore, Christ's missionary task: 'Go to *all* peoples and teach them' could not be fulfilled. If this was true then the whole question of the act of salvation was put into question. But the idea that Christ might have issued nonsensical instructions was wholly implausible. As the impossibility of crossing the equator was considered a simple matter of fact, the only possible way open for the Church was quite simply to reject the existence of the Antipodes. (53)

Since later science proves that people exist all around the Earth, it

---

47Roberts, Alexander and Donaldson, James, *Nicene and Post-Nicene Fathers, First Series: Volume II*, (Oak Harbor, WA: Logos Research Systems, Inc.) 1997.

follows that Christ's redemptive work applies to all people all over the Earth and to inhabitants of other worlds throughout the Cosmos as well. In the fourth and fifth centuries, some Catholics began developing ideas from Genesis that life originated and developed from earth and water (McMullin 155). Gregory of Nyssa developed a theory that the power of life creation was present in the very fabric of the universe only waiting for God to set the process in motion (McMullin 155). In the First Epistle of Clement to the Corinthians Chapter XX line 87 contains a reference to life beyond the ocean: "The ocean, impassible to man, and the worlds beyond it, are regulated by the same enactments of the Lord." This can be expanded to mean worlds beyond the earth are also under God's control. Lactantius (a fourth century convert to Christianity) in *The Divine Institutes* Chapter XXIII writes:

> Xenophanes most foolishly believed mathematicians who said that the orb of the moon was eighteen times larger than the earth; and, as was consistent with this folly, he said that within the concave surface of the moon there was another earth, and there another race of men live in a similar manner to that in which we live on this earth. Therefore these lunatics have another moon, to hold forth to them a light by night, as this does to us. And perhaps this globe of ours may be a moon to another earth below this. Seneca says that there was one among the Stoics who used to deliberate whether he should assign to the sun also its own inhabitants; he acted foolishly in doubting.

Archelaus: The Acts of the Disputation with the Heresiarch Manes (a Fragment of the Same Disputation) line 62: "Moreover, there are certain other worlds on which the luminaries rise when they have set on our world." Hilary and Poiters in *On the Trinity* Book 1 line 6 refers to "the Creator of Worlds" as does *The Divine Liturgy of the Holy Apostle and Evangelist Mark* section III. Moreover, the *First Epistle of Clement to the Corinthians* Chapter XXXV says "The Creator and Father of all worlds, the Most Holy, alone knows their amount and their beauty."

John of Damascus writes in *An Exact Exposition of the Orthodox Faith* Book II Chapter VII: "For with God nothing is difficult: but as the painter who has made one likeness will make ten thousand with ease, so also with God it is easy to make worlds without number and end. Rather, as it is easy for you to conceive a city and worlds without bound, so unto God is it easy to make them; rather again it is easier by far." John also writes in the same chapter: "For he that thinketh nothing of hell nor of heaven nor of ten thousand worlds in regard of his longing after Christ, how should he hunt after the glory which cometh from the many?" John of Damascus and Basil the Great (329 – 379) wrote, according to Mikhail Vasilyevich Lomonosov (1711 – 1765) of Russia, that a plurality of inhabited worlds does not violate Scripture (Crowe 160).

Saint John Chrysostom writes in *Homilies of the Gospel According to Saint John* Homily V circa section 17:

> Nay, if need were that ten thousand, or even an infinite number of such worlds be created, He remains the same, sufficient for them all not merely to produce, but also to control them after their creation." In *Homilies on the Epistle to the Hebrews* Homily II section 26 Chrysostom writes: "For the same thing which the one indirectly expressed, saying, 'In the beginning was the Word,' and 'All things were made by Him' (John i. 3), this did the other also openly declare by 'the Word,' and by saying 'by whom also. He made the worlds.' For thus he shows Him to be both a Creator, and before all ages, What then? When the prophet saith, concerning the Father, 'Thou art from everlasting to everlasting' (Ps. Xc. 2), and concerning the Son, that He is before all ages, and the maker of all things – what can they say? Nay rather, when the very thing was spoke of the Father, -- 'He which was before the worlds,' – this one may see spoken of the Son also? And that which one saith, 'He was life' (John i. 4), pointing out the preservation of the creation, that Himself is the Life of all things, -- so also saith this other, 'and upholding all things by the word of His power': not as the Greeks who defraud Him, as much as in them lies, both of Creation itself, and of Providence, shutting up His power, to reach only as far as to the Moon.

Theodoret in *The Ecclesiastical History of Theodoret* writes in Book I Chapter XI section 131 a version of the Creed: "We believe in one God, Father Almighty, the Maker of all things, visible and invisible; and in one Lord Jesus Christ, the Word of God, God of God, Light of Light, Life of Life, Only-begotten Son, First-born of every creature, begotten of the Father before all worlds; by Whom all things were made; Who for our salvation was incarnate, and lived among men etc."

Thomas Aquinas (A.D. 1224 -- 1274): Thomas says that either a literal or a metaphorical reading of Genesis is possible (McMullin 156). Thomas still leaned toward a literalist interpretation of Scripture (McMullin 156). Thomas dedicated much of his voluminous writings to reconciling Aristotelian philosophy with Christianity. Does God become less than omnipotent if he creates only the Earth and no other worlds? Because God is omnipotent, God can create an infinite number of worlds. Saint Thomas believes that "it is necessary that all things should belong to one world." For Thomas, unity yields perfection. Thus, God created the Earth perfect rather than create innumerable other imperfect worlds. Therefore, the Aristotelian position that the Earth is the only world God created is consistent with the notion of God's omnipotence (Peters, "Historical Theology" 2). It is important to observe here that Thomas is making a logical argument based on the premise that the Earth is not chaotic but ordered, not originating by a roll of divine dice but according to the divine plan that unity leads to perfection (ibid.). Thomas follows Aristotle's belief against a plurality of worlds on the grounds of natural place. Thomas argues that nothing exists outside our world because the unity of our one world is good while any division into a plurality of worlds would not be good. Thomas argues that unity is essential to perfection: "This world is called one by the unity of order whereby some things are ordered to others" because it is an unproven truth that "whatever things come from God, have relation or order to each other, and to God himself...hence it must be that all things should belong to one world" (*Summa Theologica* Part I Question 47 Article 3). Thomas argues that the Gospel of John 1:10, "the world was made by him," is a proof that God made only one world.

Aristotle's position that there was only one world was condemned by the Catholic Church in 1277 by a French bishopric council, so that the doctrine of the plurality of worlds was given the official status of not being heresy (McMullin 163). Etienne Tempier was the bishop of Paris who made this declaration, saying that to aver God's inability to create a plurality of worlds is heresy on the grounds that it restricts the power of God who is actually omnipotent (Dick, *Plurality of Worlds* 28). The result of this declaration was that theologians were now required to investigate the plurality of worlds theory so that God could overwrite Nature's laws as expounded by Aristotle or so that Aristotelian physics had to be reinterpreted to include the possibility of a plurality of worlds (ibid.).

In the thirteenth century, Godfrey of Fontaine, Henry of Ghent, and Richard of Middleton of Paris as well as William of Ware, Jean of Bassols, and Thomas of Strasbourg of Oxford all claimed that a plurality of worlds was within the realm of the possible with respect to the Christian faith. These scholars were among the first to declare that not only were other worlds possible but other worlds could revolve around other suns which God could create ex nihilo.

Many Catholics embraced the idea that an all-powerful God could create a plurality of worlds as a direct manifestation of God's power (McMullin 163). John Buridan (A.D. 1295 -- 1358), rector of the University of Paris, wrote: "...we hold from faith that just as God made this world, so he could make another or several worlds" (Peters, "Historical Theology" 3). Buridan did not wish to disagree with Aristotle, so he started with a different premise, arguing that God could create on other worlds material elements, distinct from the material elements of the earth, which obey alien laws and so are ordered in their own way (ibid.). In his argument, Buridan ignored Thomas's argument of unity and perfection. Peter Lombard's (1095 – 1165) *Book of Sentences*, an essential part of the curriculum of every masters student in the medieval era, contained in Book 1 a section entitled Distinction XLIV which asks "whether God could make anything better than he has made." The question, before 1277, became, "whether God is able to make the world better than he has made it." Thomas addressed this question in his own Distinction XLIV, written between 1254 and 1257, concluding that God would have had to create another world in order to perfect this one since God created the world perfect in the first place (Dick, *Plurality of Worlds* 31).

William of Okham (ca. 1280 – 1347) argues from Augustine's assertion that God could create a perfect man who would never sin that God can also create other beings who are different from all the species of the Earth including human beings, and so other worlds with other such beings on them, and so a better world (33). William argues with Buridan and against Aristotle that not all things naturally return to their place but will return to a place that is natural for their species. Unfortunately, William of Okham's ideas were rejected by the Church and he was excommunicated.

Nicole Oresme, Bishop of Lisieux (A.D. 1320 -- 1382) wrote a treatise entitled "De coelo de mundo" in which he disagreed forcefully with Aristotle that all things tend to gravitate towards the center of the universe (the center of the Earth), arguing that other worlds could have their own center that are not necessarily the same as the center of the Earth, thus arguing that the center of the Earth is not the center of the universe. For Oresme, God could create other worlds in defiance of the natural law expounded by Aristotle, but after the creation of that world, it would obey the same laws as the earth (Dick, *Plurality of Worlds* 36). Outside of our sphere of existence, an immaterial void exists which is "infinite and indivisible…the immensity of God and God himself" (ibid.). Oresme also says that the Lord "is infinite in His immensity, and if several worlds existed, no one of them would be outside Him nor outside his power" (cited in Dick, *Plurality of Worlds* 36). Nevertheless, while acknowledging that God could create other worlds, Oresme maintained that "there has never been nor will there be more than one world" (ibid.). Albertus Magnus, John Major, and Leonardo da Vinci all supported the plurality of worlds theory as a possibility before the Copernican Revolution. John Major (1469 – 1550) claimed that an infinite number of worlds could be a natural part of the universe, an idea also entertained by a Spanish Jew named Hasdai Crescas (1340 – 1410). Michael Crowe in *The Extraterrestrial Life Debate Antiquity to 1915* writes:

> The last quarter of the thirteenth century saw a surprising turn of events. In 1277, Etienne Tempier, Bishop of Paris, under pressure from various theologians who were troubled by the increasing dominance of Aristotelian thought, especially as interpreted by Thomas Aquinas, issued what is known as the Condemnation of 1277. In it, Tempier condemned 219

propositions and threatened those who held them with excommunication. An issue that concerned Tempier was that theologians in attempting to delineate God's relationships with the world had produced rational schemes that could be seen as denying that God *could* act in certain manners. Among the propositions condemned was number 34, which states "[t]hat the first cause [God] could not make several worlds." In other words, it seemed a short step from arguments that the Christian idea of God could be reconciled with what was known of the universe to a denial that despite God's omnipotence, God could not create more than one world. Tempier's proclamation created in the late-thirteenth and fourteenth centuries a situation in which the question of other worlds, as well as other questions about the physical world, could be discussed more openly. In fact, before the end of the thirteenth century, Henry of Ghent, Godfrey of Fontaine, Richard of Middleton, William of Ware, Jean of Bassols, and Thomas of Strasbourg had all urged that a plurality of worlds was not a theological impossibility. Moreover, in the fourteenth century, a number of the most gifted scholars discussed the question of other worlds, revealing that they were at least open to the possibility that God could have created a plurality of worlds. Among these authors were William of Ockhma (ca. 1290 -- 1349), John Buridan (d. 358), and Nicole Oresme. What is most striking in the discussions by these three authors is that although they show themselves to be open to the possibility that God could have created a plurality of worlds and although they marshal an array of powerful rebuttals to Aristotle's arguments against this doctrine, they all ultimately conclude against the pluralist position. The most highly regarded fourteenth-century discussion of this issue is that by Oresme, who served as tutor to the future King Charles V of France and eventually as bishop of Lisieux. Oresme's discussion appears in his *Le livre du ciel et du monde* (*The Book of the Heavens and the World*), which consists of a French translation of and commentary on Aristotle's *On the Heavens*. (21 -- 22)

Giordano Bruno (1548 -- 1600), an Italian philosopher, mathematician, astronomer, and occultist, developed many radical ideas of moral philosophy and natural philosophy (anticipating modern science) including the notion of an infinity of worlds. Bruno was burned at the stake at the end of the 16th century (A.D. 1600) for a variety of heresies including the idea of an infinite number of worlds but primarily for denying the divinity of Jesus Christ. Bruno wrote:

> Concerning this question [of Aristotle whether beyond this world there lieth another] you know that his interpretation of this word *world* [*mondi*] is different from ours. For we join world to world and star to star in this vast ethereal bosom, as is seemly and hath been understood by all those wise men who have believed in innumerable and infinite worlds. But he applieth the name *world* to an aggregate of all those ranged elements and fantastic spheres reaching to the convex surface of that *primum mobile*....It will be well and expedient to overthrow his arguments insofar as they conflict with our judgement, and to ignore those which do not so conflict. (cited in Dick, *Plurality of Worlds* 64)

When studying the writings of previous centuries, it is important to understand the definitions of the words they use, and *mondi* meaning "world" means different things to different people. The ancient Hebrews thought the world was surrounded by a physical dome which separated a watery chaos from the world below so that when God opened the sluicegates water fell through in a process we call rain. Bruno is right on target in questioning the meaning of the word for world. Bruno gleefully attacked Aristotelianism in favor of the plurality/infinity of worlds view in his writings in which he particularly advocated the unity of the universe and the belief that God's might in creating a perfect universe resulted in infinite individuals as well (ibid. 66).

Nicholas of Cusa (15th century; A.D. 1401 -- 1464), a Christian scholar, philosopher, cardinal, mathematician, and experimental scientist, wrote of the plurality of worlds and extraterrestrial life. Cusa believed the universe to be boundless with no absolute center towards which all things were thought to gravitate, saying that the universe's "center is everywhere and its circumference nowhere," a notion previously attributed to the nature of God (Dick, *Plurality of Worlds* 40). According to Dick, Nicholas also proposed an idea completely opposite the position attributed to Aristotle when he wrote:

> Life, as it exists here on earth in the form of men, animals and plants, is to be found, let us suppose, in a higher form in the solar and stellar regions. Rather than think that so many stars and parts of the heavens are uninhabited and that this earth of ours alone is peopled – and that with beings perhaps of an inferior type – we will suppose that in every region there are inhabitants, differing in nature by rank and all owing their origin to God, who is the center and circumference of all stellar regions. (*Plurality of Worlds* 41)

Dick says that Nicholas's ideas are an outgrowth of the Scholastic tradition (42). A contemporary of Nicholas, William of Vorilong, in answer to the question as to whether other worlds could be created that were more perfect than that of the earth, wrote, "not one world alone, but infinite worlds, more perfect than this one, lie hid in the mind of God" (43). William goes on to speak of what other commentators had been unwilling or too fearful to put into writing: "whether men exist on that world, and whether they have sinned as Adam sinned" (ibid.). William averred that such living beings "would not exist in sin and did not spring from Adam. But it is shown that they would exist from the virtue of God, transported to that world, as Enoch and Elias [Helyas] in the earthly paradise." (ibid. and also *Plurality of Worlds* 88). Hasdai Crescas (1340 -- 1410), a Spanish Jewish scholar, philosopher, rabbi, Talmudic scholar, and critic of applying Aristotelian ideas to Judaism, is a medieval theologian who expresses similar beliefs.

In conclusion, in the days of the Greeks and the early and medieval Catholic Church were many authors and laity (including the Catholic Origen, Nicholas of Cusa, and William of Vorilong) who supported the possibility of a plurality of worlds theory despite Aristotelianism. The Catholic Church, as the teacher of the infallible teachings of Christ and faith and morals, did not ever officially reject the plurality of worlds theory or the existence of extraterrestrials but indeed encouraged debate on the matter for a long time past the Copernican revolution and well into modern times.

Section 4: The Enlightenment, the Renaissance, the Protestant Revolution, and the Catholic Reformation

Johannes Kepler (1571 – 1630), German astronomer and discoverer of the three laws of planetary motion, was influenced by Bruno, although he rarely referred to him in his writings and rejected his view of an infinity of worlds, preferring the concrete and provable to Bruno's ideas of a magical world. Kepler expressed concern that the new view of the universe displaced human beings as the center and apex of God's creation by making the Earth only one world among many with intelligent beings populating other worlds:

> Well, then, someone may say, if there are globes in the heaven similar to our earth, do we vie with them over who occupies a better portion of the universe? For if their globes are nobler, we are not the noblest of rational creatures. Then how can all things be for man's sake? How can we be the masters of God's handiwork? [*Kepler's Conversation* 43 cited in Dick, *Plurality of Worlds 87* and also cited as the preface to H.G.'s Wells's *War of the Worlds* in 1897].

Kepler himself believed that human beings are the noblest of all creatures with the earth the noblest of all the planets circling the Sun. He also averred that Jupiter was inhabited because it had moons, saying that God created the moons of Jupiter for Jupiter's inhabitants just as God created the Moon for the Earth's inhabitants. I think that human beings are still the apple of God's eye even if God also blesses inhabitants of other planets. Every firstborn child experiences this feeling whenever the firstborn's parents bring home a new baby.

Tommaso Campanella (1568 -- 1639), an Italian philosopher, author, and Dominican, asserts that the heliocentric view espoused by Galileo did not include the plurality of worlds theory but rather embraced the idea that there are many subworlds within the one world. Galileo Galilei himself (1564 -- 1642), Italian natural philosopher, mathematician, and astronomer, in his studies of Aristotle, Albertus Magnus, and Thomas Aquinas, avers that Scripture speaks only of the creation of one world, so there was only one cosmos, but God could make as many worlds as he desired. Campanella wrote that the existence of water on other worlds violates the Aristotelian principle of unity and vitiates the belief that heaven is a perfect place, thus desacralizing[48] the home of angels and depriving human beings of their hope for eternal life there. Campanella further decried the notion of extraterrestrials by saying that their very existence was opposed to Scripture. Campanella moreover defended Galileo by asserting the Hebrew view that heaven was a physical vault holding back the waters of chaos, citing Scripture to support his view, particularly Genesis 1:1-10, and also citing Psalm 103:2-3 (104:2-3), "You spread out the heavens like a tent; you raised your palace upon the waters" and Psalm 148:4, "Praise him, highest heavens, you waters above the heavens" and Proverbs 7:24 (8:24), "When there were no depths I was brought forth, when there were no fountains or springs of water;." Galileo asserted that life elsewhere in the cosmos would be very different from life on Earth, an idea that he claims does not diminish the power of God (ibid. 97).

Kepler was a German Protestant while Galileo was an Italian Catholic, and the religious atmosphere surrounding their lives influenced their writings. Kepler's sense of morality was strongly influenced by Scripture, but he kept his science distinct from his religion. Galileo wrote that theologians should be solely responsible for reconciling theology with science but expressed concerns about the Catholic Church's reactions to new scientific theories anyway, a prudent position in a society in which the Catholic Church held great political power. Galileo was concerned especially about how his Church would react to the speculation of the effects of the Incarnation and Redemption on extraterrestrials and so denied that extraterrestrials existed. Galileo's friend, the Jesuit Giovanni Ciampoli, warns Galileo in 1615 that ideas about ET's had profound consequences when taking into consideration the view that ET's are not descendents of Adam nor descendents of the folk aboard Noah's Ark (Dick, *Plurality of Worlds* 90).

The science historian Colin Russell wrote that denizens of the 17th century posited that God is powerful enough to have created life

---

[48] Desacralization is the process of secularizing or rendering something less sacred.

anywhere in the cosmos he wished and that God created the universe not solely for the benefit of human beings but for all life everywhere so that the glory of God might be manifest to all his creatures universally (Wilkinson 14).

For Rene Descartes (1596 -- 1650), French philosopher, scientist, and mathematician who is considered the father of epistemology, God the Creator is great and powerful yet everything God created is not necessarily made exclusively for human beings nor do we know for what purposes they were all made. Descartes largely popularized the concept of a plurality of worlds in the 17th century. He asserted that we should not underestimate the power of God to create other worlds, a belief used by Cartesians to defend God's omnipotence in defiance of the absence of such information in the Bible (Dick, *Plurality of Worlds* 116-117). Dick says that Descartes believed God created Nature and agitated its substance to make chaotic matter and "concluded his work by merely lending his concurrence to Nature in the usual way, leaving her to act in accordance with the laws which he had established" (cited in *Plurality of Worlds* 143).

Pierre Borel, a contemporary of Descartes, wrote in "A New Discourse Proving the Plurality of Worlds" in 1657, seven years after Descartes's death, that the plurality of worlds theory was consistent with the teachings of the Bible and accorded well with the doctrine of God as Creator of all those worlds (Dick, *Plurality of Worlds* 117-118). Borel did not believe that God created all those worlds for the sake of humanity alone, implying that God made other worlds for the sake of other creatures on them (ibid. 119).

Henry More (1614 – 1687), a Neoplatonic philosopher in England, wrote in favor of atomism while maintaining that God is the First Cause who started the universe in motion. More claims that the world is not infinite but that there are an infinite number of worlds, with each star having its own system of planets with life. The notion of life on other worlds, for More, supported the theory that God is omnipotent and therefore has the power to create an infinite number of worlds, an idea that neither contradicts Scripture nor Christian theology (Dick, *Plurality of Worlds* 52). More took ideas from Rene Descartes and Giordano Bruno to argue that our Sun is a star to other worlds. I think this idea encourages faith in the immense power of God. Although More eventually broke with Descartes, he maintained his support for a plurality of worlds, arguing that God reveals to inhabitants of other worlds the good news of Christ's Incarnation and Redemption and saves them just as he saves human beings (Crowe 17).

John Wilkins, a Protestant clergyman subsequently made a Bishop of the Anglican Church and a politically powerful man, wrote *Discovery of a World in the Moone* in 1638, suggesting that the Moon may be inhabited and claiming that such a belief is consistent with both faith and reason. Wilkins argues that just because the Bible doesn't mention other worlds doesn't mean other worlds don't exist any more than the planets don't exist simply because Scripture doesn't mention them. When others argued that belief in many worlds was considered to be a heresy in ancient times, Wilkins countered by arguing that the ancients were not always right, which I think is a valid argument as evidenced by the declaration of many heretics later being declared saints. Wilkins says that most skywatchers using the telescope perfected by Galileo can see for themselves as "proof beyond exception; and certainly…man must needs be of a most timorous faith, who dares not believe his own eye" (cited in Dick, *Plurality of Worlds* 100).

Christiaan Huygens (1629-1695), Dutch astronomer, physicist, and mathematician, wrote *Cosmotheoros, or, Conjectures concerning the Celestial Earths and their Adornments*, published in 1698 three years after the author's death, in which he says "that the production of animals, and especially of man, and especially of wisdom and intelligence, is a Divine work" (cited in Dick, *Plurality of Worlds* 129). He wrote that the planets of necessity have plants and animals because this better displays divine providence (ibid. 130). He argues that human beings are not the only creatures of God who are endowed with divine substance.

Sir Isaac Newton wrote in 1713:

> This most beautiful system of the sun, planets, and comets, could only proceed from the counsel and dominion of an intelligent and powerful Being. And if the fixed stars are the centers of other like systems, these, being formed by the like wise counsel, must be all subject to the dominion of the One. [cited in Dick, *Plurality of Worlds* 142]

William Stukeley wrote to Newton (*Memoirs of Sir Isaac Newton's Life*, ed. A.H. White (London, 1936), p. 73): "God always created new worlds, always creates new worlds, new systems, to multiply the infinitude of his beneficiarys, and extend all happiness beyond all compass and imagination" (cited in Crowe xxiv).

Richard Bentley (1662 -- 1742), British clergyman, classical scholar, and regius professor of divinity at Trinity College, Cambridge, with respect to the actions of God in the Newtonian universe suggests the existence of extraterrestrials, predicting problems in ethics with respect to whether humans are the center of God's creation:

> "...we need not nor do not confine and determine the purposes of God in creating all mundane bodies, merely to human ends and uses...all bodies were formed for the sake of intelligent minds: and as the Earth was principally designed for the being and service and contemplation of men; why may not all other planets be created for the like uses, each for their own inhabitants which have life and understanding?" (Peters, "Historical Theology" 4-5).

Bentley briefly corresponded with Newton in which he suggests that belief in the Deity can be a completely rational process (*Plurality of Worlds* 144). Bentley asks Newton whether all the matter in the universe could have coalesced without the direct guidance of God, and Newton replies between December 1692 and February 1693 that divine coalescence could only have occurred in a finite universe and not in an infinite universe as proposed by Newton based on Lucretius. Nevertheless, the formation of stars and planetary systems could only have occurred by the direction of God (ibid. 144-145). While Descartes argues that God created the universe with a uniform system of physical laws, Newton argues that God may change physical laws from solar system to solar system (ibid. 147). Bentley wrote: "All Bodies were formed for the Sake of Intelligent Minds: As the Earth was principally designed for the Being and Service and Contemplation of Men; why may not all other Planets be created for the like uses, each for their own Inhabitants who have Life and Understanding" (cited in *Plurality of Worlds* 149). I believe it is consistent with Catholic theology to say that all people, ET's and humans alike, have sinned and fallen short of the glory of God and thus need Christ's saving power to attain eternal life.

Bentley participated in a series of lectures the purpose of which, according to Robert Boyle, was to prove "the Christian religion." Bentley wrote to Newton asking how he reconciled his science with his religious beliefs, and a delighted Newton wrote back four letters published in 1756, one of which contains his assertion that "the Growth of new Systems out of old ones, without the Mediation of a divine Power, seems to me apparently absurd" (cited in Crowe 22). Bentley combined Newtonianism and Christianity with the doctrine of the plurality of worlds in *Confutation of Atheism*, and his ideas spread widely (Crowe 24). Newton may have been influenced by Bentley as is evidenced by his assertion in a passage published by David Brewster in which Newton argues that, on Judgement Day, Jesus

> ...will give up his kingdom to the Father, and carry the blessed to the place he is now preparing for them, and send the rest to other places suitable to their merits. *For in God's house (which is the universe,) are many mansions, and he governs them by agents which can pass through the heavens from one mansion to another. For if all places to which we have access are filled with living creatures, why should all these immense spaces of the heavens above the clouds be incapable of inhabitants?* (cited in Crowe 24).

In fairness, it should be noted that Newton crossed out the italicized sentences above and inserted at the end the following statement: "We are also to enter into societies by Baptism & laying on of hands & to commemorate the death of X in our assemblies by breaking of bread" (ibid. 25). Newton said in a conversation with the husband of his niece, John Conduitt, that stars were suns around which orbited other planets, that these planets were populated with inhabitants, that these suns were replenished when heavenly bodies fell into them unfortunately destroying all life on them, and that extraterrestrials superior to humans "superintended these revolutions of the heavenly bodies, by the direction of the Supreme Being" (Crowe 25). Newton also said that the power of God was required to recreate ET's on these planets after these catastrophes (ibid.).

The Reverend Dr. William Derham (1657 – 1735) wrote *Astro-Theology, or A Demonstration of the Being and Attributes of God from a Survey of the Heavens* in which he claims the universe is designed by God and avers a plurality of worlds which he believes are "places of habitation, which is concluded from their being *habitable*, and well provided for *habitation* (cited in Brewster 254). Derham writes that our solar system "is far the most magnificent of any; and worthy of an infinite CREATOR…" (cited in Crowe 26)

William Whewell wrote *Of the Plurality of Worlds: An Essay* which attacks the notion of inhabitants of other worlds, and the religious implications for the Christian faith debate that followed. Among other things, Whewell contends that the Sun is somehow different from other stars so that other stars do not have the same characteristics requisite for the development of life (185 – 187). Whewell disputes the common contention of many scholars of his day that the benevolence of God necessitates the existence of life on other worlds (234). Whewell also suggests that the universe is evidence for the existence of God. He writes:

> We may remark further, that this view of God, as the Author of the Laws of the Universe, leads to a view of all the phenomena and objects of the world, as the work of God; not a work made, and laid out of hand, but a field of his present activity and energy. And such a view cannot fail to give an aspect of dignity to all that is great in creation, and of beauty to all that is symmetrical, which otherwise they could not have. Accordingly, it is by calling to their thoughts the presence of God as suggested by scenes of grandeur or splendor, that poets often reach the sympathies of their readers. And this dignity and sublimity appear especially to belong to the larger objects, which are destitute of conscious life; as the mountains, the glacier, the pine-forest, the ocean; since in these, we are, as it were, alone with God, and the only present witnesses of His mysterious working. (280 – 281)

Whewell seems to imply that the very beauty of the universe is for the benefit of human beings alone who are the apple of God's eye, but I think that it is also for the benefit of inhabitants of other worlds who are also the creations of God. The view of the heavens from Arcturus is surely not less spectacular than the view from Earth, and it would be a shame to waste such beauty on the unappreciative inanimate rocks and sand. Whewell writes, "The remotest planet is not devoid of life, for God lives there" (281). This is true, but God I believe looks through not only his own eyes but also through the eyes of intelligent beings on a wide variety of worlds, and I believe God probably "saw that it was very good" (Genesis 1).

John Ray, an Englishman, wrote of a plenitude of creatures of God throughout the universe, giving demonstrative Proof of the unlimited extent of the Creator's Skill, and the fecundity of his Wisdom and Power" (cited in *Plurality of Worlds* 151). Nehemiah Grew, a member of the Royal Society along with Ray, wrote *Cosmologia Sacra: or a Discourse of the Universe as it is the Creature and Kingdom of God* in 1701, arguing that other planets including the Moon were other earths which were populated with inhabitants to give purpose to other suns (ibid.). William Whiston wrote in 1715 that God's glory and might was demonstrated in the existence of other planetary systems. William Derham wrote *Astro-Theology: or a Demonstration of the Being and Attributes of God, from a Survey of the Heavens* in 1715 in which he argues that all the attributes of the universe are evidence for the existence of God. John Keill, a Newtonian, argues that planets revolve around other suns, "Hence we are to consider the whole Universe as a glorious palace for an infinitely great and everywhere present God; and that all the worlds or systems or worlds, are as so many theatres, in which He displays his Divine Power, Wisdom, and Goodness" (cited in *Plurality of Worlds* 155). Johann Jacob Schedult wrote *On the Probability of a Plurality of Worlds* in 1721 that worlds populated with inhabitants "make clear the wisdom, power, and goodness of the Creator, and inspire praise of the Divine" (ibid. 184).

Johann Lambert, a contemporary of Kant and Thomas Wright, published books on the plurality of worlds speculating widely on cosmological and theological implications of inhabitants of other worlds, suggesting that God created a variety of intelligent beings throughout the cosmos as an exercise of the Lord's omnipotence. Kant, Lambert, and Wright also speculated about God's purposes for our own Earth. Edward Young wrote:

One Sun by Day, by Night ten Thousand shine,
    And light us deep into the Deity.
    [*Night Thoughts,* "Night Ninth," lines 748-9].

Young also wrote, "An undevout astronomer is mad" (cited in Crowe 59) as well as:

Each of these stars is a religious house;
I saw their altars smoke, their incense rise;
And heard hosannas ring through every sphere.
(IX, 1881-1883) [cited in Crowe 85]

The great Proprietor's all-bounteous hand
Leaves nothing waste, but sows these fiery fields
With seeds of reason, which to virtues rise
Beneath his genial ray. [cited in Brewster 229]

      James Ferguson (1710 – 1776), a self-taught astronomer who influenced the great Sir William Herschel, argues that astronomy is "the most sublime, the most interesting, and the most useful" subject so that by studying it we become "clearly convinced, and affected with the conviction, of the existence, wisdom, power, goodness, and superintendency of the SUPREME BEING!" (cited in Crowe 60). Ferguson also argues in favor of other worlds inhabited by extraterrestrials. Sir William Herschel (1738 – 1822), a great astronomer, endorsed Ferguson's position that the universe contains a plurality of inhabited worlds including the Moon. E.S. Holden believed that Herschel's view of life on the Moon and other planets "rest more on a metaphysical than a scientific basis" (cited in Crowe 67).
      Johann Christoph Gottsched (1700 – 1755), a German, favors a plurality of worlds and inhabitants, arguing that extraterrestrials need not resemble human beings (Crowe 140). Johann Heironymous Schroter (1745 – 1816) observed the moon and was

    ….fully convinced *that every celestial body may be so arranged physically by the Almighty as to be filled with living creatures organized conformably to its physical plan and praising the power and goodness of God, and that the infinite grandeur of the Creator ought to be glorified in the analogous multiplicity of the physical arrangement of the celestial bodies as it is also certainly revealed in the infinite variety of their living creatures* (cited in Crowe 71).

Johann Elert Bode (1747 – 1826) wrote about inhabitants of the Sun:

Who would doubt their existence? The most wise author of the world assigns an insect lodging on a grain of sand and will certainly not permit…the great ball of the sun to be empty of creatures and still less of rational inhabitants who are ready gratefully to praise the author of their life.

Its fortunate inhabitants, say I, are illuminated by an unceasing light, the blinding brightness of which they view without injury and which in accordance with the most wise design of the all-Good, communicates to them the necessary warmth by means of its thick atmosphere. (cited in Crowe 73)

Bode further writes that "rational beings" living on other worlds "are ready to know the author of their existence and to praise his goodness" (cited in Crowe 74). Bode goes on to say that solar inhabitants are protected from the sun's intense light by the power of God (ibid. 75). He also suggests that the center of the universe is God's abode.

Jerome Lalande (1732 – 1807), French astronomer, wrote about the tense relationship between astronomy and religion:

There have been some writers, as timid as they are religious, who have condemned this system [pluralism] as contrary to religion; this was a bad way to promote the glory of the creator. If the extent of his works announces his power, can one supply any idea more magnificent and more sublime? We see with the naked eye many thousands of stars; an ordinary telescope reveals many more in every region of the sky….[I]magination pierces beyond the telescope; it sees a new multitude of worlds infinitely larger….(cited in Crowe 79)

Nevertheless, Lalande appears to have developed an intense atheism around 1800 where once he seems to have expressed an intense faith. Blaise Pascal wrote in *Pensees* "[Finally] they give them, as a complete proof [of God], the course of the moon and planets...." Adding "Nothing is more calculated to arouse their contempt" (cited in Crowe 80). Such writers seem to have great faith in God while simultaneously asserting that life on other worlds neither proves nor disproves the existence of God.

Henry Baker (1698 – 1774), a microscopist, wrote in *The Universe: A Poem Intended to Restrain the Pride of Man*:

> Nor can those other worlds, unknown to this,
> Lest stor'd with Creatures, or with Beauty be,
> For God is uniform in all his Ways,
> And everywhere his boundless Pow'r displays.
> (cited in Crowe 82)

John Henry Cardinal Newman wrote in a letter to E.B. Pusey on 13 April 1858 (*Letters and Diaries of John Henry Newman*, vol. 18, ed. C. S. Dessain (London, 1968), p. 322), after complaining about how "some scientists usurp the domain of religion" (Crowe xxiv): "Here is Dr. Brewster, I think, saying that 'more worlds than one is the hope of the Christian-' and, as it seems to me, building Christianity more or less upon astronomy." Newman also remarks in *Grammar of Assent* (1870), chapter 9: "in the controversy about the Plurality of worlds, it has been considered...to be so necessary that the Creator should have filled with living beings the luminaries which we see in the sky...that it almost amounts to blasphemy to doubt it."

Alexander Pope (1688 – 1744) supported the idea that God has created a plurality of worlds populated with inhabitants in his *Essay on Man*:

> He, who thro' vast immensity can pierce,
> See worlds on worlds compose one universe,
> Observe how system into system runs,
> What other planets circle other suns,
> What vary'd Being peoples ev'ry star,
> May tell why Heavn'n has made us as we are.
> (Epistle I, lines 23-8).

Daniel Sturmy wrote *A Theological Theory of a Plurality of Worlds* in which he argues in favor of extraterrestrials and quests for support for inhabitants of other worlds in the Bible (Crowe 35). Clergyman Isaac Watts (1674 – 1748), an English Noncomformist minister, composed a hymn which could be interpreted as arguing that Christ came only to the Earth and not to other worlds, but this doesn't mean he disbelieves inhabitants of other worlds exist, rather saying, "'tis probable that [the planets] are all Habitable Worlds furnished with rich Variety of Inhabitants to the Praise of their great Creator" (cited in Crowe 36). Thomas Wright of Durham (1711 – 1786) combines science and religion in his quest to understand God's Creation.

John Wesley (1703 – 1791), Anglican cleric, evangelist, and founder of the Methodist movement, was initially a pluralist who wrote in response to an attack on his natural theology by quoting his opponent:

> "They who affirm, that God created those bodies, the fixed stars, only to give us a small, dim light, must have a very mean opinion of the divine wisdom." I do not affirm this; neither can I tell for what other end He created them: He that created them knows. But I have so high an opinion of the divine wisdom, that I believe no child of man can fathom it. It is our wisdom to be very wary how we pronounce concerning things which we have not seen. (cited in Crowe 94)

Wesley also writes: "Nay," says the philosopher, "if God so loved the world, did he not love a thousand other worlds, as well as he did this? It is now allowed that there are thousands, if not millions, of worlds, besides this in which we live. And can any reasonable man believe that the Creator of all these, many of which are probably as large, yea, far larger than ours, would have such astonishingly greater regard to one than to all the rest?" (cited in Crowe 94-95).

Section 5:   Protestants and Catholics in Europe and across the Atlantic in America

Cotton Mather (1663 -- 1728), American Congregational minister and New England Puritan, author, and scientist who supported inoculation to prevent diseases like smallpox, also held a point of view on Many Worlds Theory (17th-18th century): Mather wrote *Wonderful Works of God Commemorated* (1690) and *Christian Philosopher* (1720). Mather argues in favor of the plurality of worlds, writing:

> Great GOD, what a Variety of *Worlds* hast thou created!...How stupendous are the Displays of thy *Greatness*, and of thy Glory, in the Creatures, with which thou has replenished those Worlds! Who can tell what Angelical Inhabitants may there see and sing the *Praises* of the Lord! Who can tell what *Uses* those marvelous Globes may be designed for! Of these *unknown Worlds* I know thus much, *'Tis our Great GOD that has made them all.* (cited in Crowe 107)

Benjamin Franklin (1706 – 1790), American scientist, author, scientist, inventor, printer, publisher, statesman, diplomat, and Founding Father who helped write the *Declaration of Independence* and influenced the *Constitution of the United States of America*, wrote in 1757 about the possibility of a collision between Halley's Comet and the Earth: "We must not presume too much on our own importance. There are an infinite number of worlds under the divine government, and if this was annihilated, it would scarce be missed in the universe" (cited in Wilkinson 15 and Crowe 109). Franklin seems to have believed not only in a plurality of worlds but also in a plurality of Gods who he claims each govern every solar system throughout the universe individually (Crowe 107 – 108).

Baron Emanuel Swedenborg (1688 – 1772), philosopher, theologian, Christian mystic, and Swedish scientist, whose followers are known as Swedenborgians or members of the Church of the New Jerusalem, and who influenced such people as William Butler Yeats and Ralph Waldo Emerson, was a visionary who claims he saw angels and resurrected humans taking care of other worlds in our solar system and elsewhere. Soame Jenyns (1704 – 1787), a politician, writer of theology, and poet wrote that the goodness of God permeates the cosmos including inhabitants of other worlds:

> Hence soul and sense, diffus'd through ev'ry place,
> Make happiness as infinite as space;
> Thousands of suns beyond each other blaze,
> Orbs roll o'er orbs, and glow with mutual rays;
> Each is a world, where, form'd with wondrous art,
> Unnumber'd species live through ev'ry part.

Edward King (1735? – 1807) favors a plurality of worlds, composing *Hymns to the Supreme Being. In Imitation of the Eastern Songs*. The beautiful poetry contains the following lines:

> Thou, O Lord, hast made all things in Heaven and in Earth:
>   and Thy tender care is over all.
> Innumerable Worlds stood forth at Thy command;
>   and by Thy word they are filled with glorious works.
> Who can comprehend the boundless Universe?
> Or number the Stars of Heaven?
> Are they not the Habitations of Thy Power?
> Filled with manifestations of Thy Wisdom, and Goodness?
> (cited in Crowe 104)

In another passages favoring a plurality of worlds, King writes, "Many worlds are nourished by it: and its glory is great" (cited in Crowe 104). King theorizes that the Sun and Stars are the habitations of the resurrected people (humans and extraterrestrials alike) of the planets in their respective solar systems. Roger Long (1680 – 1770), another pluralist, avers that God created the universe not exclusively for human beings (Crowe 104-105).

Benjamin West (1730 – 1818), writing under the pseudonym Isaac Bickerstaff, wrote in his *Bickerstaff's Boston Almanach for...1778* about Saturn:

> Strange and amazing must the difference be,
> 'Twixt this dull planet and bright Mercury;
> Yet reason says, nor can we doubt at all,

Millions of beings dwell on either ball
With constitutions fitted for that spot.
Where Providence, all-wise, has fix'd their lot.
(cited in Crowe 109)

Benjamin Banneker (1731 – 1806), a Negro farmer, mathematician, astronomer, inventor, writer, essayist, pampleteer, and writer of an almanac, who opposed slavery and war and lobbied Thomas Jefferson to improve the lot of black people, said in 1794:

View yon majestic concave of the sky!
Contemplate well, those glorious orbs on high –
There Constellations shine, and Comets blaze;
Each glitt'ring world the Godhead's pow'r displays!
(cited in Crowe 110)

Philip Freneau (1752 – 1832), American essayist, editor, and poet, known as the "poet of the American Revolution," published in his *The Monmouth Almanac, for the Year M,DCC,XCV* that inhabitants of other worlds are "all comfortably provided for by the benevolence of the Creator" (cited in Crowe 110). James Bowdoin (1726 – 1790), American politician, merchant, physicist, astronomer, and first president of the American Academy of Arts and Sciences, writes that inhabitants populate other worlds, an idea that implies the notion of "a SUPREME MIND..." (Crowe 115).

Thomas Paine in "The Age of Reason" (mid 1790's) argues that there must be a plurality of worlds (McMullin 164). Clearly, in the face of such writings, Christians needed to reconcile their faith with the plurality of inhabited worlds theory (Crowe 164).

Voltaire (1694 – 1778), French philosopher, writer, and satirist, whose real name was Francois-Marie Arouet and whose most famous work is *Candide*, favors the pluralist view and writes a science fiction story entitled *Micromegas* in 1752 in which inhabitants from Sirius (Micromegas) and Jupiter listen to a human theologian explain that, according to Saint Thomas's *Summa Theologica*, with respect to inhabitants of other worlds, "their worlds, their suns, their stars were all made uniquely for man" to which the extraterrestrials rock the ship with their gales of laughter (Crowe 121). Voltaire displays himself to be both a pluralist and a Deist, writing a prayer starting with "It is no longer to men that I address myself; it is to you, God of all beings, of all the worlds...." (cited in Crowe 122). Voltaire writes in "Dogmas":

> BY ORDER OF THE ETERNAL, CREATOR, CONSERVER, REMUNERATOR, AVENGER, PARDONER, etc., etc., be it well know to all the inhabitants of the hundred thousand millions of billions of worlds that it has pleased us to form, that we will never judge any of these inhabitants on their empty ideas, but only on their actions, for such is our justice. (cited in Crowe 123)

Charles Bonnet (1720 – 1793), a very religious scientist from Switzerland, naturalist, and philosopher, who developed a theory of evolution known as catastrophe theory, was the first biologist to use the term "evolution," and who discovered parthenogenesis in aphids, wrote that on other worlds human beings might be angels, and expressed a religious vision of the universe in "Celestial Hierarchies" in which he avers that angels are world-hoppers; he asks if the "INFINITELY GOOD BEING" would deny humans the ability to visit other planets, and his reply is, "No; because you are called one day to take your place among the CELESTIAL HIERARCHIES, you will soar, as [the angels], from planet to planet; you will go from perfection to perfection, and each instant...will be marked by the acquisition of new knowledges" (cited in Crowe 130). Bonnet mixed his belief in a plurality of worlds with this strange palingenesis (metempsychosis or transmigration of souls; literally, rebirth, regeneration), leading others to cut his theories off from Christianity proper.

Francois Xavier de Feller (1735 – 1802), a Jesuit, argues against the plurality of worlds theory and extraterrestrials in general, arguing that the Earth is the only planet with intelligent beings. On the other hand, Abbe Jean Terrasson (1670 – 1750) argues in favor of plurality and inhabitants of other worlds, claiming that the teachings of the Church including the Bible do not unequivocally deny the pluralist position (Crowe 135). He writes, "It is asked...if the eternal Word [Christ] can unite himself hypostatically to a number of men; one responds without hesitation – yes. The men would all be men-God [hommes-Dieu], men in the plural, God in the singular, because these men-God would in effect be several in number as to human nature, but they would be only one in respect to the divine nature..." (cited in Crowe 135). He also suggests that God became incarnate even on worlds which had not Fallen, claiming such inhabitants would deserve the honor even more than sinful beings (ibid.). The vast majority of authors in this era who expressed religious ideas, whether Catholic or Protestant, favored the idea of a plurality of worlds populated with inhabitants.

For Gottsched and others (including me), the idea of extraterrestrials on a plurality of worlds enhances religious faith in Christ and encourages us to laud our Creator who created such a wondrous mixture of innumerable races of intelligent beings. Ewold von Kleist (1715 – 1759), a German poet, wrote in praise of the Creator of many worlds populated with inhabitants:

> Who bids millions of suns with majesty and splendour shine?
> Who doth on their wondrous course to countless worlds their
> paths assign?
> Who endows with life each circle? Who unites the wondrous
> band?
> Thy lips' gentle breathings Lord!
> Yea, thy most high and dread command.
> (cited in Crowe 143)

Christian Furchtegott Gellert (1715 – 1769), a German poet and novelist and professor of philosophy at Leipzig, wrote that inhabitants populated planets orbiting other stars, "an infinite crowd of creatures [whom] the Lord of all nature creates, knows, and conserves!" (cited in Crowe 149).

Thomas Chalmers, as mentioned above, wrote *Astronomical Discourses* (1817) which people interpreted as an attempt to reconcile Christianity with the plurality of worlds theory. James Mitchell (1786? – 1844) wrote *Of the Plurality of Worlds* (1813), saying that arguing against pluralism "would be to impeach the wisdom of our Maker" (cited in Crowe 168). Samuel Taylor Coleridge (1772 – 1834), an English philosopher, critic, and poet, and also author of *Kubla Khan* and *The Rhyme of the Ancient Mariner*, draws the conclusion that the theory of a plurality of worlds enhances our Christian faith: "What in the eye of an intellectual and omnipotent

Being is the whole sidereal system to the soul of one man for whom Christ died?" (cited in Crowe 171).

Adam Clarke (1762? – 1832) wrote in favor of a plurality of worlds, arguing that Scripture supports pluralism, particularly with the phrase "heaven of heavens," and he cites as evidence Deuteronomy 10:14, "Think! The heavens, even the highest heavens, belong to the LORD, your God, as well as the earth and everything in it"[49] and 1 Kings 8:27 in which Solomon says, "Can it indeed be that God dwells among men on earth? If the heavens and the highest heavens cannot contain you, how much less this temple which I have built!" Clarke argues that each sun has its own planets, and God created our Sun and planets in 4004 B.C. (Crowe 173 – 174).

Jacques Necker (1732 – 1804), a Swiss banker and financial director under the French Louis XVI, favors a plurality of worlds created by God and populated with inhabitants, and he passed on this belief to his brilliant daughter, Anne-Louise-Gemaine Necker who, after marrying Baron Erik Magnus Stael von Holstein in 1786, became Madame de Stael (1766 – 1817) or the French-Swiss Baronne de Stael-Holstein, political propagandist, intellectual, novelist, playright, writer of moral and political essays, historian, poet, and literary critic, wrote *Corinne* (1807) in which she says:

> ...death will be for you only a change in habitation; and that which you leave may be the least of all. Oh innumerable worlds, which to our eyes fill the infinity of space! Unknown communities of creatures of God! Communities of his children, scattered in the firmament and arrayed under his vaults! Let our praises join to yours; we do not know your situation; we are ignorant of your first, second, and last portions of the generosities of the supreme being; but in speaking of death, of life, of times past and to come, we attain, we touch on the interests of all intelligent and sentient beings....Families of people, families of nations, assemblies of worlds, you speak with us; Glory to the master of them all, to

---

[49] The NAB note on this passage states: "Even the highest heavens: literally, 'and the heavens of the heavens'; compare the phrase, 'the third heaven,' in 2 Cor 12, 2."

the king of nature, to the God of the universe! (cited in Crowe 179)

Vicomte Francois-Auguste-Rene Chateaubriand (1768 – 1848), a French Romantic author and diplomat, is described by Edmond Gregoire as claiming that Christ traveled from world to world throughout the universe to spread his message: "From globe to globe, from sun to sun, his majestic steps had traversed all those spheres which the divine intelligences inhabit, and perhaps [peut-etre] men unknown to men" (cited in Crowe 181). Chateaubriand appears to have held the belief that other worlds were created by God for human beings to travel to and inhabit and not necessarily for extraterrestrials.

Thomas Chalmers (1780 -- 1847), mentioned above, preached on Thursday, 23 November 1815 at Tron Church, Glasgow, on the topic of Christianity and inhabitants of other worlds, and the series of sermons was published in 1817 as *A Series of Discourses on the Christian Revelation Viewed in Connection with the Modern Astronomy* (also known as *Astronomical Discourses*). The publication of these sermons had a profound effect on the pluralism and extraterrestrials debate in Christian circles. Chalmers was early on a scientist and mathematician but later in life developed a tremendous love for Christianity and preached it fervently, with the doctrines of Christ's Atonement as well as the sinfulness of human beings and our need for grace close to his heart, and his knowledge as a scientist served him well in his discussions of Christianity and inhabitants of other worlds. These published sermons were enormously popular with the general public in both Europe and America. It is worth looking at *Astronomical Discourses* in detail (Crowe 182 – 185).

In his first sermon, Chalmers cites Psalm 8:4: "When I consider thy heavens, the work of thy fingers, the moon and the stars, which thou hast ordained; What is man, that thou are mindful of him? And the son of man, that thou visitest him?"[50] (cited in Crowe 185).

---

[50] The NAB translates Psalm 8:4-5: "When I see your heavens, the work of your fingers, the moon and stars that you set in place -- What are humans that you are mindful of them, mere mortals that you care for them?" The NAB note on this verse states: "*Humans...mere mortals*: literally, '(mortal) person'...'son of man (in sense of a human being, Hebrew

Chalmers says that piously regarding the heavens is a very Christian exercise (ibid.). He also says that God regards everything from the smallest insect to human beings to extraterrestrials with great generosity, so it is both rational and pious to believe that God would "send his eternal son, to die for the puny occupiers of so insignificant a province in the mighty field of his creation" (cited in Crowe 186). He adds that our Creator "came to this humblest of its provinces, in the disguise of a servant, and took upon him the form of our degraded species, and let himself down to sorrows, and to sufferings, and to death, for us" (cited in Crowe 186).

Niceto Alonso Perujo (1841 – 1890), a Catholic canon and author of the great Dictionary of Ecclesiastical Sciences and an excellent edition of Saint Thomas's *Summa Theologica*, avers that pluralism does not contradict Catholic teachings (Crowe 422). The Reverend Thomas Dick (1774 – 1857), a Scottish minister, writer, astronomer, philosopher, and science teacher who is credited for advocating and defending the symbiosis of science and Christianity, dedicated much of his life to the pluralist theory and inhabitants of other worlds. He erroneously believed the moon and other planets in our solar system to be inhabited, but then many people of his era held this belief. He claims that the Bible supports pluralism such as Psalm 8 (cited by Chalmers). When some astronomers suggested that a single massive body exists at the center of the universe, Thomas Dick describes it as "THE THRONE OF GOD" (Crowe 197 – 198). He also suggests that angels may be material extraterrestrials (Crowe 198). One of Thomas Dick's main ideas is his attempt to harmonize science and religion (Crowe 198). He claims that inhabitants on a plurality of worlds make our Infinite Creator even more glorious (201). I believe that the existence of inhabitants of other worlds makes God even more magnificent and worthy of our worship.

Dionysius Lardner (1792/3 – 1859), an Irish popular writer of science and technology, mathematician, and professor of natural philosophy and astronomy at University College, London, in the first chapter of his *Popular Lectures* called "The Plurality of Worlds" writes: "Are those shining orbs which so richly decorate the firmament peopled with creatures endowed like ourselves with reason

---

"*adam*").' The emphasis is on the fragility and mortality of human beings to whom God has given great dignity."

to discover, with sense to love, and with imagination to expand toward their limitless perfection the attributes of Him of 'whose fingers the heavens are the work?'" (cited in Crowe 227).

Ormsby MacKnight Mitchell (1809 – 1862), a West Pointer, was an American pluralist who wrote in one of his lectures:

> Around us and above us rise Sun and System, Cluster and Universe. And I doubt not that in every region of this vast Empire of God, hymns of praise and anthems of glory are rising and reverberating from Sun to Sun and from System to System – heard by Omnipotence alone across immensity and through eternity! (cited in Crowe 234)

Ralph Waldo Emerson (1803 – 1882), a famous American Transcendentalist, wrote in his *Nature*:

> But if man would be alone, let him look at the stars....One might think the atmosphere was made transparent with this design, to give man, in the heavenly bodies, the perpetual presence of the sublime....If the stars should appear one night in a thousand years, how would men believe and adore; and preserve for many generations the remembrance of the city of God which had been shown! (cited in Crowe 235)

Isaac Asimov, an American biochemist, professor at Boston university, and famous science fiction and science writer, once wrote a story based on the last sentence of the above quotation called "Nightfall," which many believe to be the best story he ever wrote and others believe to be the greatest science fiction short story ever written by anyone. In the story, a planet surrounded by six suns has inhabitants who live in perpetual daylight, although there are ancient prophecies about a time when the world was plunged into darkness and mysterious objects called "stars" appeared and civilization was destroyed. The story relates to this book because Asimov pits the scientists against the believers of the ancient prophecies; both groups believe there are stars but neither group knows what the stars actually are. Asimov's story serves to illustrate how religious beliefs as well as scientific beliefs can develop on another world with different attributes. In *Perelandra* by C.S. Lewis, Maleldil the Young (aka

Jesus Christ) commands the first man and first woman on this world that they must stay on the movable islands on the world and not to stay overnight on immovable ground, a commandment the main character from Earth, Ransom, realizes is a different commandment from the one given to Adam and Eve because the conditions on the world Perelandra are different from those of Earth. Ransom reasons that it is not the specific commandment so much as its nature as a commandment which must be obeyed that is important, so he encourages the first woman to obey the commandment even though no reason is supplied as to why the commandment is given. Both these stories serve to illustrate that different theologies can develop on different planets from faith in the same God. Emerson himself later rejected Christianity.

Joseph Smith (1805 – 1844) founded the Church of Jesus Christ of Latter-day Saints and wrote *The Book of Mormon*, which he purportedly translated from "Egyptian, Chaldic, Asyrian, and Arabic" gold plates given him by an angel named Moroni (he gave the gold plates back to the angel, so they cannot be studied). Although *The Book of Mormon* does not contain pluralist theories, later Mormons argue that Smith was a pluralist in later documents such as *The Doctrine and Covenants* and *The Pearl of Great Price*. In *The Pearl of Great Price* is a section called "The Book of Moses" which contains purported visions and revelations given to Moses by God:

29. And he [Moses] beheld many lands; and each land was called earth, and there were inhabitants on the face thereof.

33. And worlds without number have I [God] created; and I also created them for mine own purpose; and by the Son I created them, which is mine Only Begotten.

34. But only an account of this earth, and the inhabitants thereof, give I unto you. For behold, there are many worlds that have passed away by the word of my power. And there are many that now stand, and innumerable are they unto man....

38. And as one earth shall pass away, and the heavens thereof, even so shall another come; and there is no end to my works....

The Mormon church, as I understand it, teaches that God is an extraterrestrial from the planet Kolob ("Book of Abraham") and that human beings can become gods of other worlds. The position of the Catholic Church on the Latter-day Saints is that, because the Mormons specifically and willfully deny with the validity of the contents of the Nicene Creed, which is a statement about the nature of the Trinity, the Mormon baptism is invalid on the grounds that they baptize in the name of three separate gods whom they call Father, Son, and Holy Spirit, rather than in the name of one consubstantial God which the Catholic Church calls Father, Son, and Holy Spirit. Nevertheless, Mormon views on religion and extraterrestrials make for a fascinating study all by itself. However, because I know so little about the teachings of the Church of Jesus Christ of Latter-day Saints, this is all that will be said about the Mormons.

Francois Arago (1786 – 1853), a French physicist, director of the Paris Observatory, and French politician, gave lectures on astronomy which were later published as *Astronomie populaire* in the final section of which he writes:

> Some very pious persons have imagined that to examine what will be the astronomy of an observer situated on diverse planets was to put oneself into a culpable disregard of holy Scripture. I do not share this view. In effect, in transporting an observer to different planets, and even to the center of the sun, we are not saying that he resembles the inhabitants of our globe. Besides, some very wise theologians, for example, Dr. Chalmers, have proved that nothing in the holy books forbids the supposition that the planets are inhabited. (cited in Crowe 247)

Johann Heinrich Kurtz (1809 – 1890), a Lutheran theologian who denies pluralism, argues against Chalmers and the Incarnation of God on other worlds, claiming that either inhabitants of other worlds are not fallen and therefore have no need of redemption or, if they are fallen, then Christ does not save them (Crowe 261 – 262). This, I think, is a rather bleak outlook for extraterrestrials.

Heinrich Heine (1797 – 1856), a German Jewish poet who without enthusiasm converted to Protestantism for nonreligious but pragmatic reasons, wrote in *Heine's Poetry and Prose* (London, 1934), p. 330, a touching account of a childhood dream:

> I grew entirely confused by all the information learned from astronomy, which subject even the smallest child was not spared in that period of enlightenment. I could not get over the wonder of it, that all these thousands of millions of stars were great and beautiful globes, like our own, and that one simple God ruled over all these gleaming myriads of worlds. Once in a dream, I remember, I saw God, in the farthest distance of the high heavens….He was scattering handfuls of seeds, which as they fell from heaven opened out…and grew to tremendous size, until they finally became bright, flourishing, inhabited worlds….I have never been able to forget this face; I often saw this cheerful old man in my dreams again, scattering the seeds of worlds out of His tiny window….I could only see the falling seeds, always expanding to vast shining globes: but the great hens, which were possibly lying in wait somewhere with wide-open beaks, to be fed with these worldspheres, those I could never see. (cited in Crowe 262 – 263)

William Whewell, once a pluralist (as noted above), turned against pluralism, and his work *Of the Plurality of Worlds: An Essay*, published in 1853, had a negative impact on pluralism in many circles including Christian ones. Crowe believes that Whewell's change of heart was largely due to his inability to reconcile pluralism with Christianity (267). When he was a pluralist, Whewell was obviously influenced by Chalmers (Crowe 268). He may also have been influenced by Paley who wrote that the science of astronomy "is not the best medium through which to prove the agency of an intelligent Creator [because we] are destitute of the means of examining the constitution of the heavenly bodies…," (cited in Crowe 268). In the dedication to *Astronomy and General Physics*, Whewell encourages "friends of religion" to examine positively "the progress of the physical sciences, by showing how admirably every advance in our knowledge of the universe harmonizes with the belief of a most wise and good God" (cited in Crowe 269). Whewell argues in favor of

Intelligent Design Theory, an idea he seems to believe will influence people of faith but not those who do not believe in God (ibid.).

Whewell also wrote an unpublished dialogue called *Astronomy and Religion* in 1850 in which two interlocuters, A and B, are dedicated to the debate between pluralism and its theological implications. Speaker A is disturbed by Psalm 8:3/4-4/5,[51] and B asks him to explain why, to which A replies that modern astronomy seems to decry the truth of this passage. Speaker B appears to be the voice of Whewell who asserts that A's claim that inhabitants of other worlds denigrate God's saving act on Earth by Christ disturbs B who begins to doubt the compatibility of extraterrestrials and Christianity (Crowe 278 – 279). Whewell's doubts were rooted in religious concerns, but he tried to combine scientific as well as religious reasons for his rejection of pluralism (Crowe 280 – 281). His major concern seems to have been related to the Incarnation and Redemption of people on Earth by Christ. He seems to suggest that one may accept either Christianity or pluralism but not both, just as Thomas Paine asserted, but, unlike Paine, Whewell comes down clearly on the side of Christianity. Interestingly, Whewell encourages his readers to refrain from speculating about inhabitants of other worlds until it is determined by astronomers that planets around other stars exist. It is noteworthy that astronomers in the late 20th century did exactly that, and no serious astronomer or scholar today denies that other planets orbiting other suns exist.

Sir David Brewster (1781 – 1868) opposed Whewell and engaged in a public debate with him that was followed by the academic public. Brewster criticizes Whewell for his intelligent design theory which Brewster feels limits the power of God. Brewster defends pluralism because he claims it demonstrates God's power (Crowe 301). Brewster read Isaiah 45:12 to support his theory that Scripture supports intelligent beings inhabiting a plurality of worlds: "For thus saith the Lord that created the heavens, God himself that formed the earth, and made it; he that established it, created it not in vain, he formed it to be inhabited" (cited in Crowe

---

[51] Psalm 8:4-5: "When I see your heavens, the work of your fingers, the moon and stars that you set in place -- What are humans that you are mindfu of them, mere mortals that you care for them?"

303). Brewster argues that if the worlds are not inhabited then God would have formed them in vain, further claiming that the verse supports the view that the prophets of the Bible were familiar with other inhabited worlds (ibid.). Brewster was fervent in his beliefs to an extreme that troubled even his supporters.

Interestingly, both Brewster and Whewell were devout men who each believed that their respective positions were the more religious than the other for opposite reasons. Brewster's natural theology caused him to believe that it would be impious to fail to believe inhabitants exist on a plurality of worlds, while Whewell thought it would be impious to believe the opposite position. Thus, the debate in the 19th century raged on between two aging patriarchs, the public following the debate, well, religiously.

According to Richard Simpson (1820 – 1876), a British Catholic writer and literary scholar, the Roman Catholic Church had not up to that time made any *de fide* proclamations either in favor of the theory that other worlds are populated with inhabitants or against it (Crowe 337). Crowe writes: "Although St. Augustine and St. Philastrius of Brixen included this doctrine in lists of heresies, St. Clement of Rome, Clement of Alexandria, St. Irenaeus, Origen, and St. Jerome all affirmed it (337). Simpson disagrees with the Brewster book by saying that Brewster's suggestions that the Incarnation may have taken place on numerous inhabited planets borders on "Gnosticism" (ibid.).

Richard Anthony Proctor (1837 – 1888) was a prolific English astronomical writer whose religious views he rarely expressed, although Crowe notes that he criticizes certain pluralists "whom he describes as overestimating the degree to which God's design for the universe can be known" (Crowe 374). Although Catholic for a time, Proctor eventually left the Church on the grounds that he was told his theories were incompatible with the teachings of the Catholic Church. Crowe says that he rarely expressed his beliefs so it is not known how he ever attempted to reconcile Christianity with pluralism (375).

In America, both Catholics and Protestants discussed the issue of pluralism and inhabitants of other worlds, including Mark Twain and Walt Whitman, though these particular giants of literature did not write within the realm of orthodox Christianity (Crowe 446). Whitman embraced pantheism in conjunction with pluralism as well as transmigrational doctrines (Crowe 446 – 447). Whitman may have been influenced by Thomas Paine who was a friend of Whitman's father (Crowe 447) as well as Paine's *Age of Reason*. Whitman was very anticlerical and antichurch (Crowe 447). Mark Twain, also a pluralist, was also anti-Christian and pessimistic (Crowe 448).

In America, although Protestants disputed Darwinism in the late 19th century, they in general found no theological difficulties with pluralism (Crowe 450). The Mormons, the Seventh Day Adventists, and the Swedenborgians, as well as disciples of Thomas Lake Harris (1823 -- 1906), an American poet, mystic, and spiritualistic prophet, embraced pluralism enthusiastically. Mainstream Protestants were not as enthusiastic, but numerous authors including a Baptist, a Methodist, a Congregationalist, and two Presbyterians wrote on the subject favorably (Crowe 450). Rev. Edwin T. Winkler (1823 – 1883) wrote in favor of the view that Christ's redemptive work extends to inhabitants of other worlds throughout the universe (Crowe 450). Rev. Adam Miller (1810 – 1901) favors pluralism as well as the notion that humans after death populate other planets (Crowe 450 – 451). Enoch Fitch Burr (1818 – 1907), a pluralist and Congregationalist minister, cites the Bible in *Celestial Empires* to support his contention that "God, his holy angels…, the spirits of saved men, ... Satan, the evil angels, and the lost souls…have their proper homes on glorious materialisms *somewhere* out yonder in the profound of space" (cited in Crowe 451). Rev. William Leitch (1818 – 1864), a Presbyterian, says that the Bible does not directly support pluralism but does not deny it either (Crowe 452). Leitch believes the Incarnation of Christ is unique to the Earth and also rejects the idea that the merits of Christ's atoning sacrifice applies to extraterrestrials (Crowe 452).

Rev. Augustine F. Hewit (1820 – 1897), the superior general of the Paulists, suggests that currently the plurality of worlds are uninhabited, according to Scripture, but after the final judgement will be inhabited by resurrected humans (Crowe 456 – 457).

If life is an extremely unlikely occurrence bordering on the impossible, then it follows that some divine impetus is necessary for life to occur at all. Darwinism tells us how life evolves but says nothing about how life began. Experiments by reputable scientists have established the veracity of the theory that life arises from previous life and does not arise from spontaneous generation. Nevertheless, many scientists seem to hold to the theory that life arose on Earth by spontaneous generation even while simultaneously asserting that spontaneous generation no longer occurs. This position is inconsistent with science as well as theology.

Rabbi Hayim Perelmuter, former President of the Chicago Board of Rabbis and a professor at the Catholic Theological Union in Chicago, says that modern Judaism would embrace the discovery of inhabitants of other worlds wholeheartedly because it would expand the Jewish understanding of the universe. Perelmuter writes, "We Jews have had to adjust to all kinds of things in history, including Nazi Germany and the difficulties with Israel. I am sure we could adjust to space beings emerging from flying saucers as well" (Peters, "Contemporary Theology" 4). Many Christian theologians and popular writers share Perelmuter's view that members of different faiths will adjust to the existence of extraterrestrials without their faiths disintegrating.

Rabbi Norman Lamm is a modern scholar who refers to medieval Jewish thought to express his belief that Jews should examine "a Jewish exotheology, an authentic Jewish view of God and man in a universe in which man is not the only intelligent resident, and perhaps inferior to many other races" (cited in Dick, *Life on Other Worlds* 250 – 251). Lamm argues that God is expansive enough to create and love innumerable inhabitants of innumerable worlds. For Jews, the existence of extraterrestrials expands our knowledge of God and his universe while not denigrating the importance and uniqueness of humanity.

Fundamentalists in their literature have sought to demonize UFOs, and this may reflect how Fundamentalists will react to actual extraterrestrials. Fundamentalists give the impression that Christianity is more fragile than it actually is (Peters, "Introduction" 2). I suspect that, when we encounter intelligent beings from other worlds, most religious people, including Fundamentalists, will react with intelligence and calm reason as they seek to find out what they believe and as they seek to explain human religious belief systems to them.

Chapter 11

Religion and Science

God does not play dice.
                – Albert Einstein

Theology is the queen of the sciences. It is the study of God as revealed in His Word. From it flows the knowledge of the discovery of secrets imbedded in God's creation. Theology is the study of what God has revealed to Man about Himself and His creation.
                -- Christian Apologetics and Research Ministry Webmaster
                www.godonthe.net/evidence/dictiona.htm

The mystery of the Incarnation grants insight into the mysteries of the universe in light of a sense of order in creation and the power it gives to sustain us in the midst of sin and suffering so that we experience an interiorization of morals and values and faith in the mysteries of the Cross and resurrection. God gives us minds capable of using reason both to question and to discover the secrets of the inner workings of his universe. Religion and science have much to say to each other, and, in this chapter, we will discuss the sometimes violent interplay of the different modes of thought imbedded within each discipline.

Two revolutions in the history of humanity have forever altered our ways of experiencing reality in both its material and spiritual forms: the scientific revolution and the rise of Christianity. The opposite of Christianity is not science but heresy, and the opposite of science is not Christianity but ignorance. Like dogs and cats, science and religion are not natural enemies, but they are not necessarily natural friends either. The epistemologist may argue that, like Socrates, we can know nothing but only reach conclusions of reasonable certainty based on observation, hypotheses, tests, and logic. However, it may be said that there is no such thing as scientific knowledge because what we think we know is really only strong or weak beliefs and not asseverations.[52]

What is science? What is religion? What are the consequences of the scientist and the theologian engaging in dialogue? Nothing other than the discovery that science and religion are two different sides of the same coin. In that vein, I will attempt to define science and religion in the hopes of experiencing a vision of truth that many scientists and theologians only dream about.

Religion is a system of beliefs developed by human beings (and perhaps extraterrestrials, but that is still unknown) not only from reason but also from revelation such that religious information (whether objectively true or false) purports to be special and vitally important with respect of the nature of the universe and humanity's role in it along with the relationship of human beings (and possibly extraterrestrials) to the universe's creator and/or other divine beings involved in the spiritual maintenance of the universe. However, there is a wide divergence of claims among different religions and religious persons as to what this information is, and what assurance we have that it is true. Religion is the dispensation and reception of beliefs believed by the recipient to contain information about the divine realm and people's relationship to it. Religious belief entails the reception of information that may or may not be true.

Religious belief is radically different from ordinary knowledge and how we discover it: C.S. Lewis wrote, "Most people don't believe in heaven in quite the same way they believe in Australia." In many religions, the sort of information that is regarded as crucial consists of reported revelations of the word of God. The differences between revealed beliefs and ordinary knowledge is remarkable: Scientific knowledge is gathered from generally acceptable evidence, experimental data, records, public experience, and facts, whereas religious beliefs are gathered from eyewitnesses who report religious information, such as prophets who report prophecy as written in the Bible. Furthermore, the test of whether the Bible is a source of religious beliefs boils down to personal experience or faith in the truth of someone else's personal experience of the divine. There are historical problems about when the various books of the Bible were

---

[52] Asseverations means here positive, solemn, and emphatic declarations that are regarded as absolutely true.

written, who wrote them, and the like, but these are different sorts of problems from whether the Bible is a source of religious beliefs. How do we make this determination?

We begin by studying the religious epistemology of different faith traditions in an effort to determine whether religious belief constitutes justified true belief. We may begin with Christian epistemology: does Christianity not only have but teach religious knowledge? Is there a difference between Catholic epistemic justifications for true belief and Protestant epistemic justifications for true belief? One major difference between Calvinist epistemology and Catholic epistemology lies in the approach to Original Sin because, although both traditions agree that the Fall harmed natural human faculties, the position of Catholics is that the Fall primarily damaged the will and only secondarily the intellect, which for epistemologists is the root of knowledge, for the intellect is the developing and holding of knowledge. Moreover, the Catholic position is that reason is a powerful source of ethical knowledge. Natural knowledge differs from yet complements revealed knowledge.

Both moral and metaphysical knowledge are reflections of our knowledge of human nature, and human reason gives us such knowledge. Catholicism also rejects evidentialism, a Reformed belief used to attack Catholicism and which maintains, in the words of W.K. Clifford, "It is wrong always, everywhere, and for anyone to believe anything upon insufficient evidence." Even so, some Catholic evidentialists maintain that religious beliefs (including, according to some, revealed truths) are supported by adequately justified evidence, leading to justified true belief.

Anyone can write a book and declare that the book contains religious information, but how do we know whether this is true? The answer is that we cannot know whether it is true; rather, we can only believe that it is true. The truth-value of a declaration that a book contains religious truth cannot be established via ordinary knowledge, but rather personal faith in the truth-value of the declaration. Thus, faith is necessary for religious belief but not sufficient.[53] No

---

[53] In standard logic, a necessary condition is one which must be satisfied for the statement to be true, whereas a sufficient condition is one which, if satisfied, makes the statement true. In other words, the statement If P then

historical investigation can establish the truth-value of any declaration of religious beliefs. Whether Moses was correct in his assertion that he received religious information (whether true or false) from a divine source (God) cannot be historically or scientifically determined, at least by current science. Whether Moses dispenses religious beliefs that are truthful declarations is a matter of belief. Carl Sagan, on the other hand, in a fictional work, postulated that God may have hidden a secret code in the value of pi that gives us religious information about the nature of the divine realm, and if we ever discover this code and accurately decode the information contained in it to dispense to people, that would be proof of God's existence. However, our current scientific knowledge of pi has not yet revealed such religious knowledge. The difference between an ordinary book of ordinary historical knowledge, like Caesar's Gallic Wars, and a religious book, is that one purports to contain religious beliefs while the other does not because it contains no information about the divine realm that is necessary for belief. The standards we apply to determine historical information and scientific information do not help us to determine if some particular book or person such as a prophet dispenses religious beliefs. Thus, to determine the truth-value of declarations of religious beliefs requires instead some element of faith or religious experience; that is, these things are necessary for beliefs to be religious in character, and containing information about the divine realm is sufficient for it to be religious belief.

Let us suppose that an archaeologist discovers a document that itself purports to contain religious information. We can question the finder, examine and study the contents of the document, and subject it

---

Q means that P is a sufficient condition of Q, whereas in the statement If Q then P, then P is a necessary condition of Q. For example, for whole numbers greater than 2, that the number must be odd is a necessary condition of the number's quality as prime but not a sufficient condition (there are odd numbers that are not prime). Moreover, that a number is evenly divisible by 10 is a sufficient condition to know that it is divisible by 2, while the conclusion, that the number is divisible by 2, is a necessary condition of the hypothesis, because, if the hypothesis is that a number is divisible by 10, it necessarily follows that it is divisible by 2. Finally, the statement P if and only if Q is equivalent to If P then Q and If Q then P, meaning that P is both necessary and sufficient for Q. For instance, if a number's last digit in 0, then it is evenly divisible by 10, and if a number is evenly divisible by 10, then its last digit is 0.

to historical and scientific tests about its origin and meaning, but we cannot subject the contents of the document to chemical tests or obtain scientifically empirical information about the contents. Rather, we can only rely upon non-empirical evidence such as extraordinary signs or miracles that distinguish this document from others and lead us to believe that the document contains significant religious information. Thus, the document is not necessary to personal belief in the divine realm, but belief in the divine realm is necessary to accepting the text as containing meaningful religious truth. Furthermore, acceptance of the nature of the document as religious requires one's personal conviction, belief, faith, or religious experience that the document contains the revealed word of God. Just because we accept the truth-value of a document does not de facto make it an ark of religious beliefs; rather, one must have personal conviction or faith that the document contains religious beliefs, or experience a divine revelation that this is so, or believe the divine revelation of others who claim that this is so.

The Bible contains religious documents because certain people Jews/Christians/Muslims) believe it contains religious beliefs (a necessary but not sufficient condition) and members of institutions such as churches, synagogues, or mosques proclaim that the documents called the Bible contain religious information describing the nature of the universe and people's relationship to it and the divine realm. Furthermore, the information in the Bible is dispensed to people as religious beliefs and is received by people as religious beliefs. Therefore, Christianity, Judaism, and Islam are said to be religions because each organization dispenses religious beliefs to its members who receive it as the vitally important information of the divine realm and people's relationship to it. Some variations of Buddhism are not properly religions because they have no belief in a personal god or gods, which are necessary to a realm being divine by definition, whereas other variations of Buddhism do have such a belief that is dispensed to and received by people. Some forms of Buddhism are, like Confucianism, therefore more properly called philosophies since they entail beliefs about how to live but do not express humanity's relationship to the divine.

Alvin Plantinga states that the evidentialist objects that belief in God is not properly "basic," an objection rooted in foundationalism, which asserts that a proposition P is "basic" for

Cynthia Anne Miller Smith

person S if it is self-evident or incorrigible (the position of modern foundationalists), or if it is self-evident or "evident to the senses" (the position of classical foundationalists). Plantinga rejects both modern foundationalism and classical foundationalism on the grounds that both are "self-referentially incoherent" ("Is Belief in God Properly Basic" 135). Plantinga asserts that the Reformed position is that belief in God is properly basic and is not groundless. Plantinga also argues that we have a natural disposition as creatures of God to see the handiwork of the universe as evidence for God; now, this sounds like something Saint Thomas would say. Why is belief in the Great Pumpkin not properly basic? Plantinga defends his position by asserting that just because he rejects foundationalism does not mean that he accepts just anything as properly basic. In my opinion, he doesn't adequately address why we should believe in the Christian God but not the Great Pumpkin. I think that the Catholic position refutes Plantinga's rejection of foundationalism on the grounds that reason tells us that God created the universe because God designed our minds to use reason to develop belief in God, and God did not design our minds to believe in the Great Pumpkin. For this reason, many religions have similar moralities that may be construed as properly basic even while having different ideas about the nature of God. For this reason, revelation is an important complement to reason, as both Saint Thomas and Saint Augustine would agree.

Ralph McInerny suggests that not only do Christian beliefs influence philosophy but the lack of beliefs also influences philosophy, so that lack of belief is not simply a negation that leaves pure reason in its wake (266). He says that if reason is not influenced by faith then reason is an "existential vacuum" that leaves nothing in its wake. Christian philosophy, if it exists, serves to reinforce the notion that reason complements faith and vice versa. The position of modern Thomists seems to be that knowledge or reason is what scholarship is comprised of, so that to rest scholarship on the foundation of Christian belief is to deprive scholarship of its very definitional nature (McInerny 267). Plantinga's rejoinder is that faith is in and of itself a type of knowledge, a position Saint Thomas agrees with, and that beliefs based on faith comprise theology (hence religious knowledge) and not philosophy (essentially the Augustinian position).

218

Plantinga's position that faith is a type of knowledge is found in both Calvin and Thomas, but what is knowledge? For Plantinga, knowledge is thinking a truth for which one has adequate justification (what Plantinga calls "warrant"). For Plantinga, a belief has warrant if one's senses are functioning correctly, but how do we know whether our senses are functioning correctly? For Calvin, a belief is true whether one comes to know the truth belief from reason or faith. I'm not sure Thomas would disagree. The "Sensus divinitatis" is a phrase used to denote beliefs resulting in knowledge derived from the natural mental faculty of reason granted us by God as an intrinsic quality of our human nature. Unfortunately, according to Thomas, that nature has been damaged by the Fall and therefore cannot save, so that for the believer it is necessary to supplement this natural knowledge with revealed knowledge in order for the knowledge to be salvific. So, not only do we have natural knowledge of God obtained by reason, we have revealed knowledge of God divulged by Prophets and the Church inspired by the Holy Spirit.

What is the difference between knowledge of the Sensus Divinatatis and the Testimony of the Holy Spirit, that is, revealed knowledge? Does the created universe give us knowledge of God? If faith is a type of knowledge, it is still a different type of knowledge than natural knowledge. When natural knowledge and revealed knowledge coincide, everything is fine, but what about objectors who claim that natural knowledge contradicts revealed knowledge? The Catholic/Thomistic position seems to be that natural knowledge and revealed knowledge cannot contradict one another by definition, so any apparent discrepancies between the types of knowledge are caused by human nature's Fallen tendency to fail to comprehend adequately what is true knowledge.

Reason leads to beliefs about the natural universe that are distinct from beliefs derived from revelation, so faith and philosophy do not mix, as it were, according to Plantinga. He seems to suggest that what we know by reason is epistemically[54] superior to what we know by revelation. Perhaps the Catholic notion of "mystery" is baffling to the pure reason theorist on the dubious grounds that, given enough time, humans can learn all that is learnable and ultimately

---

[54] Epistemically means relating to knowledge or knowing; in other words, cognitive. (From the Greek word *episteme* meaning "knowledge.")

know all that is knowable (a divine characteristic). Epistemology is not simply the study of knowledge but the study of the limits of human knowledge, so that, no matter how long we may live, we will not ever be able to know all that is knowable. Thus, we must rely on both reason and testimony to make sense of the universe around us. Knowledge based on testimony (such as the Pythagorean Theorem) we may believe is true because expert mathematicians claim it is true and not based on whether we really understand it. Even scientists accept as true a very great deal of scientific knowledge based on testimony (that is, ideas in papers published in reliable journals). It can be argued that theology is a science.

The Fathers of the Catholic Church including Augustine go to great lengths to defend Christian dogmas and thereby indirectly show how revealed truth harmonizes with reason, that is, how religious knowledge harmonizes with natural knowledge. The position of many Catholics today is that faith and reason are in harmony so that religious knowledge does not contradict natural knowledge and vice versa. The senses, in this view, are primarily trustworthy, while perfect knowledge is intellectual knowledge based on sense data which we can rise above to reach general conclusions about the nature of the universe and its creator. We know we exist by intuition (Descartes's Cogito ergo sum), we know God exists by demonstration, and we know the universe exists by sensation. The Catholic believes the religious information dispensed by the Catholic Church to be true knowledge because religious knowledge is based on justified true belief resting on reliable testimony (Oral Tradition and Written Tradition or Scripture), while the Protestant believes the religious information of the Bible to be true knowledge based on justified true belief resting on reliable testimony (Sola Scriptura). Nevertheless, the veridicality[55] of religious information, that is, whether it constitutes knowledge based on true belief, ultimately rests on faith. Moreover, it can be argued that much scientific information is judged to be knowledge based on testimony (publications in reliable journals). Thus, religious knowledge and scientific knowledge complement one another.

---

[55] Veridicality means truthful, that is, corresponding to facts and not illusory; real, genuine.

As sentient beings, we are enormously indebted to the testimony of others whom we regard as reliable for a great deal of what we generally call "knowledge" (Coady 13). Without testimony, our level of knowledge would be no better than our stone age ancestors. The question is what testimony we accept for different types of "knowledge." We accept the testimony of scientists and mathematicians for scientific and mathematic knowledge, and we accept the testimony of prophets and religious people for religious knowledge. Scientists and mathematicians may argue that the testimony of scientists and mathematicians is a more reliable form of knowledge than religious knowledge because experiments can be reproduced for the discerning public, whereas religious experiences cannot generally be exactly reproduced by experiment in quite the same way. Thus, geometric proofs and scientific experiments can be repeated to prove the veridicality of scientific or mathematical knowledge, whereas prophets or religious persons typically cannot reproduce religious experiences for which the claim of religious knowledge is based.

If a person is dying, courts often regard the dying person's last words as true on the theory that people do not lie when they are about to die. However, this is true only for certain types of testimony. For example, if a dying person said, "John Doe shot me," his testimony would be regarded as having veridicality, but if a dying person said, "I have squared the circle," his testimony would not be regarded as having veridicality because it has been proven by mathematicians writing in reputable journals that the circle cannot be squared. The testimony of religious martyrs is often regarded as having veridicality with respect to religious beliefs but not with respect to scientific or mathematical beliefs (Coady 52 – 53). Thus, scientific and mathematical knowledge is distinct from religious knowledge in that scientific and mathematical knowledge can be empirically verified whereas religious knowledge cannot be empirically verified, but, if accepted as true, must be accepted as justified true belief on the grounds that the testimony of the testifier is veridical for non-empirical reasons.

Thomas Aquinas refuses to say that knowledge is ever based on testimonial evidence because, following the ancient Greeks, Thomas perceived knowledge as coming from a person's ability to reason correctly from prime axioms.[56] Thus, for Thomas, religious belief is not actually knowledge, and the only way for a person to develop true knowledge is through scientific reasoning (Coady 16). Our reliance on the testimony of others for our beliefs is, for Thomas, a kind of faith (Coady calls this "natural faith") endemic to our society (ibid.) and part of the reason why our society continues to function as a collective whole without disintegrating into a knowledgeless mass of confusion. While Thomas regards faith as a necessary component of religious belief, he falls short of calling it "knowledge," a term he reserves for beliefs derived from the use of reason (Coady 17).

Saint Augustine argues that a knower may not transmit to anyone else his knowledge (Coady 18). Augustine suggests that knowledge exists only in the mind of knowers who use reason to derive justified true belief, and that knowledge cannot be transferred to others by testimony alone, no matter how reliable the authority (ibid.). Augustine holds that we know by reason and by sense data but not by contact with other minds. Augustine also suggests that sense data only produce belief and not knowledge, though the belief may have great utility (ibid.). Augustine's attitude seems to be two-fold: sense data and testimony produce valuable beliefs but not knowledge, and another sense in which sense data and testimony do produce a kind of knowledge (ibid.). Augustine writes: "What we know, therefore, we owe to reason, what we believe, to authority" (Coady 19). Augustine thus makes a distinction between scientific knowledge determined by reason and empiricism, and religious belief based on authoritative testimony such as is found in Scripture. Augustine argues that much of our knowledge is based on testimony, such as when and where we were born, that is not based on sense data, yet that we regard as true belief. Thus, the distinction between true knowledge and true belief is very thin, leading one to conclude that empirical knowledge is true not simply on the basis of testimony and religious belief is true not simply on the basis of testimony but inclusive of testimony. Nevertheless, Augustine does assert in some

---

[56] Axioms are generally accepted propositions or principles, maxims, rules, or laws that are accepted universally by convention. Prime axioms are in the subject of logic primary principles, maxims, rules, or laws that are commonly accepted as a general matter on the basis of their intrinsic worth as self-evident and undisputed truths.

obscure writings that testimonial evidence does give us a kind of knowledge (Coady 20), leading him to say, "if it is not inappropriate to say that we also know what we firmly believe, this arises from the fact that we are correctly said to see mentally what we believe, even though it is not present to our senses" (ibid.). Coady says that no matter how much we want to believe something that is false is true, it will never be true (21). Religious belief has foundations of testimony just as scientific belief has foundations of both testimony and experimentation.

To believe the truth and to shun error are two different approaches to epistemic knowledge. William James suggests that these two approaches are consistent, but they are as different as saying a glass of water is half full or half empty and has significant consequences in terms of our approach to what we believe we know. It is possible to shun error by declining to hold any beliefs at all, like Socrates who claimed to known nothing, but this is akin to avoidance of telling lies by declining to speak at all (Coady 112). James says, "the risk of being in error is a very small matter when compared with the blessings of real knowledge" (ibid.), so one might say that justified true belief in God is more desirable than any kind of belief that is contrary to faith in God (as in Pascal's Wager). Generally, James seems to think that the benefits of believing in God are greater than the potential adverse consequences of not believing in God, but this flies in the face of "It is wrong always, everywhere, and for anyone to believe anything upon insufficient evidence" (Clifford, ibid.). So, to believe incorrectly is construed as morally wrong, but believing testimonial evidence leading to justified true belief is morally right. The question for everyone, believer and non-believer alike, is whether the testimony is reliable, with believers generally attributing the quality of truth to testimony and non-believers generally attributing the quality of error to the same religious testimony, each giving different reasons for their conclusion. Thus, the question as to whether religious knowledge is possible is just as fundamentally unanswerable to the unbeliever as is the question as to whether knowledge in general is possible to one who holds to the brain-in-a-vat hypothesis (that is, the belief that I am a brain-in-a-vat and all of you readers of this book along with the entire universe are merely figments of my imagination. This belief is often called solipsism, from the Latin solus (alone) plus ispe (self)).

John Locke wrote that because God is a God of truth God would not ask us to believe anything that cannot be determined or learned by natural reason (Pojman 510). Since faith and reason both consistently produce true belief for Locke, faith must be defended with evidence to be considered religious knowledge. The contention of many religious believers is that evidence for faith includes verifiable and reliable testimony of witnesses to religious experiences. Locke writes,

> Revelation is natural reason enlarged by a new set of discoveries communicated by God immediately, which reason vouches for the truth of, by the testimony and proofs it gives, that they come from God. So that he that takes away reason, to make way for revelation, puts out the light of both, and does much the same, as if he would persuade a man to put out his eyes, the better to receive the remote light of an invisible star by telescope. (cited in Pojman 511)

Thus, for Locke, testimony provides evidence of God by natural reason that is natural revelation. Reason and faith thus complement one another nicely. For William James, who is not an evidentialist like Clifford, our will to believe must supersede our desire for evidence of the unseen (Pojman 519).

In conclusion, religion is the giving or receiving of religious beliefs. Religious beliefs contain information derived from personal faith, conviction, or personal experience of the divine and contain information that is regarded as true and vital to an understanding of the nature of the universe and the role of humanity in it with respect to the divine realm. Religion often entails believing that certain information obtained via testimony contains religious beliefs on the basis of faith in the truth-value of the person or document giving the information that is claimed to be religious belief, which is personal conviction, faith, or personal experience of the divine. While there is a wide divergence of opinion concerning the truth-value of the religious beliefs of different religions, religion itself is properly defined as the dispensation of religious beliefs in which people have faith as a necessary condition of divine truth. The ancients asked, "What is truth?" Religious beliefs must have the quality of truth in order to count as religious knowledge, so religious beliefs must be consistent with empirical beliefs, for, as Arthur C. Clarke, cited earlier, once noted, "any faith which cannot survive collision with truth is not worth many regrets."

Chapter 12

Science and Christianity

The God whom science recognizes must be a God of universal laws exclusively, a God who does a wholesale, not a retail business. He cannot accommodate his processes to the convenience of individuals.
-- William James, *The Varieties of Religious Experience*, 20

All our scientific and philosophic ideas are altars to unknown gods.
-- William James, *The Dilemma of Determinism* [1884]

Anybody who has been seriously engaged in scientific work of any kind realizes that over the entrance to the gates of the temple of science are written the words: *Ye must have faith.* It is a quality which the scientist cannot dispense with.
-- Max Planck, *Where Is Science Going?* [1932]

Cast your bread upon the waters; after a long time you may find it again.
-- Ecclesiastes 11:1

Many anti-Christians assert that Biblical myths have been thoroughly debunked because they believe that there is a complete, perfect, and irreconcilable conflict between science and Christianity. It is obvious to me that people who believe that science and Christianity are irreconcilable understand neither science nor theology. No empirical evidence refutes the teachings of the Catholic Church, either Oral Tradition or Written Tradition (Scripture).

By definition, Tradition and Scripture never theologically conflict. Scripture contains historical errors because the Bible is not a history textbook. Similarly, Scripture contains scientific errors because the Bible is not a science textbook. Finally, Scripture contains no theological errors because the Bible *is* a *theology textbook.* Sometimes Scripture is historically inconsistent, but it is not theologically inconsistent. The point of the Joseph story is to tell how God showed his power by blessing Joseph and his family and is not about whether Joseph was sold to the Ishmaelites or rescued from the cistern by the Midianites – the inspired editor imperfectly meshed together two different traditions for the story (cf. Genesis 37:28; 37:36; 39:1). Trying to make the stories consistent is a little like trying to keep Star Trek episodes consistent – it frustrates you and annoys the writers and producers.

Some people claim that in the war between science and the Catholic Church, science won at the expense of the teachings of the Church. This is nonsense. In point of fact, the Catholic Church has gone on record as having formally stated that they have no quarrel with science. There never was a bloody war between science and faith. Faith and science complement one another. Trying to create a dichotomy between faith and science is a useless enterprise. Religion without science is lame; science without religion is blind (Einstein was right). The Catholic Church teaches that science is compatible with Oral Tradition and Scripture. Pope Leo writes:

> The Catholic Church has always taught that "no real disagreement can exist between the theologian and the scientist provided each keeps within his own limits....If nevertheless there is a disagreement....it should be remembered that the sacred writers, or more truly 'the Spirit of God who spoke through them, did not wish to teach men such truths (as the inner structure of visible objects) which do not help anyone to salvation'; and that, for this reason, rather than trying to provide a scientific exposition of nature, they sometimes describe and treat these matters either in a somewhat figurative language or as the common manner of speech those times required, and indeed still requires nowadays in everyday life, even amongst most learned people." (Providentissimus Deus 18)

In the Catholic Catechism, the Church teaches:

> Though faith is above reason, there can never be any real discrepancy between faith and reason. Since the same God who reveals mysteries and infuses faith has bestowed the light of reason on the human mind, God cannot deny himself, nor can truth ever contradict truth. Consequently, methodical research in all branches of knowledge, provided it is carried out in a truly scientific manner and does not override moral laws, can never conflict with faith, because the things of the world and the things of the faith derive from the same God.

> The humble and persevering investigator of the secrets of nature is being led, as it were, by the hand of God in spite of himself, for it is God, the conserver of all things, who made them what they are. (CCC 159)

The Catholic Church has no fear of science or scientific discovery. Similarly, the theory of evolution does not violate Catholic theology or any Catholic teachings including Scripture. A Catholic may believe that the stories of Creation in Scripture are mythical in character and not violate Catholic teachings. Whether Scripture contains scientific errors is irrelevant to Catholic theology. For example, if a writer of a cookbook made a reference to sunrise and sunset, should one conclude that the text was scientifically inaccurate, since everyone knows it is not the sun that rises and falls but rather the Earth that revolves around the sun spinning on its axis? The Bible contains many different types of literature including legal documents, history, poetry, folk tales, parables, gospels, myths, letters, and apocalyptic literature. Poetry is filled with symbols and metaphors, and to interpret a poem literally is often to miss the point the poet is trying to convey. To read poetry as if it contained science lessons would be just as big a mistake as reading a science textbook as if it contained religious knowledge. Science and theology complement one another but are not the same. The first eleven chapters of Genesis are a kind of poetic prose that is mythical in character, but the tales are profoundly true on a deep level that must not be confused with history. We should be sensitive in the Bible to poetic symbol and imagery to avoid the mistake of reading Scripture as though it were a science textbook and vice versa.

We should not search for scientific knowledge in a theology textbook anymore than we should search for theological knowledge in a science textbook. Some scientists are very poor writers and make grammatical mistakes in their essays. If we treated a poorly written science paper as if it were a textbook of English grammar, we would find a number of glaring errors. Does that mean the scientific information in the science textbook is flawed because it contains grammatical errors? No. Nor does the Bible contain theological errors simply because the stories told, which teach theology not science, reflect an imperfect understanding of some scientific principles.

When I was in school, we were taught that, before you read a text, you should know who the author is and who the intended audience is in order to properly understand the text. Scientists write science textbooks for science students, and so science textbooks may contain theological errors because they are not theology textbooks. The Bible is a library of books that often tell violent stories about violent times in an effort to teach theological and moral truths. I read in a high school biology textbook about the scientific experiments on Jews conducted by the evil Joseph Mengele, and what those experiments told us about human biology and human genetics. The morality of these experiments was appalling, but the science textbook is not a moral textbook and so contains appalling morality. Does that make the scientific knowledge Mengele gained invalid? No. Similarly, the Bible's scientific errors or historical errors do not make the theology of the Bible erroneous.

For human beings, empirical uncertainty in the face of the omniscience of God leads to the belief that our senses are so limited that our very perceptions are very fallible while the perceptions of God are infallible. God not only sees our hearts but also speaks to us in the language of the heart. God, because he has illimitable consciousness, experiences certain truth because Christ is the truth: "I am the way and the truth and the life: No one comes to the Father except by me" (John 14:6). Jesus is the divinely revealed truth which is the very imprint of the Father leading to freedom from sin and death via the experience of divine knowledge.

Some regard the omniscience of God as incompatible with free will. Those who believe it is a paradox understand neither omniscience nor free will. It is like questioning whether light is a wave or a particle – it depends on the way one looks at it. Can God create a human with a free will such that the free will actions of the human are not presciently known or believed? Can God create randomness in the sense that God does not know the future? This question is a lot like asking "Can God create a rock so heavy that he cannot lift it?" God's knowledge of the universe he created is total and without error. He thought it and brought it into being with his Word (Logos). God sustains the universe with his being. He knows every sparrow that falls and every butterfly's wing that flutters. Nothing anyone of us can do can surprise God who knows our hearts intimately and completely and infallibly, who experiences all of our deepest desires as his own, and from whom no secrets are hidden. The Psalmist tells us:

> LORD, you have probed me, you know me:
> You know when I sit and stand;
> You understand my thoughts from afar.
> My travels and my rest you mark;
> With all my ways you are familiar.
> Even before a word is on my tongue,
> LORD, you know it all.
> Behind and before you encircle me
> And rest your hand upon me.
> Such knowledge is beyond me,
> Far too lofty for me to reach.
> (Psalm 139:1-6)

For Saint Thomas, reason and faith are compatible, but we know with high or low probabilities of truth while we believe religious truth. Perhaps God, like Socrates, knows nothing but believes everything that is religious truth, and so reveals religious truth to humans. However, such a view might be placing undue limitations on the power of God. We should not and cannot limit God with our own limitations. With the proper materials and tools, the scientist, some believe, can learn all that is learnable, while others maintain that only God has this power, yet perhaps God grants us the power to learn everything of importance and place this knowledge in libraries for the dissemination of the curious and the devout. Christians believe that we do have freedom of choice. In the Old Testament, Ecclesiasticus/Sira 15:14-20 tells us:

> When God, in the beginning, created man,
> > he made him subject to his own free choice.
> If you choose you can keep the commandments;
> > it is loyalty to do his will.
> There are set before you fire and water;
> > to whichever you choose, stretch forth your hand.
> Before man are life and death,
> > whichever he chooses shall be given him.
> Immense is the wisdom of the LORD;

> he is mighty in power, and all-seeing.
> The eyes of God see all he has made;
> he understands man's every deed.
> No man does he command to sin,
> to none does he give strength for lies.

Some argue that we do not really know what knowledge is with respect to God. To deny God knowledge of the minds of human beings (and perhaps inhabitants of other worlds) on the altar of free will is to deny God's omniscience. To claim that God is an atemporal being does not really make a path out of this dilemma. If God existing in eternity knows our hearts and thoughts and free choices before we make them, then God is demonstrating temporal knowledge via atemporal means. In this sense, I see no conflict between human free will and divine omniscience. Since God is omniscient, he knows all potential futures based on every thought and action possible to sentient creatures. While contemplating this issue, I find solace in the same way that Isaiah found solace: "God indeed is my savior; I am confident and unafraid. My strength and my courage is the LORD, and he has been my savior" (12:2). To trust in God is to trust that he understands each one of us well enough to guide us in all ways at all times.

God is truth. Truth is not a thing which exists outside of God but is immanent within God. It can be argued that there are no paradoxes in God, only paradoxes within ourselves because of our fallen nature. Is this contrary to reason? God will not require us mortal beings to believe anything contrary to reason, even though some mysteries are beyond our comprehension. Certainly, some mathematical theorems are mysterious to me and appear contrary to reason, especially where infinities are involved, but that does not mean that we should disbelieve the equations involving infinities simply because we do not understand them. The mysteries of God are not problems to be solved but realities to be experienced. On Judgement Day, God will, I believe, judge us on the basis of our faith and works and not on how finely tuned our understanding is of the technical niceties of Christian theology. Embrace the mysteries boldly. God is just and kind.

In terms of omniscience, for any agent x, "x is omniscient" equals, for every statement s, "if s is true, then x knows that s and does not believe that not-s." Essentially, if a particular statement is true, then God knows it and does not believe it to be false. How does this apply to God's foreknowledge? If "it is raining today" is a true statement, then yesterday the statement "it will rain tomorrow" is true also. Then, according to omniscience theory, God knows it and does not believe otherwise. Again, if the statement "it will rain five days from now" is true, then God knows it. God knowledge or divine knowledge is not perceptual in the same way that we gain knowledge from our senses and reason but is rather conceptual knowledge. God's knowledge is self-contained and perfect and immutable and innate. The very ideas of "looking ahead" or "seeing the future" are terribly anthropomorphic[57] ideas that we apply poorly to God.

Not all propositions are true or false. Some propositions are pure nonsense. One cannot expect a sensible answer when the question itself is contradictory. It is like asking God to explain to us the meanings of the oddities and absurdities of *Alice's Adventures in Wonderland*. Can God's omnipotence limit God's omniscience? The religious answer may be that, yes, God can, but God does not because God is consistent and true.

There are several theories regarding how the universe functions. In one theory, the universe sprang spontaneously out of "nothing" as a kind of quantum fluctuation and blindly follows the laws of physics, which, like the wind, no one knows whence it comes or where it goes, and everything that happens in the universe is a result of pure chance. In a second theory, God created the universe by the process of the Big Bang, following in its wake the laws of physics, and, like a blind watchmaker, has let it run its course ever since with no divine interference. In yet a third theory, God created the universe and, like a gardener, tends it carefully, gently nudging it with occasional miracles to keep it functioning properly, and also gently nudging his intelligent creatures (humans and perhaps inhabitants of other worlds) with divine guidance and occasional miracles to keep us on the straight and narrow path. Clearly, I fall into the third theory.

---

[57] Anthropomorphic refers to the practice of referring to nonhumans as having human characteristics; often, as here, anthropomorphic refers to attributing to God characteristics normally associated with human beings or mortals. (From the Greek *ho anthropos* meaning "human being" and *morphe* meaning "form" or *metamorphosis* meaning "to transform" or "to change form, shape, or substance."

There is no empirical proof one way or the other for believing any one of the above three theories. Each one requires a certain kind of faith. To believe that God created the universe from nothing makes more sense to me than to believe that the universe sprang from nothing as a result of a quantum fluctuation. By a similar token, to believe that God created life only on Earth and nowhere else in the universe requires an enormous stretch of blind belief that in a galaxy of millions of stars and planets in a universe of millions of galaxies only one planet was chosen by God to be the seat of life.

To state that any one of the above three theories of the universe's origin is correct beyond the shadow of a doubt is to support the unsupportable. As Paul said, "Faith is the realization of what is hoped for and evidence of things not seen. Because of it the ancients were well attested. By faith we understand that the universe was ordered by the word of God, so that what is visible came into being through the invisible" (Hebrews 11:1-3). Some scientists and non-theists will argue that God is not detectable by any measuring instrument that we know of, but theists and theologians will point out that God is detectable, just not by conventional means such as a God-meter made in a physics lab. Since Christians accept by faith that God created the universe and tends it regularly like a loving Gardener, talking to his creations in whispers of the Wind, we are therefore more willing to accept what Scripture teaches us about his ways and commandments and spiritual realm as well as his involvement in the creation of his universe and his creatures, great and small, terrestrial and extraterrestrial. Many scientists today do not now believe or at least are not so certain that science can answer all the questions that we have about the universe and any possible stellar neighbors, nor do scientists have the answers to life, the universe, and everything. The notion that science and technology can solve all of our problems and answer all of our questions is a kind of wishful thinking that went the way of the dinosaurs quite some time ago. Good riddance.

Science and religion are two different ways of looking at the universe and use different terminology to describe similar data. The Christian religion teaches the revelations of the Christian God. Moreover, the Apostle Paul tells us in 1 Corinthians 2:10b-16:

> For the Spirit scrutinizes everything, even the depths of God. Among human beings, who knows what pertains to a person

except the spirit of the person that is within? Similarly, no one knows what pertains to God except the Spirit of God. We have not received the spirit of the world but the Spirit that is from God, so that we may understand the things freely given us by God. And we speak about them not with words taught by human wisdom, but with words taught by the Spirit, describing spiritual realities in spiritual terms. Now the natural person does not accept what pertains to the Spirit of God, for to him it is foolishness, and he cannot understand it, because it is judged spiritually. The spiritual person, however, can judge everything but is not subject to judgment by anyone. For "who has known the mind of the Lord, so as to counsel him?" But we have the mind of Christ.

The point Paul is making, it seems to me, is that the natural universe is described using natural terminology (or the language of science, if you prefer), whereas the spiritual universe or "spiritual realities" are taught by the Spirit "describing" them "in spiritual terms." When talking science, we use the language of mathematics; when talking religion, we speak the language of the Spirit. We may be describing the same data, one in natural terms and one in spiritual terms. With sensitivity to the niceties of language, we can avoid the temptation of discussing spiritual realities in natural terms along with the opposite tendency of discussing the natural universe in spiritual terms. There is a bridge. It can be crossed both ways.

As a spacefaring people, limited though our spacefaring is, we should work towards human spiritual evolution so that we will present a presence of honor and integrity when one day we begin to interact with inhabitants of other worlds. We will grow in the estimation of God when we begin to prepare fresh ideas and noble theologies for presentation in the court of the greater universe. Let us consider again the theological and Biblical ramifications of inhabitants of other worlds. If, as Father Greeley has suggested in his science fiction works, angels are extraterrestrials with extraordinarily long lifespans, then it might follow that angels use spaceships. I tend to believe that angels are spiritual beings who do not need spaceships. Nor does God. As Captain Kirk wisely asked in "The Final Frontier": "What does God need with a spaceship?" The same can be said of the Blessed Virgin Mary and all the saints. When Our Lady appears to faithful Christians, it is for the purpose of discernment, not answers to questions on particle physics. When we speak about inhabitants of other worlds, we should think of them as spiritual beings like us who have desires and aspirations beyond the material realm. Perhaps extraterrestrials will have theistic scientists and atheistic scientists just like we do, and we may find ourselves engaging in lengthy discussions of natural realities and spiritual realities. We may have much to learn from one another. We should not assume that anyone's science can be so advanced that the universe no longer contains mysteries, especially in the spiritual realm. The Bible, like some officials in the government or agents of the CIA, neither confirms nor denies extraterrestrial life. God is infinite and, like Walt Whitman, contains multitudes.

Human beings, as inhabitants of one of many planets created by God, give glory to God in the highest heaven, although the place to search for God may more properly be within the human heart. Extraterrestrials no doubt have hearts and souls and spirits and bodies – all creations of God – and they may love their Creator with a passion prophets prophesy about and seers proclaim in a universe filled with the passionate art of the divine artist. As the Psalmist tells us: "The heavens declare the glory of God; the sky proclaims its builder's craft. One day to the next conveys that message; one night to the next imparts that knowledge" (19:1-3). Even so, sentient beings alone, whether on Earth or other worlds, have the power given them by God to give this glory to God as a conscious act of free will. If the heavens tell of the power of God, prophets and seers and apostles and disciples and divines praise the greatness of the power of God. Each one of the inhabitants of the many worlds in God's universe praise their Creator by giving him the glory that is due so great an artist and lover of souls. As Unamuno would say, God created the universe for each one of us on whatever planet orbiting whatever star. The goal of creation is to know the mind of God and to experience his mysteries.

The notion that God created all planets besides Earth to be lifeless voids borders on the absurd. No one writes a book for his own eyes alone; people write books because they want people to read their ideas. No artist draws a picture for his eyes alone; people draw pictures so other people might enjoy them. Similarly, the artist who is God does not create for his eyes alone; God creates so that his creations might experience the mysteries of his universe even while exploring it, studying it, and loving it as we love its creator. Jesus said, "You are the light of the *kosmos*. A city set on a mountain cannot be hidden. Nor do they light a lamp and then put it under a bushel basket; it is set on a lampstand, where it gives light to all in the house. Just so, your light must shine before others, that they may see your good deeds and glorify your heavenly Father" (Matthew 5:14-16). God loves his creation, especially, I think, his sentient creatures. Indeed, Scripture tells us, "For God so loved the *kosmos* that he gave his only Son, so that everyone who believes in him might not perish but might have eternal life" (John 3:16).

How do we reconcile the existence of extraterrestrials with the redemption of Christ? Many theologians and authors declare openly that there is no conflict because Christ has redeemed the inhabitants of all worlds of whom "all have sinned and are deprived of the glory of God" (Romans 3:23). Indeed, Scripture also assures us that "For Christ, while we were still helpless, yet died at the appointed time for the ungodly. Indeed, only with difficulty does one die for a just person, though perhaps for a good person one might even find courage to die. But God proves his love for us in that while we were yet sinners Christ died for us" (Romans 5:6-8). Paul also quotes Isaiah 52:15 in Romans 15:21b): "Those who have never been told of him shall see, and those who have never heard of him shall understand." Perhaps extraterrestrials shall see and understand. Perhaps we shall see and understand God's love for all his creatures wherever they may be found. Paul also assures us in Colossians 1:15-20:

> He is the image of the invisible God,
>> the firstborn of all creation.
> For in him were created all things in heaven and on earth,
>> the visible and the invisible, whether thrones or
>> dominions or principalities or powers;
>> all things were created through him and for him.
> He is before all things,
> And in him all things hold together.
> He is the head of the body, the church.
> He is the beginning, the firstborn from the dead,
> That in all things he himself might be preeminent.

For in him all the fullness was pleased to dwell,
And through him to reconcile all things for him,
Making peace by the blood of his cross [through him],
Whether those on earth or those in heaven.

Jesus is the Incarnate Verb because his name is a verb meaning "Yahweh saves." Scripture assures us that all who have faith in Christ and believe that Jesus died and was raised from the dead will be saved, and, if extraterrestrials believe this, then they will be saved as well. The only question we have is whether extraterrestrials currently have this knowledge or whether God expects us to bring this knowledge to them. Christ is the center and head of all creation and all creatures as well as the Catholic Church. The way God chooses to disseminate divine knowledge among the many worlds is currently unknown, but, when we find out, we should act in accordance with the teachings of Jesus explicated in the Tradition and Scripture of his Catholic Church.

The last feast of the liturgical year is the Feast of Christ, King of the Universe, and in the liturgy we remember the universal scope of his kingdom and the universal call of all his creatures, whether inhabitants of the Earth or inhabitants of other worlds. We also remember Christ as King of our lives in the daily Mass. Should we bring the daily Mass to other worlds, we will remember Christ as King of their inhabitants as well.

Chapter 13

Reason and Faith and Scripture

I myself believe that the evidence for God lies primarily in inner personal experiences.
>   -- William James, *Pragmatism*, 2

There St. John mingles with my friendly bowl
The feast of reason and the flow of soul.
>   -- Alexander Pope, *Imitations of Horace, II, II, l. 159*

Reason is God's crowning gift to man.
>   -- Sophocles, *Antigone, l. 672*

Reason in man is rather like God in the world.
>   -- Saint Thomas Aquinas, *Opuscule 11, De Regno*

Come now, and let us reason together saith the LORD: though your sins be as scarlet, they shall be as white as snow; though they be red like crimson, they shall be as wool.
>   -- Isaiah 1:18, KJV

Saint Thomas Aquinas brought to the Church and the West a system of thought which almost single-handedly caused the Renaissance and instilled a respect for the use of reason in philosophical discourse and religious studies. His legacy endures in the twenty-first century. Catholics today embrace rational discourse in studying and disseminating and drawing conclusions about the nature of the universe as well as about the nature of Scripture and Tradition. Since human beings are a natural part of the universe, it follows that studying the sacred stories, mythologies, histories, apocalyptic literature, letters, Gospels, and theological dialogues of our Christian faith and culture will lead us to a greater appreciation and respect for both our religious and scientific heritage. When we engage in cultural exchanges with inhabitants of other worlds, we will want them to know that our religions, philosophies, and literature are just as important as our scientific theories and technological breakthroughs. We on Earth remember the Romans and Greeks as much for their religion and art and literature as for their architecture and science. As Edgar Allen Poe once wrote, "Thy naiad airs have brought me home / to the glory that was Greece and the grandeur that was Rome" (*To Helen*). We humans are a wide variety of cultures at various stages of technological and spiritual development. No doubt some extraterrestrials will be more interested in our science and technology while others will be more interested in our mythologies, literature, religions, and cultures. Some regard mathematical theories and equations as more poetic than poetry, while some regard poetry as saying things about reality that mathematical equations only dream about.

Christians believe that Jesus makes available within ourselves the power to do good and accomplish great things, including the ability to explore space, travel to distant stars, communicate our deepest thoughts, aspirations, truths, and the most desperate desires of our hearts. If we desire to conquer space, we must know that Jesus made it there ahead of all of us. Astronauts and cosmonauts will simply follow in his wake.

If non-Christian inhabitants of Earth as well as non-Christian inhabitants of other worlds can be saved, then why have faith? If we can use reason to realize truth and the nature of reality, then why have faith? Faith is much more than intellectual assent to theological truths. The Apostle Paul tells us,

> But what does it say?
> "The word is near you, in your mouth and in your heart" (that is, the word of faith that we preach), for, if you confess with your mouth that Jesus is Lord and believe in your heart that God raised him from the dead, you will be saved. For one believes with the heart and so is justified, and one confesses with the mouth and so is saved. For the scripture says, "No one who believes in him will be put to shame." For there is no distinction between Jew and Greek; the same Lord is Lord of all, enriching all who call upon him. For "everyone who calls on the name of the Lord will be saved." (Romans 10:9-13)

However, Paul, I think, does not mean that simply assenting to the theological truths that Jesus is Lord and that God raised him from the dead is all there is to being a Christian. We must demonstrate our faith with works, otherwise our faith is not really faith at all. James tells us, "You believe that God is one. You do well. Even the demons believe that and tremble" (2:19). During the ministry of Jesus, demons possessing people whom Jesus exorcised would shout out as they were being expelled, "You are the Son of God!" (e.g., Mark 3:11 et al.). In Mark 1:24, an unclean spirit cried out, "What have you to do with us, Jesus of Nazareth? Have you come to destroy us? I know who you are – the Holy One of God!" The demons knew who Jesus was, they recognized his power, they respected his authority, and yet they did not have faith in Jesus because, again, faith is more than simple intellectual assent to theological truth. Faith is trust in the person in whom one has faith. As a Catholic, I trust Jesus completely. In fact, I trust him so completely that I have made him Lord of my life, not of my own accord but because he called me, and I responded to his call. Will inhabitants of other worlds respond to the call of Christ as I have and as millions of other people on the Earth have done? We shall see. However, what we should not do is deny them the right to hear the Word simply because they are not descendants of Adam and Eve or Noah.

In general, the Catholic Church teaches that salvation is only through Christ. However, it is possible to believe that the benefits of Christ's death and resurrection are available to both inhabitants of the Earth and inhabitants of other worlds who may not explicitly recognize their dependence on Christ. For Catholics, Jews who lived before Christ can be saved, while Jews and other non-Christians who lived after Christ can still be saved because God will judge them on Judgement Day on the basis of their faith and works, and if their faith is rooted in an obvious trust in whatever higher power they asseverate, then, if God chooses to save non-Christians, it is not our place as Christians to question God's generosity.

The philosophy of modern science prohibits the development of the theory that God exists through the "scientific" principle that no theory is "scientific" or philosophically valid unless it can be disproved. According to basic science and standard inductive logic, theories can be proven false but cannot be proven true; theories have only high or low probabilities of truth. Thus, the statement "God exists" cannot be falsified even in principle, and therefore, according to some scientists, the statement is not scientific but metaphysical. However, this argument has no bearing on whether God really exists or not. At one time, the passenger pigeon was thought to be extinct, but later passenger pigeons were rediscovered and thriving. Some scientists argue that we have no proof one way or another about the existence of God. However, the nature of reality is that whatever is real is true regardless of scientific theories to the contrary. If God is real, then no scientific proofs to the contrary are valid. If God is not real, then no scientific proofs to the contrary are valid. The statement "There is no God" is not a scientific statement, and "Is there a God?" is not a scientific question because God is spiritual in nature and belongs to the ethereal plane or the spiritual realm, although the spiritual realm is ubiquitous in the material realm.

The Incarnation of the Logos changes all that. The Logos, a spiritual being existing in the ethereal plane or spiritual realm, intruded, in a sense, on the material realm by becoming flesh, that is, mortal. The statement that Jesus of Nazareth was "manifested in the flesh" would be a grandiloquent pious platitude if not for its truth. In 1 Timothy 3:16, Paul tells us: "Undeniably great is the mystery of devotion, Who was manifested in the flesh, vindicated in the spirit, seen by angels, proclaimed to the Gentiles, believed in throughout the *kosmos*, taken up in glory." Christ himself is the mystery of our devotion. The One who was manifested in the flesh is God. John tells us a similar thing when he writes that "No one has ever seen God. The only Son, God, who is at the Father's side, has revealed him" (1:18). Another reference is 2 John 7: "Many deceivers have gone out into the *kosmos*, those who do not acknowledge Jesus Christ as coming in the flesh; such is the deceitful one and the antichrist." This statement does not make sense unless we acknowledge that Jesus Christ is God. The fleshly Logos prayed to God the Father who continued to exist in the spiritual realm, acknowledging his greatness, and asseverating that the spiritual Father is greater than the incarnate Son just as the spiritual realm is a better place than the material realm, even though it is in the material realm that we gain temporal experience and material knowledge as well as spiritual knowledge by studying the material universe as scientists and by studying the spiritual universe as theologians.

In quantum theory, the distinction between the material realm and the spiritual realm becomes fuzzy. God is not like a triumvirate acting in unison, like identical triplets singing a song together. God is truly One. Yet God has manifested himself as Father, Son, and Holy Spirit in many ways and at many times. The greatest of his manifestations was in the form of his only begotten Son, Jesus Christ.

Christians freely acknowledge that attempts to explain the mystery of
God in Christ is vain because the mystery is by definition one which
reason cannot solve. Divine mysteries are not problems to be solved
but realities to be experienced. Many theologians have attempted to
define the nature of God, but all of them ultimately fail because God
cannot be reduced to definitions by theologians nor mathematical
equations by scientists. The Deity defies definition and laughs in the
face of analysis. In some ways, quantum theory defies definition and
laughs in the face of analysis. We have come full circle. In
attempting to understand our universe, we have come to the
disquieting revelation that the universe defies explanation or is, in
other words, as mysterious and unfathomable as its creator.

The three Persons of the Trinity are the persona through which
the One God has manifested himself to inhabitants of the Earth and
possibly to inhabitants of other worlds as well as to the angels, risen
and fallen. Fallen angels recognize the power of God and may even
respect the power of God, but they do not worship God for reasons we
do not yet fully understand. Good angels are messengers of God just
as saints are often used as messengers of God. Angels proclaim the
message of the Gospel, yet Scripture warns us to be cautious: "But
even if we or an angel from heaven should preach (to you) a gospel
other than the one that we preached to you, let that one be accursed!"
(Galatians 1:8). The Son of God is our ultimate Rabbi (a word
meaning "Teacher" or perhaps literally translated "My Great One").
All three Persons of God care for the creatures of the universe with a
passion. Paul tells us in Scripture, specifically, 2 Corinthians 13:13:
"The grace of the Lord Jesus Christ and the love of God and the
fellowship of the holy Spirit be with all of you." Each of the Persons
of the Trinity has gifts to give us. The Scottish call the Holy Spirit
the "Giftie," and the appellation is well-deserved. When we are
clothed with the Spirit, nothing is impossible. The Spirit gives us
gifts of patience, perseverance (such as the perseverance I have been
given to write this book), love, faith, hope, kindness, and wisdom, et
al. Paul tells us, "But grace was given to each of us according to the
measure of Christ's gift" (Ephesians 4:7). Through the persona of
Jesus the grace of God became manifest so that his grace could be
distributed and implemented. Through the persona of the Holy Spirit,
the Spirit of Christ (Romans 8:9), God communicates not only the
Body and Blood of Christ but also his Word (Oral Tradition and

Written Tradition/Scriptures) to the *kosmos* in which dwell
inhabitants of all the worlds. Through the persona of the Father, the
Head of the Godhead, God directs his love, even if it is sometimes
"tough love" in the form of discipline. Yet the author of the letter to
the Hebrews tells us:

> You have also forgotten the exhortation addressed to you as
> sons:
> > "My son, do not disdain the discipline of the Lord
> > Or lose heart when reproved by him;
> > for whom the Lord loves, he disciplines;
> > He scourges every son he acknowledges."
>
> Endure your trials as "discipline"; God treats you as sons. For
> what "son" is there whom his father does not discipline? If
> you are without discipline, in which all have shared, you are
> not sons but bastards. Besides this, we have had our earthly
> fathers to discipline us, and we respected them. Should we not
> [then] submit all the more to the Father of spirits and live?
> They disciplined us for a short time as seemed right to them,
> but he does so for our benefit, in order that we may share his
> holiness. At the time, all discipline seems a cause not for joy
> but for pain, yet later it brings the peaceful fruit of
> righteousness to those who are trained by it. So strengthen
> your drooping hands and your weak knees. Make straight
> paths for your feet, that what is lame may not be dislocated but
> healed. (12:5-13)

To all believers, some of these manifestations appear instantaneous
and simultaneous because God is ubiquitous yet centered in our
hearts. David the King tells us that he welcomes the discipline of the
LORD (Psalm 51, particularly verse 10, "Let me hear sounds of joy
and gladness; let the bones you have crushed rejoice"). Just as Israel
was disciplined for 40 years in the desert in order to prepare the
people of God for the Promised Land, so also inhabitants of the Earth
may well be being disciplined by God for millennia in order to
prepare the people of God for evangelizing lands in other star
systems.

Death is a material event in the material universe, and many people fear death, although Saint Francis of Assisi taught us to embrace Sister Death without fear. When Scripture tells us "He will wipe every tear from their eyes, and there shall be no more death or mourning, wailing or pain, [for] the old order has passed away" (Revelation 21:4), what does God mean? That the fires of hell will be quenched and hell itself destroyed? Scripture also tells us, "The last enemy to be destroyed is death" (1 Corinthians 15:26) because death is a force in the *kosmos* that Jesus has conquered by his work on the Cross and resurrection. Death was, before Christ, the ultimate consequence of the sins of all inhabitants of the Earth and perhaps all the inhabitants of other worlds. Yet the Good News is that Christ of the spiritual realm has intruded upon the material realm and its darkest consequence – death – so that the death of the material body is not permanent because, according to Catholic teachings, we will rise with our bodies on the last day:

> For just as in Adam all die, so too in Christ shall all be brought to life, but each one in proper order: Christ the firstfruits; then, at his coming, those who belong to Christ; then comes the end, when he hands over the kingdom to his God and Father, when he has destroyed every sovereignty and every authority and power. For he must reign until he has put all his enemies under his feet. The last enemy to be destroyed is death, for "he subjected everything under his feet." But when it says that everything has been subjected, it is clear that it excludes the One who subjected everything to him. When everything is subjected to him, then the Son himself will [also] be subjected to the one who subjected everything to him, so that God may be all in all. (1 Corinthians 15:22-28)

Nowhere in God's universe will eternal sin reign in the sense of causing permanent death because the sacrifice of Jesus was perfect and sufficient. God can handle our free will because he is perfect and immutable. Scripture assures us that

> In him we have redemption by his blood, the forgiveness of transgressions, in accord with the riches of his grace that he lavished upon us. In all wisdom and insight, he has made

known to us the mystery of his will in accord with his favor that he set forth in him as a plan for the fullness of times, to sum up all things in Christ, in heaven and on earth. In him we were also chosen, destined in accord with the purpose of the one who accomplishes all things according to the intention of his will, so that we might exist for the praise of his glory, we who first hoped in Christ. (Ephesians 1:7-12)

The Psalmist prays: "The LORD is with me to the end. LORD, your love endures forever. Never forsake the work of your hands!" (138:8). Ecclesiasticus/Sira assures us "The works of God are all of them good; in its own time every need is supplied" (39:16). Finally, the Bible tells us, "The Lord does not delay his promise, as some regard 'delay,' but he is patient with you, not wishing that any should perish but that all should come to repentance" (2 Peter 3:9). By "all," we might very well include both inhabitants of the Earth and inhabitants of other worlds. We should also be patient even while exhorting America to expand its space program to develop interstellar flight so that we can communicate with our space brothers and sisters.

In the coming Kingdom of the Christ, Israel, the elected nation, and the Catholic Church, the elected community of faith, are seen via prophecies and visions as subjects of the Kingdom even while Christ rules through the Catholic Church, while at the Parousia the Pope, as the Living Representative of Christ on Earth, will hand over the reign of the Church to Christ who has ever been its ruler. As the Bride of Christ, the Catholic Church shares in the reign of Christ. On Judgement Day, all Catholics will stand with our community in the presence of God, and God will invite all other Christians as well as non-Christians who are baptized by desire to stand with our community, too. Then, the Church will truly be one. We will all be one with God.

In the age to come, the Gospel will be preached to all creatures in heaven, both on the Earth and scattered throughout the *kosmos*. Luke 9:30-31 tells us of Christ's Exodus: "And, behold, two men were conversing with him, Moses and Elijah, who appeared in glory and spoke of his exodus that he was going to accomplish in Jerusalem." Upon Christ's Exodus including his Passion, crucifixion, death, resurrection, and ascension, his disciples were commissioned to preach the glad tidings to all creatures throughout the *kosmos*.

Salvation causes perfection in the souls of believers, for Christ commands us, "So be perfect, just as your heavenly Father is perfect" (Matthew 5:48). The Lucan parallel tells us "Be merciful, just as (also) your Father is merciful" (Luke 6:36). One who is merciful for the sake of Christ will be shown mercy and granted perfection of soul. As children of the Promise, all disciples from whatever planet of origin will be made perfect in Christ.

The divine call extends to Jews and Gentiles and, eventually, extraterrestrials who may be construed as the new Gentiles. Scripture tells us about the mission of the Catholic Church, which is a great mystery:

> When you read this you can understand my insight into the mystery of Christ, which was not made known to human beings in other generations as it has now been revealed to his holy apostles and prophets by the Spirit, that the Gentiles are coheirs, members of the same body, and copartners in the promise in Christ Jesus through the gospel." (Ephesians 3:4-6)

It is entirely possible that inhabitants of other worlds will come to share in this great mystery so that they become coheirs of the Promise, members of the same Body, and copartners in the promise in Christ Jesus through the gospel. In this new era, Christians will be formed in people regardless of their physical forms because they are *hnau*, God's creatures. In this new relationship between inhabitants of the Earth and inhabitants of other worlds, the Catholic Church will make no distinction between hnau who are homo sapiens and hnau who are extraterrestrials, just as Jesus makes no distinction between Jew and Greek, male and female, slave and free, because we will all be "one in Christ Jesus" (Galatians 3:28). We will be able to say to inhabitants of other worlds with confidence, "And if you belong to Christ, then you are Abraham's descendant, heirs according to the promise" (Galatians 3:29). We can say to extraterrestrials boldly that, just as we once were, all of them "were at that time without Christ, alienated from the community of Israel and strangers to the covenants of promise, without hope and without God in the *kosmos*. But now in Christ Jesus you who once were far off have become near by the blood of Christ" (Ephesians 2:12-13).

Moreover, we who are inhabitants of the lowly Earth will say to our space brothers and sisters: "Blessed be the God and Father of our Lord Jesus Christ, who has blessed us in Christ with every spiritual blessing in the heavens, as he chose us in him, before the foundation of the *kosmos*, to be holy and without blemish before him" (Ephesians 1:3-4). Christians throughout the *kosmos* will experience Christ who gives us supernatural standing and character simply because we are his disciples. Extraterrestrials along with their earthly counterparts identically need the same grace of God as Paul tells us in Romans 3:9b: "for we have already brought the charge against Jews and Greeks alike that they are all under the domination of sin," etc. Yet grace will be offered to extraterrestrials and humans alike, as it says in Romans 10:12-13: "For there is no distinction between Jew and Greek; the same Lord is Lord of all, enriching all who call upon him. For 'everyone who calls on the name of the Lord will be saved.'" Although both humans and extraterrestrials have sinned, the good news is that God forgives us in Christ so that resurrection unto eternal life is within our grasp:

> This I declare, brothers: flesh and blood cannot inherit the kingdom of God, nor does corruption inherit incorruption. Behold, I tell you a mystery. We shall not all fall asleep, but we will all be changed, in an instant, in the blink of an eye, at the last trumpet. For the trumpet will sound, the dead will be raised incorruptible, and we shall be changed. For this which is corruptible must clothe itself with incorruptibility, and this which is mortal must clothe itself with immortality. And when this which is corruptible clothes itself with incorruptibility and this which is mortal clothes itself with immortality, then the word that is written shall come about:
> "Death is swallowed up in victory.
> Where, O death, is your victory?
> Where, O death, is your sting?
> The sting of death is sin, and the power of sin is the law. But thanks be to God who gives us the victory through our Lord Jesus Christ. (1 Corinthians 15:50-57)

The Catholic Church has been given a new, heavenly purpose by God: to spread the Good News of God in Christ to Jews and Greeks,

humans and extraterrestrials, as Paul tells us in Colossians 3:11:
"Here there is not Greek and Jew, circumcision and uncircumcision,
barbarian, Scythian, slave, free; but Christ is all and in all." The love
we must demonstrate for both ourselves and our space brothers and
sisters will be for all of us "the bond of perfection" (Colossians 3:14).
The Catholic Church is more than simply an ever-growing assembly
of redeemed individuals gathered from not only the four corners of
the Earth but also gathered from other worlds scattered throughout the
kosmos and coming from all ages of time but is also the Bride of
Christ, the incarnate Logos, who will forever bear his human nature
because of the riches and the depths of love God has for his creation
and his creatures of whatever planet of origin.

Humans and extraterrestrials alike may ask many similar
questions:

1. Why was the veil in the Temple rent in two?
2. Why did the Spirit descend on Mary and the Apostles at Pentecost?
3. Why is Christ the Head of the Catholic Church?
4. In what way does Christ minister to hnau in heaven?
5. Why did Christ manifest himself in order to the Israelites, the Gentiles, and, finally, to the inhabitants of other worlds?
6. Why does the Holy Spirit dwell within the Baptized?
7. Why will there be a New Jerusalem filled with the redeemed?
8. Why do the Baptized receive the grace of Jesus Christ?
9. Why the Incarnation? Why the Crucifixion? Why the Resurrection?
10. Why do Christians believe the mysteries of the Catholic Church given by Christ?
11. Why are the Baptized born again by definition and become "new creations"?
12. Who is Jesus and why do we worship him?
13. Why did the Catholic Church declare Oral Tradition and Written Tradition (the entire Bible) the Word of God?

14. Why do Catholics believe the doctrine of the consubstantiality of the Trinity?
15. Why will the Master on Judgement Day separate the sheep from the goats?
16. Why did Christ say the greatest commandment is to love God and the second greatest commandment is to love one another?
17. What does it mean to be a disciple of Jesus Christ and to accept him as one's personal Lord and Savior?
18. Why do Christians confess their sins to God in the presence of priests?
19. Why are there seven sacraments? What are the sacraments for?
20. Why does God cause the bread and the wine to transubstantiate into the Body and Blood of Christ? Why do we call receiving the living presence of the living God Communion?
21. Why do we believe that Jesus Christ is God?
22. Why did God create the universe?
23. Why did God create hnau?
24. Why did the Blood of Christ bathe the universe?
25. Why do we have faith in Christ, in his Father, and in his Holy Spirit?

These questions are worth serious thought and serious discussion, especially if extraterrestrials ask them of us, and most especially if it becomes clear that God is capable of administering other economies of salvation, and gives the call to hnau scattered amidst the stars. We are infinitely blessed by God because we who are Baptized have received the fullness of the Holy Spirit. Because the Spirit contains within itself the fullness of the Tradition of the Catholic Church, it follows that when we are Baptized we also de facto receive the fullness of the Tradition of the Christian faith. What we do not receive in Baptism is the teaching authority of the Catholic Church to interpret that Tradition and hand it on to others. Every time we hear the Word of God preached to us or read the Bible, we are simply rediscovering the Tradition infused at our Baptism within our souls and spirits along with grace. Jesus assures us that God is not stingy or niggardly[58] in his gifts: We receive the fullness of the Holy Spirit when we are Baptized. Paul assures us in 2 Corinthians 1:21-22: "But the one who give us security with you in Christ and who anointed us is God; he has also put his seal upon us and given the Spirit in our hearts as a first installment." Also, 2 Corinthians 5:5: "Now the one who has prepared us for this very thing is God, who has given us the Spirit as a first installment." If extraterrestrials receive the Spirit just like human Christians, then, Paul tells us in Romans 8:14-17:

> For those who are led by the Spirit of God are children of God. For you did not receive a spirit of slavery to fall back into fear, but you received a spirit of adoption, through which we cry, "*Abba*, Father!" The Spirit itself bears witness with our spirit that we are children of God, and if children, then heirs, heirs of God and joint heirs with Christ, if only we suffer with him so that we may also be glorified with him.

Moreover, if extraterrestrials become believers and request to be baptized because they have received the Holy Spirit, then, we may be as astonished at the request as the circumcised Jewish believers were, but as a believer I believe many if not most Christians would respond as Peter did, as Luke tells us in Acts of the Apostles 10:44-48:

> While Peter was still speaking these things, the holy Spirit fell upon all who were listening to the word. The circumcised believers who had accompanied Peter were astounded that the gift of the holy Spirit should have been poured out on the Gentiles also, for they could hear them speaking in tongues and glorifying God. Then Peter responded, "Can anyone withhold the water for baptizing these people, who have received the holy Spirit even as we have?" He ordered them to be baptized in the name of Jesus Christ.

---

[58] The word niggardly means meanly parsimonious, miserly, or one who is not disposed to spending his wealth on anything much less giving it away. Also, sparing in the use or disposal of resources or immaterial things.

The Spirit groans for inhabitants of other worlds as much as it groans for inhabitants of the Earth, and both we and extraterrestrials no doubt groan with creation for the resurrection, the total redemption of our bodies for eternal life in heaven. Perhaps extraterrestrials in the rest of creation are waiting for us as, indeed, the Apostle Paul assures us:

> For creation awaits with eager expectation the revelation of the children of God; for creation was made subject to futility, not of its own accord but because of the one who subjected it, in hope that creation itself would be set free from slavery to corruption and share in the glorious freedom of the children of God. We know that all creation is groaning in labor pains even now; and not only that, but we ourselves, who have the firstfruits of the Spirit, we also groan within ourselves as we wait for adoption, the redemption of our bodies. For in hope we were saved. Now hope that sees for itself is not hope. For who hopes for what one sees? But if we hope for what we do not see, we wait with endurance. In the same way, the Spirit too comes to the aid of our weakness; for we do not know how to pray as we ought, but the Spirit itself intercedes with inexpressible groanings. (Romans 8:19-26)

I believe it is possible for extraterrestrials to experience adoption by God and conform by grace to the image of the incarnate Son of God because as part of creation they are groaning for God and the Spirit intercedes with inexpressible groanings for them also.

Saint Seraphim[59] of Sarov (1759 -- 1883), a Russian Orthodox monk, priest, one-time ascetic, mystic, and wonder-worker of the Monastery of Sarov, who was declared a saint by the Russian

---

[59] Seraphim, in Hebrew (Isa 6:2 WTT), is a plural, meaning literally "fiery" or a "fiery serpent" or a poisonous serpent (fiery from the burning effect of the poison) and is a mythical six-winged creature and majestic being typically identified as the highest of the nine choirs of angels. The other choirs of angels are the cherubim (variously in the Old Testament and see also Hebrews 9:5), thrones, dominions (dominations), principalities, powers (Colossians 1:16; Acts 8:10; Romans 8:38; 1 Corinthians 15:24) or celestial powers (or celestial authorities) and celestial rulers (Ephesians 1:21; 3:10; Colossians 2:10; 2:15), archangels (1 Thessalonians 4:16; Jude 1:9), and angels (variously throughout the Old Testament and the New Testament).

Orthodox Church in 1903, once said, "Save yourself, and thousands around you will be saved." Before Christians spread the Gospel to outer space, we should be examples of the Christian faith and life here on Earth.

Genesis 9:8-17 tells us:

> God said to Noah and to his sons with him: "See, I am now establishing my covenant with you and your descendants after you and with every living creature that was with you: all the birds, and the various tame and wild animals that were with you and came out of the ark. I will establish my covenant with you, that never again shall all bodily creatures be destroyed by the waters of a flood; there shall not be another flood to devastate the earth." God added: 'This is the sign that I am giving for all ages to come, of the covenant between me and you and every living creature with you: I set my bow in the clouds to serve as a sign of the covenant between me and the earth. When I bring clouds over the earth, and the bow appears in the clouds, I will recall the covenant I have made between me and you and all living beings, so that the waters shall never again become a flood to destroy all mortal beings. As the bow appears in the clouds, I will see it and recall the everlasting covenant that I have established between God and all living beings – all mortal creatures that are on earth." God told Noah: "This is the sign of the covenant I have established between me and all mortal creatures that are on earth."

The above passage is the heart of the covenant between God and all inhabitants of the Earth, whether sentient or of animal intelligence or of plant life or even of bacteria. The covenant God made with Noah and his descendants applies to all inhabitants of the Earth, particularly humanity, since all human beings are descended from Noah. The laws and rules associated with God's covenant with Noah do not necessarily apply to sentient inhabitants of other worlds. Yet, if other worlds have atmospheres and clouds and rain and rainbows, what are we to think? Many scientists believe that water is an essential component of life, and, where there is water and rain, there are rainbows. Thus, perhaps God's covenant with Noah applies to beings who are not his descendants but are still children of the Promise.

Some materialists believe that the acquisition of information that science can bring causes scientists to develop their own sense of beauty in a sensible universe, whereas theologians and believers in Christ believe that the key to a truly religious faith is a converted heart and a regenerate soul. Scientists believe that the acquisition of scientific knowledge has its own rewards and that scientific knowledge has its own beauty, but, then, so do many things. Why does science matter at all? This is a question many theists ask, and scientists give a variety of answers, some just as puzzling and mysterious to the scientific laity as some theological treatises are to scientists who are members of the theological laity. A friend of mine who is a Ph.D. in chemistry once said to me that what I have written in this book is practically in a foreign language to him. Certainly, many scientific treatises are written in a foreign language to me, although I try to keep up with the latest developments in science by reading scientific magazines and journals including *Scientific American* and *Nature* as well as *Biblical Archaeology Review.* Scientists and astronomers who quest for the Star of Bethlehem write works that are just as important as theologians who quest for the religious meaning of the Star of Bethlehem. Is the Star a myth or is it a part of history? Assuming that Leverdierre is right and myths are profoundly true stories that speak to universal aspects of life and reality, to moments in time which cannot be historically described, then the answer to the question is as mysterious as the Incarnation of the mystical Logos. That the Logos became incarnate can no more be described scientifically than a supernova can be described theologically, although Madeleine L'Engle may have put it best in *A Wrinkle in Time* when she wrote that, when a star dies, it screams, too.

Franz Shubert or Schubert (1797 -- 1828), a master Austrian composer and practicing Catholic who composed many beautiful musical scores for the Mass, once wrote, "It is with faith that one first comes into the world, and it long precedes intelligence and knowledge; for in order to understand anything, one must first believe in something ... Intelligence is nothing but analyzed faith" (Deutsch 337). What is the result of scientists analyzing faith? Can faith truly be analyzed? Is attempting to analyze faith a waste of time? Is attempting to theologize science a waste of time? Many people assume that scientists and theologians have nothing to say to each other that is worthwhile. I believe such discussions are very much worthwhile and can contribute greatly to humanity's store of knowledge. Norman Cousins once declared: "The word faith is not generally regarded as a primary term in the scientist's lexicon, yet ... Faith is the vital ingredient in the Cyclops project" (i.e., communicating with extraterrestrial races via microwave transmission). While nature is not definitionally chaotic, because there is an order of things in this universe, neither should it be reduced to a scientific formality in the sense that both science and mysticism can be construed as the vehicle of the artistic expression of the divine that is at once inexplicable and uniquely transcendent, like the music of the spheres. The creative impulse of God creates a correspondence between the artistic expression of the beautiful universe in spiritual, angelic, and divine musical language and the scientific expression of the functional universe in mathematical language. Mathematical equations can be just as beautiful as music scores. Thus, God calculates the mathematical formula for light and scientifically engineers it by singing "Let there be light!" J. Harvey writes "The Mirror of Ambiguity" in "The Language of Electro-Acoustic Music" (in 1987) in which he claims that the purpose of music is "concerned with transcending that dichotomy, with healing Descartes's ontological separation of self and world and Kant's epistemological separation of self and certain knowledge, both formative of today's dominant paradigms (and difficulties)." Samuel Taylor Coleridge writes:

> And what if all of animated nature
> Be but organic harps diversely fram'd,
> That tremble into thought, as o'er them sweeps
> Plastic and vast, one intellectual breeze,
> At once the Soul of each, and God of All?
> (*The Eolian Harp, l. 44*)

Coleridge also writes perhaps his most famous poem, *Kubla Khan*, which is the product of an opium dream. The first stanza describes a creative power that is unnatural in the universe while the second stanza describes a creative power in harmony with the universe. The first stanza can be thought of as a song in tune with mortal human's creation, while the second stanza can be thought of as a song in tune with divine creation. It is the second stanza where the narrator describes passionately the music he experiences, but it is the first stanza that sets the tone -- it may be thought of as the narrator experiencing poetry without music and poetry with music, which music is described on a page in a fascinating revelation. More than any other poem, it is unique in describing creative music in a way that inspires the narrator with feverish delight that both enraptures and passionately moves the narrator to fantastic heights not for the faint of heart:

> In Xanadu did Kubla Khan
> A stately pleasure-dome decree:
> Where Alph, the sacred river, ran
> Through caverns measureless to man
> Down to a sunless sea.
> So twice five miles of fertile ground
> With walls and towers were girdled round:
> And there were gardens bright with sinuous rills,
> Where blossomed many an incense-bearing tree;
> And here were forests ancient as the hills,
> Enfolding sunny spots of greenery.
> But oh! that deep romantic chasm which slanted
> Down the green hill athwart a cedarn cover!
> A savage place! as holy and enchanted
> As e'er beneath a waning moon was haunted
> By woman wailing for her demon-lover!
> And from this chasm, with ceaseless turmoil seething,
> As if this earth in fast thick pants were breathing,
> A mighty fountain momently was forced:
> Amid whose swift half-intermitted burst
> Huge fragments vaulted like rebounding hail,
> Or chaffy grain beneath the thresher's flail:
> And 'mid these dancing rocks at once and ever
> It flung up momently the sacred river.
> Five miles meandering with a mazy motion
> Through wood and dale the sacred river ran,
> Then reached the caverns measureless to man,
> And sank in tumult to a lifeless ocean:

And 'mid this tumult Kubla heard from far
Ancestral voices prophesying war!
The shadow of the dome of pleasure
Floated midway on the waves;
Where was heard the mingled measure
From the fountain and the caves.
It was a miracle of rare device,
A sunny pleasure-dome with caves of ice!

A damsel with a dulcimer
In a vision once I saw:
It was an Abyssinian maid,
And on her dulcimer she played,
Singing of Mount Abora.
Could I revive within me
Her symphony and song,
To such a deep delight 'twould win me,
That with music loud and long,
I would build that dome in air,
That sunny dome! those caves of ice!
And all who heard should see them there,
And all should cry, Beware! Beware!
His flashing eyes, his floating hair!
Weave a circle round him thrice,
And close your eyes with holy dread,
For he on honeydew hath fed,
And drunk the milk of Paradise. (*Kubla Khan*)

Coleridge also assures us, "No man was ever yet a great poet, without at the same time a profound philosopher" (*Biographia Literaria, 14*). The war in the poem could represent humanity's constant battle between barbarism and our veneer of civilization. The music may represent the music of the spheres through which and by which God created the universe with humanity's greatest musicians being a pale comparison. Arthur William Edgar O'Shaughnessy (1844 -- 1881), a British poet, has similar sentiments in his poem that when composed he called simply *Ode*:

We are the music-makers,
And we are the dreamers of dreams,
Wandering by lone sea breakers,
And sitting by desolate streams;
World-losers and world-forsakers,
on whom the pale moon gleams:
Yet we are the movers and shakers
Of the world forever, it seems.

With wonderful deathless ditties
We build up the world's great cities,
And out of a fabulous story
We fashion an empire's glory:
One man with a dream, at pleasure,
Shall go forth and conquer a crown;
And three with a new song's measure
Can trample an empire down.

We, in the ages of lying
In the buried past of the earth,
Built Nineveh with our sighing,
And Babel itself with our mirth;
And o'erthrew them with prophesying
To the old of the new world's worth;
For each age is a dream that is dying,
Or one that is coming to birth.

God's creative power is a kind of music that both causes the material universe to be and carves out its structure, yet the divine music does not simply shape the spiritual dimension -- it reveals it. Celestial music is the fabric of the universe, played and sung with great fecundity and a complexity that belies an underlying simplicity, leading us to wonder at the immanence of God in that universe that we can only try to explain the nature of scientifically but can experience mystically. Attempting to define music in words on a page is ultimately unsatisfying compared to experiencing the music with attentive listening and swaying to the exquisite beat and feeling heightened emotions with each rising crescendo, intense rhythm, and harmonic progression. Thus, God's revelation of creation in Genesis and other books of the Bible is best described in poetry or poetic prose or song because human words are only an imperfect reflection of divine words which may be lyrics and notes, chords, and melodies in a symphony we will hear in full only at the end of time.

Will extraterrestrials have music? What will it sound like? What will our music sound like to them? Shakespeare wrote, "Good night, sweet prince, and flights of angels sing thee to thy rest" (Horatio in *Hamlet* Act V Scene ii 359-360). Do angels sing inhabitants of other worlds to sleep, too?

Paul Schanz (1841 – 1905), a theologian of the Catholic faith from Tubingen in southwestern Germany, supports Joseph Pohle's views when he writes in *Apologie des Christentums*:

> …when it is said that Christ died for all men, it means after all the men on earth and no other….the Schoolmen taught in opposition to Anselm, that the Incarnation was not an absolute necessity. Some, however, held that even apart from sin the Incarnation formed part of God's eternal plan; nor did several Incarnations seem to them impossible….Why not [then] admit other possibilities for rational beings in other planets? Perhaps they did not fall in their progenitor and head; maybe they fell and were redeemed by an Incarnation of their own or in some other way….(cited in Crowe 434)

Giuseppe Pohle (Joseph Pohle) himself, a German theologian, also writes in his "The Celestial Realms and Their Inhabitants," Cologne 1904, p. 457): "It seems to be the purpose of the Universe that the celestial bodies are inhabited by beings who reflect the glory of God in the beauty of their bodies and worlds as man does, in a limited way, in his world." Pohle also says, "The hypothesis of the plurality of inhabited worlds is totally favourable to the glory of the Lord. God creates for His glory, and any glory is possible without intelligent beings, able to know the creation of the Lord" (cited in Balducci). Pohle also writes: "It seems to be accordingly with the aim of the world that inhabitable celestial bodies are settled by creatures that recognize the glory of God in the physical beauties of their worlds, in the same way man does with his smaller world" (cited in Balducci). Christians need to step up to the plate and examine, disseminate, and propound theories on the religious and scientific ramifications of the whole extraterrestrial question. We have come to the realization that the mysterious ways of God and his universe include ideas and beings who think those ideas consist of dramatic revelations, both scientific and divine, that we would be fools to ignore.

The only revolution that had a more significant impact on human civilization than the scientific revolution was the original Jesus movement within Judaism and its expansion to the Gentiles. It is possible that the impact of Christianity will have a greater effect on extraterrestrial/Earth relations than scientific and technological exchanges.

Noumena is a plural word (singular noumenon) meaning objects or events as they appear in and of themselves regardless of how they are perceived by the senses of hnau (from the Greek neuter of the present passive participle of noein meaning "to think" or "to conceive" and ultimately from nous meaning "mind"). Every object has a location and a speed, but, according to Heisenberg, it is not possible to know both location and speed at the same time, although objects do have both simultaneously – they simply cannot both be *known* simultaneously. Since God is omniscient, does God know both the location and speed of every object in his universe? Or is this just as logically impossible as whether God can create an object too heavy for him to lift? Does God know the noumena of everything in the universe, and is this knowledge necessary for the universe to continue to exist? This greatly bothered Einstein who famously said "Der Alte wurfelt nicht" ("God doesn't play dice"). Because we are limited by time, space, and the laws of physics, we can perceive only velocity or location even while the act of observing itself directly affects the observed. God, however, is not so limited because he exists in eternity and is not bound by time and space. We know reality only as we are capable of observing it. The same may be said for God only on an infinite scale.

The clockwork universe of earlier centuries caused many people to embrace the new science at the expense of the old faith, but, in the twenty-first century, many scientists are taking back their rejection of faith and, by embracing both, are revealing a new approach to the study of reality in which the material universe complements the spiritual universe and vice versa. Science and theology are both moving away from their previous divorce back into a marriage rekindled by the fire of discovery. However, if the marriage is to last, communication between the two must be vigorous and open to challenges lest one or the other find itself a widow. As noted earlier, when theology and science have been wedded in the past, new scientific theories lead to leaving the older theology behind along with the older science. We do not need new theology. Rather, we need a marriage that is so strong that both science and theology may continue to embrace one another like young lovers every time science advances in maturity and every time theology brings a fresh look at both the material and spiritual universe. Science and theology are thus interdependent and complementary without sacrificing their marriage on the altar of the goddess of discord.

Science and theology often pierce one another's veils to reveal an underlying structure to both material and spiritual reality that it is possible only poets really understand. If it's true that science without theology is blind, it is equally true that theology without science is like the resurrection without the crucifixion – it does not make sense. Science sometimes has corrective insights into theology, and theology sometimes has corrective insights into science. Science and theology are like different windows on the truth. Together, they are like the elephant examined by the blind men – some say the elephant is like a snake (the trunk) or a wall (the side) or pillars (the legs) or rope (the tail). When science looks at reality, the scientist sees a material universe and tries to make sense of it. When theology looks at reality, the theologian sees both a material universe and a spiritual universe teeming with material and spiritual beings ripe for the harvest. Theologians see reality in terms of ultimate purpose (to know the mind of God and to worship the Creator). Scientists who lack theology sometimes see the universe as without purpose and fail to make sense of it. For those who see death as the ultimate end with no resurrection in sight, the universe is indeed a materially full but spiritually empty place. Einstein was convinced that there is an order of things in this universe, and that our observations of reality should reflect that order. If the material universe has order, then so does the spiritual universe. One does not preclude the other. Determination and tenacity in the pursuit of truth propel our knowledge forward and preserve both our faith and science in the cause of progress.

Science and theological theories often pass in and out of favor and flow with the times. Sometimes new theories are abandoned and old theories resurrected. For the Franciscan, doubt can lead to faith just as, for the scientist, doubt can lead to new discoveries and theories. Doubt may be construed as an essential element in the growth of a scientist and theologian to mental maturity. The pursuit of truth via doubt, such as Cartesian doubt, can transform our understanding of reality into meaningful theories as well as transform our faith into a meaningful relationship with God. The theory that extraterrestrials exist is based on the doubt of the scientist and theologian that, in the vast expanse of the universe, we humans are on Earth alone the seat of intelligent life. Doubt leads to speculation, speculation leads to quests for truth, and such quests lead to experiments and programs like SETI in our efforts to learn the true and the real. Sometimes the quest is just as important as the achievement of the goal.

Faith can be informed and enriched by scientific exploration just as science can be informed and enriched by theological exploration. The exaggerated faith many people have in science spills over into religious expression with the idea that science is more "the Truth" than Jesus is the Truth. In some ways, Americans esteem science too much in our Western culture, often to the point of idol worship. Science, for all its virtues, cannot save anyone from their sins for eternal life in heaven. Science is amoral, neither helping nor hindering people's attempts to work out their own "salvation with fear and trembling" (Philippians 2:12b). When science is viewed as an amoral tool, science treats religion with the respect which it deserves. Science will discover the existence of extraterrestrials, but religion will make sense of the discovery.

Theologians can respond broadly to advances in science and technology either by rejection or by accommodation. The scientific worldview permeates our culture so thoroughly that we are often not aware of the profundity of its impact on our society. The culture and days described in Scripture are so far removed from our modern technological culture that we often have difficulty grasping the depth of the wide gulf separating us from our spiritual ancestors, the Israelites. In this book, I am attempting to examine the Bible in light of scientific research, a tactic I believe will bear fruit for our understanding of both the material universe and the spiritual universe. Such an approach should give us new insight into our Christian faith, a practice I believe will be fruitful in terms of enabling us to respond to the human quest for who we are, where we have come from, and where we are going, as well as what kinds of creatures of God we might become in our search for other intelligent creatures like ourselves.

Although, historically, a profound disunity between science and religion has, in the past, promulgated deep misunderstandings, a broader examination of the two fields in which we attempt to see not only the forest but the trees will result in a unifying dialogue that will breech the gulf. While the scientist traditionally approaches the study of the universe with broad materialistic goals in mind, the Christian theologian approaches the study of the universe with broad spiritual goals in mind even while working to make the material universe a better place. While the scientist approaches the universe from the outside in, the theologian approaches the universe from the inside out, starting with the ancient Israelites, then Jesus, one human being among many, who forever altered our view of time and space in a way as profound as Einstein's discovery of the special and general theories of relativity and his brilliant insight that $E = mc^2$.

The theologian starts from Jesus and works his way out into the universe, whereas the scientist starts with the universe and works his way in. Christianity starts with a particular event, the Incarnation, whereas the scientist starts from a broad understanding of the universe that may culminate in the discovery that the spiritual universe intruded upon the material universe in the Incarnation of the Logos. The scientist takes reality as axiomatic in the same way the theologian takes the Incarnation as axiomatic. Philosophers may begin with the Cartesian Cogito ergo sum (I think therefore I am), which is an axiom and not a syllogism.[60] The scientist may deduce that God is a real

---

[60] A syllogism in logic is a three-statement argument with exactly three terms (major term, minor term, and middle term) consisting of two premises (major premise and minor premise) and a conclusion which follows necessarily from the premises. For example: 1. All human beings are mortal creatures. 2. Socrates is a human being. 3. Therefore, Socrates is a mortal creature. In this syllogism, "mortal creature" is the major term appearing in the major premise, "Socrates" is the minor term appearing in the minor premise, "human beings" is the middle term, appearing in both premises but not the conclusion. If the premises are true, and the conclusion follows from the premises and is also true, then the argument is both valid and sound. This is an example of simple or categorical logic or deductive reasoning. Deductive arguments as a form typically reason from the general to the specific.

part of the universal equation from the axiomatic premise that the universe is real, whereas the theologian may deduce that the universe is real based on the axiomatic premise that God is real. The two different approaches give us two different windows on the truth.

The scientist may argue that, if extraterrestrials exist, we should try to find ways to communicate with them via the language of mathematics, while the theologian may argue that we should try to find ways to communicate with them via the language of theology or theological myths and rituals. C.S. Lewis, in discussing theology, writes that telling stories often explains concepts better than logical arguments. He may have derived this idea from his friend J.R.R. Tolkien, author of *The Lord of the Rings*, who told him that myths from whatever cultures were God's method for generating theological ideas that would later become clear as truth in the stories of Jesus Christ. Thus, the stories of the resurrections of various gods and other characters in ancient tales of many different cultures were precursors to the actual and real resurrection of Christ: In other words, Christ is the culmination of the myths that people told before him, which sealed with the Holy Spirit who inspired in these tales the promise of the resurrection of all in Christ. In general, language is a tricky construct, whatever the language is, and, when we discover inhabitants of other worlds, we will doubtless have to find a Rosetta Stone[61], whether of mathematics or any other language, to communicate. To use Robert A. Heinlein's word from his novel, *Stranger in a Strange Land*, we must truly grok[62] one another and the universe in which we find ourselves if we are to hope to bring to one another the good news of salvation. A major goal of this book is to

---

[61] The Rosetta Stone is a famous stone tablet on which is inscribed sentences written in Greek, demotic, and hieroglyphics; the stone dates around the second century B.C. and was found in 1799 near Rosetta in Egypt and now resides in the British Museum. After Jean-Francoi Champollion deciphered it in 1822, linguists were able to decipher Egyptian hieroglyphics and interpret innumerable early records of Egyptian civilization. In modern language, Rosetta Stone refers to any key used to comprehend some previously undecipherable writing or language.
[62] Grok means to understand something so thoroughly that the observer actually becomes part of the observed. The human struggle to grok the universe is an eternal quest in the grand scheme of reality in which we try to understand our relationship to what we observe. Reality is not an illusion.

bridge the divide between science and theology by encouraging a dialogue culminating in a scientific plunge into the depths of Christianity rooted in Tradition and Scripture and a theological plunge into the depths of the universe rooted intrinsically in God's creative Logos who became flesh to show hnau the way to heaven.

Chapter 14

Time and the Kingdom of God

For God created man to be immortal, and made him to be an image of his own eternity.
> -- *The Wisdom of Solomon* 2:23

All that we see or seem
Is but a dream within a dream.
> -- Edgar Allan Poe, *A Dream Within a Dream* [1827, revised 1849], l. 10

They who dream by day are cognizant of many things which escape those who dream only by night.
> -- Edgar Allan Poe, *Eleonora* [1841]

And all my days are trances,
And all my nightly dreams
Are where thy gray eye glances,
And where thy footstep gleams --
In what ethereal dances,
By what eternal streams.
> -- Edgar Allan Poe, *To One in Paradise, st. 4*

To every thing there is a season, and a time to every purpose under heaven.
> -- Ecclesiastes 3:1

What is time? Time is a thing which has no substance yet is a rational concept or perhaps a rational entity. We properly speak of the spacetime continuum since time and space, like soul and spirit, can be distinguished but not separated. For the theologian, time might best be thought of as a mystical entity but not in the sense of nonrational. For the scientist, time might be best thought of as a rational entity but not in the sense of nonmystical. Like viewing light as a particle or a wave, it depends on the way one looks at it. Yet time is as real as the pages of the book you are reading and just as impossible to ignore. Rev. Dr. Claus Westermann (b. 1909), a German Old Testament scholar, in his study of the concept of time in the Biblical creation tradition, has indicated that, in Genesis 1:1, God created time before space. Westermann writes:

> In his description of the creation of the light he has given the
> separation into time precedence over the separation into space
> and so has made possible the succession of the works of
> Creation in days. Then in his presentation of the creation of
> the world he has given precedence to the category of time,
> which come about by the separation of light and darkness,
> over the category of space,…And so he has firmly established
> something quite basic for the understanding of the world and
> man in the Old Testament in the context of Creation:
> existence in time has a priority over the existence of material
> things. (Westermann, *Creation* 43)

In the Scriptural creation stories, God creates time by his own choice,
and creates the material universe within that time while maintaining
the spiritual universe in eternity. As noted earlier, the universe has
both a temporal and a physical beginning. Time is embedded within
creation in such a fashion that the universe will have a temporal end
but not necessarily a physical end. Perhaps that is what the Catholic
Church means in the doxology: "Glory be to the Father, and to the
Son, and to the Holy Spirit. As it was in the beginning, is now, and
ever shall be, world without end. Amen." The *kosmos* will never end
though the material universe may merge with the spiritual universe in
a great dance the nature of which our feeble senses cannot detect nor
our feeble minds fathom.

What do scientists mean when they say time is real? What do
theologians mean when they say time is real in the material universe
but is experienced mystically while in the spiritual universe time is
not so much arrested as nonexistent? Qoheleth assures us:

> There is an appointed time for everything,
>> and a time for every affair under the heavens.
> A time to be born, and a time to die;
>> a time to planet, and a time to uproot the plant.
> A time to kill, and a time to heal;
>> a time to tear down, and a time to build.
> A time to weep, and a time to laugh;
>> a time to mourn, and a time to dance.
> A time to scatter stones, and a time to gather them;
>> a time to embrace, and a time to be far from embraces.

A time to seek, and a time to lose;
    a time to keep, and a time to cast away.
A time to rend, and a time to sew;
    a time to be silent, and a time to speak.
A time to love, and a time to hate;
    a time of war, and a time of peace.
(Ecclesiastes 3:1-8)

The ultimate reality of time rests in the Godhead who created it by willing it and sustains it and will ultimately destroy it in favor of eternal life for the chosen.

What does time mean to Jesus? For Jesus, as for us, the crucifixion is the center of all of space and time. To be united with Jesus in the crucifixion and resurrection is to transcend the time that Jesus permeates. The beginning as described in Genesis 1 is incomprehensible to our limited understanding of the nature of reality. Jesus often speaks in parables and figurative language to describe what essentially cannot be described in words. We can only glimpse what the risen Christ sees as one all-encompassing now. Light and darkness form an intricate web spun by God in the beginning to make sense of a universe that once was the chaos of pure darkness. We cannot understand this supernal light anymore than we can really understand the darkness of the crucifixion or the light of the resurrection – we can only experience them mystically to hope to gain insight into the mind of God.

Time and space are interwoven like light and darkness, like the crucifixion and the resurrection, and like the revelations of Oral Tradition and Written Tradition. Indeed, light and darkness, crucifixion and resurrection, Tradition and Scripture, are all woven together just as time and space are woven together to give us what we choose to call, for lack of a better term, reality. But, again, what is real? The real and the true are revealed by the Son of God in his work on the cross and his resurrection unto eternal life. For this reason, all of creation is bound up in the life, death, and resurrection of Christ, and extraterrestrials are woven into this picture as surely as the inhabitants of the Earth. As Christians, we remember these divine events regularly in the Mass, in the Sacrament, and every time Christ is made manifest in our lives. Surely, it is our duty to spread this good news to inhabitants of other worlds.

Time is divided into three parts: past, present, and future. In terms of the Christ events, there was the past (preparation for the coming of Christ), the present (an ever-present explosion of divine power in the cross and its emptying), and the future (apocalyptic expectation and the Parousia). It is possible that the Apocalypse and Parousia will occur only after all of space has been explored and conquered by hnau. Then, the last thing to be conquered will be time, just as the last thing Christ conquered was death. Upon contemplating our history, we come away with a new vision for the future – a vision that will catapult humans and perhaps extraterrestrials into a new age of faith, hope, and love. As creations of God, we may stretch, pull, metamorphose, and distend both our universe and ourselves, but God will not allow us to permanently divide, fracture, alienate, or destroy his universe or its many inhabitants because it is his universe to transform in his own way, according to his own pleasure, and in his own time.

For the scientist and the theologian, primeval matter was bound up in the great dance in the beginning of time when light and shadow interpenetrated the stuff of the universe. The Genesis story begins in medias res when God was in the process of separating light from shadow, creating order out of chaos. The Logos, proceeding from the Father, caused this order to be shaped into what we now know as the universe with its galaxies and solar systems. As the Logos caused the creation of life on the Earth, so the Logos probably caused life to develop on other worlds as well.

Is the evolution of life on the Earth unique or did it follow some kind of universal pattern? Will the convergence of evolution cause other species on other worlds to develop similar body structures with the five senses?

To understand Jesus, we must place him in his chronological context: that of first century Israel, a nation beset by the vicissitudes of the Roman Empire and the asperity of Pontius Pilate, the Roman governor of Judea. Again, to grasp the nature of Jesus and his message, we must grasp his time and the way to view time with respect to Jesus. Within the temporal dimension of the life of Jesus on Earth, we must understand the three basic time periods in terms of eschatology:

1   The past clears the way to reveal the present: "This is the time of fulfillment" (Mark 1:15a).

2   The future clears the way to reveal the present: "The Kingdom of God is at hand" (Mark 1:15b).

3   The present demands immediate reaction and participation: "Repent, and believe the Gospel" (Mark 1:15c).

The message of Jesus is temporal in that it demands participation on the part of believers in the present now and yet is atemporal in the sense of timeless because the Gospel is eternal, having been formed before the creation of the *kosmos*. The message of Jesus is also universal in scope, applying to all inhabitants of all worlds in a spatial sense for all yesterdays, todays, and tomorrows in a temporal sense. Jesus, in a sense, redefined time itself because he demands of his disciples an immediate response to his call such that the disciple's past, present, and future are all interwoven in this one act of accepting Jesus as the disciple's personal Lord and Saviour and acting on that faith daily. The Eucharist transcends and permeates all of space and time. So also does Baptism transcend space and time because the baptized is born again in the waters and Spirit of Baptism, having died with Jesus and risen again as Christ rises within the disciple. The event of rebirth is, for every disciple, a moment which cannot be historically described but only mystically experienced. When infants are baptized, they know what the unbaptized adults have forgotten. When we reach out into space, overcoming the barriers of lightspeed and time, we may discover that extraterrestrials need the message of the Gospel as much as we do. Inhabitants of other worlds may know as much as we do about God and his work on Earth or they may know nothing so that we need to instruct them or they may know what we have forgotten and need to relearn.

     For many inhabitants of the Earth, time is rooted in the past, for others, time is rooted in the future, while, for still others, time is rooted in the present. For Jesus, time is rooted in eternity. The present is closer to eternity than either the past or the future. This is why Jesus demands of us daily conversion to Christ, just as Bernard of Clairvaux intimated. When time is rooted in eternity, Jesus re-

269

establishes the wholeness and unity of time as a thing of immediacy requiring instantaneous responses on the part of his disciples. Those who live in the present rooted in eternity are truly disciples of Jesus and children of the Promise because they respect the past and do not fear the future, trusting in God's providence. The only fear worth having is fear of God in the sense of respect for the One who controls everyone, whether inhabitants of the Earth or inhabitants of other worlds. As Jesus said, "And do not be afraid of those who kill the body but cannot kill the soul; rather, be afraid of the one who can destroy both soul and body in Gehenna" (Matthew 10:28). Also, Scripture tells us several times: "The fear of the LORD is the beginning of wisdom; prudent are all who live by it" (Psalm 111:10a); "The fear of the LORD is the beginning of knowledge; wisdom and instruction fools despise" (Proverbs 1:7); "The beginning of wisdom is the fear of the LORD, and knowledge of the Holy One is understanding" (Proverbs 9:10); "The beginning of wisdom is fear of the LORD, which is formed with the faithful in the womb" (Ecclus/Sira 1:12). This fear of the Lord means a healthy respect for his power, yet that is not all the Lord requires of us. As James tells us, "You believe that God is one. You do well. Even the demons believe that and tremble" (2:19). Fear of the Lord must be rooted in a basic trust or it means nothing. To deal with possible extraterrestrials, we will require a basic trust in God upon whom we rely for our daily sustenance: "Give us this day our daily bread" (Matthew 6:11 and Luke 11:3). Of course, this bread of which Jesus speaks is not that which enters into our mouths and goes out into the latrine but is the food of God, that is, as Jesus instructs us, "to do the will of the one who sent me and to finish his work" (John 4:34). Indeed, Scripture also tells us, "You have been told, O man, what is good, and what the LORD requires of you: Only to do the right and to love goodness, and to walk humbly with your God" (Micah 6:8). Should we do this when we encounter extraterrestrials, and obey the Golden Rule, we will be doing well in the eyes of God. Jesus expresses the view that we should regard every moment in time as an opportunity to serve God by loving our fellow human beings (and one day other fellow hnau) in his Our Father, parables, healings, miracles, and teachings about the Kingdom.

The Our Father wraps up the wholeness and unity of time in one neat little package. The Our Father is divided up into sections:

1. The invocation in which we call upon our God as supplicants
2. Sanctification of God's Name in which we declare our faith
3. Supplication that the Kingdom be present in the now along with the will of God
4. Supplication for basic divine sustenance
5. Supplication for forgiveness of past sins as well as a promise to forgive others
6. Supplication for God not to abandon us to temptation
7. Supplication for God to "deliver us from evil"
8. Supplication to let it be so, that is, "Amen."

There are six supplications while there are only two statements in which God is invoked and his name hallowed. This is because we need God so much that we must constantly beg him to give us succor as it says in the song:

He is coming in the glory of the morning on the wave,
He is wisdom to the mighty, he is succor to the brave,
So the world shall be his footstool,
     and the soul of time his slave.
Our God is marching on.
(Julia Ward Howe, *Battle Hymn of the Republic*, st. 6)

These supplications express our desire for God to present within us and around us in the present time connected to eternity, perhaps best expressed in the doxology, "Glory be to the Father, and to the Son, and to the Holy Spirit. As it was in the beginning, is now, and ever shall be, world without end. Amen." The doxology is a prayer of faith in God and in his power to create good things and sustain them eternally.

The Our Father reveals the attitude of Jesus towards time as a kind of qualitative reality instead of a quantitative thing. What is more important to Jesus than how much time we have is the quality of the time we spend in this mortal life with the immortal God. The meaning of our temporal existence is serve God in time in preparation for serving God in eternity, and the way we serve God is by serving one another and by loving one another. The Our Father is a temporal aid to gaining eternal life. The eternal nature of the crucifixion and resurrection liberates us from sin in a way that opens the door for the mystical experience of God. Jesus tries to explain this to his disciples in his Kingdom teachings in which he declares that the Kingdom of God is here and now: Luke 17:20-21: "Asked by the Pharisees when the kingdom of God would come, he said in reply, 'The coming of the kingdom of God cannot be observed, and no one will announce, "Look, here it is," or, "There it is." For behold, the kingdom of God is among you.'" Also, Luke 11:20: "But if it is by the finger of God that [I] drive out demons, then the kingdom of God has come upon you." Finally, Matthew 11:12: "From the days of John the Baptist until now, the kingdom of heaven suffers violence, and the violent are taking it by force." If we fail to see the Kingdom, we fail to experience God mystically. It is perhaps by the violence of the cross that the Kingdom has become present for us both in this world and in many others. In the cross, past, present, and future become united in one Kingdom, the Kingdom of God.

We cannot avoid the presence of God by running away, hoping that time is on our side. In fact, time is on God's side, and apocalypticism is the way of the future made by God and connected to the present via the past. We can rediscover the past but not relive it. Jesus tells us to live in the present, not the past, even while not forgetting the past. Jesus tells us in Luke 9:60b in response to a man who wished to bury his father before discipling himself to Jesus, "Let the dead bury their dead. But you, go and proclaim the kingdom of God." Jesus must come first in our lives or we cannot embrace the Kingdom in eternity. To someone else who wanted to experience a long farewell to his family, Jesus brings into the present Kingdom by telling him, "No one who sets a hand to the plow and looks to what was left behind is fit for the kingdom of God" (Luke 9:62). As in attempting to find one's way in a maze, "back" does not work. For Jesus, one must trust in God wholeheartedly and without reservation, the way a child trusts a loving parent, so that he said, "Let the children come to me; do not prevent them, for the kingdom of God belongs to such as these. Amen, I say to you, whoever does not accept the kingdom of God like a child will not enter it" (Mark 10:14b-15). The teachings of Jesus are eternal: "Heaven and earth may pass away, but my words will not pass away" (Matthew 24:35).

Jesus is eternal because the Kingdom is eternal. We must remember this if we wish to bring the Kingdom of God to inhabitants of other worlds.

Is God fair? Some people think that God sits on his throne in heaven with a tally book in his hand keeping track of all the pluses and minuses that go on in the *kosmos* for the purpose of making sure that everything works out to some arbitrary point of zero that mere mortals seem to think is "fair." This is nonsense. God is not "fair." God is generous. In the parable of the workers in the vineyard, the Master hires men to work in his fields in the morning, afternoon, and evening, and gives to all the same wage. The ones who bore the heat of the day regarded the Master as "unfair," but the Master said, "(Or) am I not free to do as I wish with my own money? Are you envious because I am generous?" (Matthew 20:15). Many people are envious because God is generous. As a Catholic, I believe that, if God chooses to bring non-Christians into heaven with him, then it is not our place as Christians to question God's generosity. Similarly, if the blood of Jesus bathes the universe filled with inhabitants of many worlds, it is not our place as Christians to question God's generosity in bringing extraterrestrials into heaven with him. The power of Jesus transcends and permeates all inhabitants of all worlds throughout the universe. We should be glad.

As noted earlier, when faith knowledge and scientific knowledge are placed side by side, the view often causes the belief that a dichotomy exists between the two disciplines so that faith and science appear to be out of touch with each other. In a sense, the Kingdom brings the two disciplines together because faith is based on inward true and certain knowledge while science is based on outward objective and tentative knowledge. The dialogue between science and faith is often brisk, and disagreements are common. However, when scientists look upon the universe as God's Kingdom and when the theologian looks upon the universe as a feat of engineering, then rational discourse is possible. After all, God's Kingdom is a feat of engineering, and God is the Engineer of engineers. In fact, God is a hell of an engineer. The universe is magnificent both as a Kingdom and as a work of engineering. We must explore this universe as part of our very nature and, in the process, discover the Kingdom within ourselves and other hnau.

While faith can be objective in terms of analyzing reality as the creation of God, science can also be very subjective in terms of scientists developing ideas based on personal beliefs and convictions. Many theologians and scientists believe life exists on other worlds, but this is a personal belief that is not yet based on any kind of scientific data, although the belief can be construed as stemming from logic: If Earth is the only planet with life in a galaxy amidst millions of galaxies, God is certainly a very wasteful engineer to waste so much space. If scientists have nothing to say about faith, it is more likely than not that their scientific views are extremely limited, perhaps by not only prejudice but the willful suspension of faith on spurious grounds. Science, as a discipline, has inherent limits by its very nature, and it is extremely doubtful that science will ever be able to explain the nature of God or the mysteries of God's universe. Scientific instruments can only measure what they are designed to measure, and, if space contains inexplicable unknowns, that is, mysteries, then it is possible that only theology will be able to capture their essence.

Science and theology are not natural enemies. Unfortunately, they're not natural friends either. Science and theology are neither one foreign constructs, but both are created by God, directed by God, and given the status of truth by God. Truth is knowledge obtained either by means of science or theology, although different windows on the truth sometimes yield different kinds of knowledge. The complementary nature of science and faith must not be overlooked by the discerning mind and heart. Science uncovers the comprehensibleness in the design of the universe and makes it fathomable to our limited intellects. Theology complements this practice by explaining not how but *why* God created the universe. Science attempts to identify the source of that comprehensibleness in a way that can lead to God the creator. Theology attempts to identify the source of that comprehensibleness in a way that transcends the structure of the universe to render its hnau accountable for the way the inhabitants of the many worlds have obeyed the commandment to take care of it (cf. Genesis 1:28-29).

Theology and science would both be rewarded for complementing one another by each accepting its potential as well as its limits. Theology is the study of God while science is the study of God's creation, the universe and everything in it. It is possible that to understand creation is to understand the God who created it. As Einstein said, "I want to know the mind of God." Does the eternal nature of God and the temporal nature of his creation create a dichotomy between science and theology? Not necessarily. Theology is the rational side of the Christian faith, whereas science is often the rational side of hnau inquisitiveness. As natural theologians, we are inquisitive about God and his creation. As spiritual scientists, we are inquisitive about God and his creation. However, God is not a natural part of the universe, and this creates problems for many scientists whose own beliefs are to study nature and not the supernatural, which is the realm of metaphysics. The natural theologian also has problems in studying nature absent the spiritual realm, which they regard as essential to the structure of the universe. For the natural theologian and the spiritual scientist to communicate, they must both recognize the limits and frailties of hnau nature. Some things will always remain mysterious, and both kinds of seekers of truth must recognize that this is not a bad thing.

Science by its very nature develops theories that either contradict or supersede preceding theories, and theology by its very nature develops theories that build upon previous theories while not contradicting them per se. This is known as Tradition. Science has traditions but does not regard them as infallible, whereas Christian Tradition is indeed infallible as is its offshoot the Bible, both of which are the Word of God. Tradition clarifies Scripture, whereas scientific traditions are made to be changed, updated, and modified. Every time I read the Bible, I learn something new, and every time I look at the stars at night, I experience the mysteries of God anew. I dream of encountering extraterrestrials, and perhaps they dream of encountering other hnau as well. To discover extraterrestrial life will create a crisis among both scientists and theologians, and I have no doubt that people of both traditions will rise to the occasion to develop theories, explanations, and conclusions based on the data. Some people will be fearful, but Jesus said, "Take courage, it is I; do not be afraid" (Matthew 14:27; Mark 6:50; cf. John 6:20 and 14:27 and Revelation 1:17). Indeed, the Psalmist assures us in a song of ascents, "Like Mount Zion are they who trust in the LORD, unshakable, forever enduring" (125:1b). As long as we trust in the Lord, everything will happen according to the Lord's plan, although it should be noted that discipleship to Jesus brings both joy and sorrow, and we should be prepared for both, trusting in the Lord to bide his time.

Ultimately, Jesus Christ is the Truth, and both scientists and theologians quest for the truth in their explorations of reality. Nature is an imperfect reflection of this truth, a divine expression of the love of God. God both transcends and permeates his creation, often in unfathomable ways yet always with a keen eye on redemption. God panentheistically exists within the universe and also exists in eternity outside the material realm. As mortal hnau, we can only grasp truth partially because truth is ultimately a spiritual and mysterious thing, and wisdom is acting on the truth, even when we only partially understand it. Jesus Christ is the ultimate reflection of both God and divine reality in the panentheistic sense. Any understanding of nature without God is inauthentic. The theological implications of intelligent life on other worlds are a renewed appreciation for the diversity of God's creation by all hnau on Earth and other worlds, respect for who we are as the people of God, what we have been, and what me must become in our quest for the ultimate reality, and the development of the strong conviction that, because we are not alone in God's universe, we must seek out and relate to other creatures who may have beliefs and aspirations similar to our own or very different. We must evangelize yet with respect for the beliefs of other cultures and religions because, as C.S. Lewis once wrote, "Most religions are vague prophetic distortions of the one true God and his Messiah." This may never be more true than in any encounters with inhabitants of other worlds. We have a hard enough time getting along with ourselves. It may be that God wants us to conquer ourselves before we are allowed the gift of encountering intelligent beings on planets orbiting other stars.

We must learn to distinguish between real truth and ostensible truth. Metaphysics teaches us theological truth that science only dreams about. Panentheism teaches us the importance of God transcending reality to bring us truth, no matter how mysterious. Panentheism teaches us that God in a very real way is distinct from the material universe and yet permeates it, spreading his goodness across the vast reaches of interstellar space and time. God transcends the spatial and temporal to enable us to experience the divine eternally. God is immanent and personally present in his creation, constantly involving himself in the affairs of hnau of all planets.

Scientists and theologians who synthesize science and theology to develop a kind of theological unified field theory give us a cosmic view such that each complements the other perfectly. As long as we recognize Christ as the immanent divine presence in the universe who sustains it, cultivates it, and nurtures and redeems its hnau, we will all be complementary scientists and theologians.

Science and theology can embrace in a way that serves the interests of both with neither losing its identity as a true expression of reality. Science and theology coalesce to produce an understanding of the contiguous nature of the past, the present, and the future, especially in terms of the eternal cross and resurrection of Christ. Science and theology must involve each other in a dialogue of give and take in order for both to be presentable to cultures who may understand neither science nor Christian theology. As scientists and theologians we must experience the unity of reason and mystery or find ourselves left behind and possibly lost in our quest for the ultimate reality. Jesus will search for his lost lambs amidst the *kosmos*, but the search presupposes that the lambs wish to be found. Jesus may find us, but we must respond to his call or remain forever lost in the wilderness.

Chapter 15

Inhabitants of Other Worlds and the Theology of the Cross and Creation

...But, of old, there was One whose suffering changed an instrument of torture, degradation, and shame, into a symbol of glory, honor, and immortal life....
-- Harriet Beecher Stowe, *Uncle Tom's Cabin* (Chapter 40)

The chief triumph of Christianity is that it changed the cross from the symbol of all that is degrading and most shameful into the symbol of all that is grandest and most sacred. The point is that what was dishonorable transformed into honorable, what was inglorious transformed into glorious, and what was a symbol of death transformed into the symbol of eternal life. Natural theology assures us that the universe has a purpose, and that purpose is to serve as proof of the glory of God for the benefit of all hnau throughout the *kosmos*. The universe also serves the purpose of providing the place where the Logos chose to become incarnate, also for the benefit of hnau. God created the Earth for the purpose of providing a place where the glory of God might become manifest on the cross, the center of all of space and time. Richard Bentley writes:

> All Bodies were formed for the Sake of Intelligent Minds: As the Earth was principally designed for the Being and Service and Contemplation of Men; why may not all other Planets be created for the like uses, each for their own Inhabitants who have Life and Understanding. (cited in Dick, *Plurality of Worlds* 149)

The cross of Christ was the purpose of Jesus on Earth to effect the salvation of hnau throughout his *kosmos*. Similarly, the purpose of the *kosmos* was to bring about the crucifixion of Jesus for the redemption of hnau. The resurrection of Christ is the unification of the material universe with the spiritual universe.

How will inhabitants of other worlds react to the religious instruction that the cross is the way to heaven? The Apostle Paul tells us: "The message of the cross is foolishness to those who are perishing, but to us who are being saved it is the power of God" (1 Corinthians 1:18). The cross is the power and the glory of God. Paul continues: "For Jews demand signs and Greeks look for wisdom, but we proclaim Christ crucified, a stumbling block to Jews and foolishness to Gentiles, but to those who are called, Jews and Greeks alike, Christ the power of God and the wisdom of God" (1 Corinthians 1:22-24). The cross glorified Jesus and brings glory to those who are steeped in its mysteries. When we encounter extraterrestrials, should we say to them "For I resolved to know nothing while I was with you except Jesus Christ, and him crucified" (1 Corinthians 2:2)? If extraterrestrials already know about the cross, then we may find Earth being evangelized, but, if they know nothing of the cross, then it will be our job to explain it to them and encourage them to steep themselves in its mysteries.

Mysticism is the study and experience of the mysteries of God. The mystery of the cross is the mystery of God and the power of God. The crucified Christ tells us what power is and what glory is. A mystery is a manifestation of God. The exalting power of God is found only in the emptying of Christ on the cross who emptied himself of his Godness in order to manifest the glory and power of God as in Philippians 2:7: "Rather, he emptied himself, taking the form of a slave, coming in human likeness; and found human in appearance, he humbled himself, becoming obedient to death, even death on a cross." When I pray, I try to immerse myself in the wounds of God and experience the mystery found in the cross. "He was bearing our sins in his own body on the cross, so that, free from sin, we might live for righteousness. By his wounds you have been healed" (1 Peter 2:24). Jesus saves us daily so we should daily convert to Christ, as Sira says, "Delay not your conversion to the Lord, put it not off from day to day" (Ecclus/Sira 5:8). We consume him in the Eucharist, and so he consumes us, for "Our god is a consuming fire" (Hebrews 12:29 and cf. Deuteronomy 4:24). Therefore, we should imitate Christ, who had such zeal for God's house that it consumed him (John 2:17 and Psalm 69:10). "God proves his love for us in that while we were still sinners Christ died for us" (Romans 5:8). The cross is a great and powerful mystery; who can understand it? We can only experience the mystery and be thankful because the mystery of the cross is not a problem to be solved but a reality to be experienced.

I came across the following definition of mysticism from Webster's Online Dictionary:

> [eccl. Hist.] The doctrine of the Mystics, who professed a pure, sublime, and wholly disinterested devotion, and maintained that they had direct intercourse with the divine Spirit, and acquired a knowledge of god and of spiritual things unattainable by the natural intellect, and such as cannot be analyzed or explained.

> [philos.] The doctrine that the ultimate elements or principles of knowledge or belief are gained by an act or process akin to feeling or faith. From WordNet ® 1.6 Database (wn)

> Mysticism. A religion based on mystical communion with an ultimate reality.

I find these to be interesting definitions. I think that mysticism is the experience of mysteries. In the Christian faith, mysticism is the experience of the mysteries of God. Scripture discusses different types of mysteries:

Dan. 2:17-19: Daniel went home and informed his companions Hananiah, Mishael, and Azariah, that they might implore the mercy of the God of heaven in regard to this mystery, so that Daniel and his companions might not perish with the rest of the wise men of Babylon. During the night the mystery was revealed to Daniel in a vision, and he blessed the God of heaven:....

Daniel 4:6 Finally there came before me Daniel, whose name is Belteshazzar after the name of my god, and in whom is the spirit of the holy God, I repeated the dream to him: "Belteshazzar, chief of the magicians, I know that the spirit of the holy God is in you and no mystery is too difficult for you; tell me the meaning of the visions that I saw in my dream."

Mark 4:11   [Jesus] answered them, "The mystery of the kingdom of God has been granted to you. But to those outside everything comes in parables, so that 'they may look and see but not perceive, and hear and listen but not understand, in order that they may not be converted and be forgiven.'"

Ro. 11:25-27 I do not want you to be unaware of this mystery brothers, so that you will not become wise [in] your own estimation: a hardening has come upon Israel in part, until the full number of the Gentiles comes in, and thus all Israel will be saved, as it is written:
> "The deliverer will come out of Zion,
> he will turn away godlessness from Jacob;
> and this is my covenant with them
> when I take away their sins."

Romans 16:25 [Now to him who can strengthen you, according to my gospel and the proclamation of Jesus Christ, according to the revelation of the mystery kept secret for long ages but now manifested through the prophetic writings and, according to the command of the eternal God, made known to all nations to bring about the obedience of faith, to the only wise God, through Jesus Christ be glory forever and ever. Amen.]

1 Cor. 2:1-2 When I came to you, brothers, proclaiming the mystery of God, I did not come with sublimity of words or of wisdom. For I resolved to know nothing while I was with you except Jesus Christ, and him crucified.

1Co. 15:51-52 Behold, I tell you a mystery. We shall not all fall asleep, but we will all be changed, in an instant, in the blink of an eye, at the last trumpet. For the trumpet will sound, the dead will be raised incorruptible, and we shall be changed.

Eph. 1:8b-10   In all wisdom and insight, he has made known to us the mystery of his will in accord with his favor that he set forth in him as a plan for the fullness of times, to sum up all things in Christ, in heaven and on earth.

Eph. 3:1-6   Because of this, I, Paul, a prisoner of Christ [Jesus] for you Gentiles -- if, as I suppose, you have heard of the stewardship of God's grace that was given to me for your benefit, [namely that] the mystery was made known to me by revelation, as I have written briefly earlier. When you read this you can understand my insight into the mystery of Christ, which was not made known to human beings in other generations as it has now been revealed to his holy apostles and prophets by the Spirit, that the Gentiles are coheirs, members of the same body, and copartners in the promise in Christ Jesus through the gospel.

Eph. 3:8-10   To me, the very least of all the holy ones, this grace was given, to preach to the Gentiles the inscrutable riches of Christ, and to bring to light [for all] what is the plan of the mystery hidden from ages past in God who created all things, so that the manifold wisdom of God might now be made known through the church to the principalities and authorities in the heavens.

Eph. 5:32   This is a great mystery, but I speak in reference to Christ and the church.

Eph. 6:18-19   With all prayer and supplication, pray at every opportunity in the Spirit. To that end, be watchful with all perseverance and supplication for all the holy ones and also for me, that speech may be given me to open my mouth, to make known with boldness the mystery of the gospel for which I am an ambassador in chains, so that I may have the courage to speak as I must.

Col. 1:24-27   Now I rejoice in my sufferings for your sake, and in my flesh I am filling up what is lacking in the afflictions of Christ on behalf of his body, which is the church, of which I am a minister in accordance with God's stewardship given to me to bring to completion for you the word of God, the mystery hidden from ages and from generations past. But now it has been manifested to his holy ones, to whom God chose to make known the riches of the glory of this mystery among the Gentiles; it is Christ in you, the hope for glory.

Col. 2:1-3   For I want you to know how great a struggle I am having for you and for those in Laodicea and all who have not seen me face to face, that their hearts may be encouraged as they are brought together in love, to have all the richness of fully assured understanding, for the knowledge of the mystery of God, Christ, in whom are hidden all the treasures of wisdom and knowledge.

Col. 4:2-4   Persevere in prayer, being watchful in it with thanksgiving; at the same time, pray for us, too, that God may open a door to us for the word, to speak of the mystery of Christ, for which I am in prison, that I may make it clear, as I must speak.

2 Thess. 2:7   For the mystery of lawlessness is already at work. But the one who restrains is to do so only for the present, until he is removed from the scene.

1 Tim. 3:8-9   Similarly, deacons must be dignified, not deceitful, not addicted to drink, not greedy for sordid gain, holding fast to the mystery of the faith with a clear conscience.

1 Tim. 3:16   Undeniably great is the mystery of devotion,
        Who was manifested in the flesh,
        vindicated in the spirit,

seen by angels,
proclaimed to the Gentiles,
believed in throughout the world,
taken up in glory.

Christians who become one with God in the sacraments are mystics by definition. Mystics experience the mysteries of the cross and resurrection in episodes of indescribable joy and abandon. Mystics do not simply *know* Jesus as Lord; mystics *experience* Jesus as Lord. To bring Jesus to hnau of other worlds is to spread the joy. Yet, as noted above, discipleship to Jesus brings both joy and sorrow. It is not always easy to be a Christian, especially in the face of a hostile *kosmos*. The *kosmos* entertains believers and nonbelievers, mystics and nonmystics, scientists and nonscientists, theologians and nontheologians. New Christians may find themselves martyred for the sake of their faith in the name of Jesus. This is unsurprising, though it causes sorrow and anguish. We should, in such cases, imitate Jesus himself, "the leader and perfecter of faith. For the sake of the joy that lay before him he endured the cross, despising its shame, and has taken his seat at the right of the throne of God" (Hebrews 12:1-2).

Some people erroneously believe that the Jews alone crucified Jesus in collusion with the Romans. I say that we all chose to free a murderer and demand the crucifixion of the eternal Son of God. One of the most powerful experiences I have had was a Good Friday Mass in which I got in line with others to approach a man-sized cross with nails on the altar, genuflecting three times on the way to symbolize the three times Jesus stumbled, while singing "Were you there when they crucified my Lord?" and then picked up a hammer and hammered the nail to signify that I crucified Christ with my sins, and then kissed the cross to signify that I believe Jesus forgives me for crucifying him with my sins. Jesus criticized the Pharisees for saying "If we had lived in those times, we would not have killed the prophets." Of course they would have. Many of us would like to believe that, had we been in the crowd, we would not have yelled for his crucifixion, but in fact we would have done just that. Jesus "was handed over for our transgressions and raised for our justification" (Romans 4:25). John tells us in his letter that if we say we do not sin, "we deceive ourselves, and the truth is not in us," (1 John 1:8) nor is

Christ truly in us. We must acknowledge our sins, acknowledge that we crucified Christ with our sins, believe that he rose for our justification, and live not for ourselves but for Christ who lives in us. To believe that others crucified Christ but not I is to preach restoration of health without medicine, treatment with a band-aid without cleansing the wound, revival without passion, recovery without palliative time, remission of sins without conversion, absolution without repentance, victory without spiritual warfare, acquittal without trial, vindication without divine judgement, and Easter without Calvary. By his stripes we are healed. By his death we experience eternal life: "Where, O death, is your victory? Where, O death, is your sting?" (1 Corinthians 15:5). Saint Francis, of all noncanonical writings, may have expressed it best in his famous prayer:

> Lord, make me an instrument of your peace.
> Where there is hatred, let me sow love.
> Where there is injury, pardon,
> Where there is doubt, faith,
> Where there is despair, hope,
> Where there is darkness, light,
> And where there is sadness, joy.
> O Divine Master,
> grant that I may not so much seek
> To be consoled, as to console;
> To be understood, as to understand,
> To be loved, as to love;
> For it is in giving that we receive –
> It is in pardoning that we are pardoned;
> And it is in dying that we are born to eternal life.

I think in history books many people are called great who were not and many great people are absent. What about Jesus? What makes Jesus a "great person"? Let us not say because he was the Son of God since not everyone knew that when he walked the streets of Israel. Jesus, in the pages of the Bible, is very charismatic and tells the truth, both of which earned him many disciples as well as enemies. Many people adored him and yet many people despised him. But what made him "great"? He taught with authority, he healed the sick, exorcised demons, preached the good news to everyone, performed miracles, raised the dead, was crucified, died, buried, and rose again in fulfillment of the Scriptures. If we had lived in Israel two thousand years ago, would we have considered Jesus a "great person"? It seems to me that when your words survive for thousands of years, the words must be great. "Heaven and earth will pass away, but my words will not pass away" (Matthew 24:35; Mark 13:31; Luke 21:33). Jesus did not flaunt his power or his greatness. "He was spurned and avoided by men, a man of suffering, accustomed to infirmity, One of those from whom men hide their faces, spurned, and we held him in no esteem" (Isaiah 53:3). God often chooses the weak and despised to exalt and to show forth God's power and greatness. A great man is not seduced by fame. Jesus taught his words of power, letting the words speak for themselves.

So, it seems to me that, if people remember your words generations after you have passed on because those words made sense and electrified them, that's a great part of what makes one great. That Jesus rose from the dead is evidence that he spoke great words worth remembering. Interestingly, the disciples often did not understand what Jesus told them because his words only made sense after his resurrection when Jesus opened the hearts of his disciples to comprehend his greatness. So, the words of Jesus only make sense in the light of the resurrection. Nevertheless, many people, from kings and peasants to revolutionaries and saints have found the words of Jesus great. Mohandas K. Gandhi was one who found the words of Jesus great and yet was not a Christian. The words of the Bible are great and have great power all by themselves whether you believe the Bible to be the Word of God or not. Similarly, the words of Jesus are great whether you consider him to be the Son of God or not. Others have spoken great words, too, but only Jesus sealed his words with the power of faith and hope and love. Words have power. Jesus taught us what greatness is in the scandal of the cross and the power of the resurrection. Thus, it is more than his words that make him great but also his works.

Greatness is not to be found in fame and fortune. The preacher, Qoheleth, tells us, "Though I said to myself, 'Behold, I have become great and stored up wisdom beyond all who were before me in Jerusalem, and my mind has broad experience of wisdom and knowledge'; yet when I applied my mind to know wisdom and knowledge, madness and folly, I learned that this also is a chase after wind" (Ecclesiastes 1:16-17). I am also reminded of Ozymandias about whom Percy Bysshe Shelley wrote; inscribed on a pillar was the following verse:

> My name is Ozymandias,
> King of Kings;
> Look on my works,
> Ye mighty, and Despair!

Ozymandias is pushing up daisies. Many people like Ozymandias are seduced by their own fame and fortune, not realizing that death awaits all who fancy greatness. Jesus did not seek fame and fortune but achieved greatness with humility. Philippians tells us that Jesus,

> Who, though he was in the form of God,
> did not regard equality with God something to be grasped.
> Rather, he emptied himself,
> taking the form of a slave,
> coming in human likeness;
> and found human in appearance,
> he humbled himself,
> becoming obedient to death, even death on a cross.
> Because of this, God greatly exalted him
> and bestowed on him the name that is above every name,
> that at the name of Jesus every knee should bend,
> of those in heaven and on earth and under the earth,
> and every tongue confess that Jesus Christ is Lord,
> to the glory of God the Father.
> (2:6-11)

Everyone has the potential for greatness, but only those who seek the Kingdom of God will find it in abundance.

The Tradition of the Catholic Church is the Word of God, and the Bible is the Word of God because the Bible is part of the Tradition of the Catholic Church. Tradition came first, and Scripture followed. To forsake Tradition is to forsake Scripture, since Scripture is part of Tradition. Protestants sometimes complain that this is circular and self dependent. It is no more circular than the belief that the Bible is the Word of God because the Bible says that the Bible is the Word of God (although the Bible does not say this explicitly and there is no inspired table of contents for Scripture). What matters is not just that you believe Tradition and Scripture but your response to the call of Jesus Christ in your life. Jesus Christ is my personal Lord and Savior, and I have taken my place in the world as a soldier for Christ. I have done this not so much because I love Jesus but because Jesus loves me, and Jesus responds to me in the way that I respond to Jesus. If you've ever noticed in the Bible, Jesus always responds to people in the way that they respond to him. Jesus asks, "What do you want me to do for you?" and the blind man says, "I want to see," so Jesus makes mud with his spit, places it on the man's eyes, he washes, and he can see. A centurion asks Jesus to heal his servant from a distance, and Jesus does so. As we ask Jesus, so he responds to us. Jesus responds to our faith because he is faithful. I have not so much chosen Jesus as Jesus has chosen me from the foundation of the world, and I cannot help but proclaim his message as found in the Tradition and Scripture of the Catholic Church. You may accept or reject that Word of God as you please; we have free will. Jesus is our Rabbi/Teacher and we are his disciples/students. I have accepted the call of my Savior, and I must proclaim what I believe, because if I didn't the very stones would shout.

Our duty as human beings studying God and his universe is to find out by experiential learning how God operates his universe to the best of our ability. God gave us a sense of curiosity for a reason. As Catholics, we may posit that we cannot know God and his universe by physical experience alone.

The Weak Anthropic Principle asserts that our region of space necessarily is one in which observers can exist; the Strong Anthropic Principle asserts that the universe is one in which observers can exist. It can be argued that the universe exists because God observes it and created other observers. Thus, observers are a necessary function of the universe. The very existence of the universe depends upon life, that is, living things that observe the universe. God has chosen to create the laws of physics of the universe so that observers could evolve in it. The Teleological Principle demands that God create the universe for the sake of observers who evolve in it.

The notion that God explains the universe's life-generating character very succinctly answers the problem of why intelligent life evolved on earth and perhaps elsewhere in the universe. God's explicit reasons for bringing into existence living beings who could observe the universe around them may be unfathomable, but the Bible give us insight into the mind of God, implying that the nature of God as light and love explains why God created light for observers to see by and love for observers to experience in terms of their relationship to God and one another.

Does the God hypothesis have serious competition? Some would have us think so. God tidily explains many problems of the nature of reality. We must be observing in a universe in which living observers exist. Do we exist for the purpose of observing the universe and perhaps also of observing God in our own limited way? Anthropocentrism dictates that we believe other life forms are similar to those on Earth. God made humans in God's spiritual image, not physical image. Divine selection may explain our existence better than any other theory. In other words, the universe seems tailor-made for observers because God indeed tailor-made the universe for us observers.

Life demands a divine sustainer. What about life elsewhere in the universe? If, as some theorists claim, life is abundant in the universe, then where are they and why have they not visited Earth? Perhaps life develops easily but intelligent life is a little harder to manage, except with divine assistance. Is our human life highly unusual? Do other forms of life elsewhere in the universe require divine assistance as well?

What should we think of Stephen Hawking's suggestion that the Big Bang Theory in conjunction with Quantum theory has "no place for a Creator"? Should we think Hume and Kant successfully refuted the idea of Intelligent Design? For neoplatonists, God is the word for the principle that the universe exists because of the ethical need for it. For Einstein, time could not have been created by a temporal being. So, God is eternal. Theorists like Hawking tend to treat the coming-into-being of the universe as a what rather than a why. All in all, I think God is real and necessary as Creator of our universe because we are both necessary observers.

I have heard some scientists claim that mathematics is the universal language with which we will communicate with extraterrestrials. I think this is a mistaken belief, but only in a technical sense. Stephen Hawking uses imaginary numbers in his equations to avoid the singularity of the big bang with his model, a practice some object to on the theory that only real numbers produce real results. This is based on a very flawed understanding of mathematics. To object to imaginary numbers is to object to all numbers because numbers do not really exist; numbers are a figment of the human imagination that we use for the purpose of solving certain problems in our universe and about the nature of the universe. Thus, although I've seen some assert that $5 + 3 = 8$ is a truth regardless of the universe in which one finds oneself, I counter that in a ring of numbers including 1 and 2 and 3 and 4 and 5, $5 + 3 = 3$. If you're not familiar with ring theory, a clock is a ring comprised of 12 numbers from 1 to 12. If it's 8 o'clock and you add 6 hours, it's 2 o'clock, so in this ring $8+6=2$. So, mathematical rules are not laws of physics but are primarily determined by popular vote among mathematicians and scientists who keep what is useful and works and discard what is not useful and does not work. Bertrand Russell (1872 -- 1970), a British philosopher, logician, epistemologist, educator, social reformer, and writer on the topic of philosophy of mathematics, who received the Nobel Prize for Literature in 1950, wrote: "Mathematics may be defined as the subject in which we never know what we are talking about, nor whether what we are saying is true" (*Recent Work on the Principles of Mathematics [1901]*. In *International Monthly, vol. 4, p. 84*). Russell also wrote, "Mathematics takes us still further from what is human, into the region of absolute necessity, to which not only the actual world, but every possible world, must conform" (*The Study of Mathematics*). As a practical matter, the mathematical rules which prove useful are retained, and the mathematical rules that do not produce useful results are discarded. Rules of mathematics may differ from one culture to another, so I see no reason to believe that our mathematics will be a universal language that intelligent beings from other worlds will be able to recognize, at least without some measure of translation.

Does understanding mathematics and equations mean we have knowledge? There is no such thing as false knowledge. Certainly, we can be mistaken in thinking that we have knowledge, however. False belief is not knowledge by definition. There cannot be complete justification for a false belief. The strong conception of knowledge says that we must have complete justification for a belief to count as knowledge. However, since our sense data can be unreliable, we cannot really know anything for certain, so knowledge is impossible. The weak conception of knowledge asserts that a belief must have strong or reasonable justification for truth but not absolute certainty. The problem with the weak theory is that no proponent of the theory seriously puts a percentage on the probable truth of a belief. Congress requires a 51% majority to pass a bill, and the Constitution requires a 2/3 majority for others on the theory that Congress needs to determine the amount of passion for an unusually important idea before it passes muster. Similarly, how passionate should we feel about a belief before it qualifies as knowledge? No one knows. Thus, the strong conception of knowledge requires us to be supermen whereas the weak conception of knowledge requires us to be wishy-washy. Mathematicians might say undecidability means we cannot know which version is right. So the uncertainty principle. I'm not sure I find that comforting.

Inductive reasoning is central to science but is by definition uncertain. Thus, scientists must be wishy-washy by definition. Religious knowledge is of a different order. In a real sense, there's no such thing as scientific knowledge or empirical knowledge, since such knowledge is not possible, but there is religious knowledge which is true by the definition of the Catholic Church. If the Catholic Church denies a statement is true, then it is not true despite all the logical reasoning in the universe (assuming the statement denying the validity of a claim is proclaimed by the Pope ex cathedra in conjunction with the Magisterium about a nonscientific matter involving the faith and morals of the Church). Some may ask what happens if the Church changes its mind about something, and the answer is that the Church has not, does not, and will not change its positions on matters of faith and morals, which the Catholic Church teaches infallibly. It's like asking a Sola Scriptura Protestant what happens when the Bible contradicts the Bible? It doesn't happen, so the question is academic.

Public revelation ended with the death of the last apostle. Many things that we believe are not found directly in Scripture, some not even indirectly. For example, all Christians believe the doctrine of the consubstantiality of the Trinity, but this doctrine is found nowhere in the pages of Scripture. Scripture does not contradict the doctrine, but it does not define it either. One of the functions of the Catholic Church is to define Christian doctrine authoritatively. The purpose of both Tradition and Scripture is to bring us to faith in Christ

Jesus. When we encounter extraterrestrials, one of the functions of the Catholic Church will be to bring knowledge of Tradition and Scripture to inhabitants of other worlds so that they may become Christians and worship alongside us.

Tradition defines Scripture, and Scripture supports Tradition in the following verses:

Ecclus/Sira 8:9 — Reject not the tradition of old men which they have learned from their fathers; From it you will obtain the knowledge how to answer in time of need.

1 Corinthians 11:2 — I praise you because you remember me in everything and hold fast to the traditions, just as I handed them on to you.

1 Corinthians 11:23 — For the tradition I received from the Lord and also handed on to you is that on the night he was betrayed, the Lord Jesus took some bread, etc.

1 Corinthians 15:3 — The tradition I handed on to you in the first place, a tradition which I had myself received, was that Christ died for our sins, in accordance with the scriptures, etc.

1 Thessalonians 2:13 — When you received God's word, which you heard from us, you accepted it, not as the word of men, but, just as it truthfully is, as the word of God, which is also at work in you believers.

2 Thessalonians 2:15 — Therefore, brothers, stand firm and hold fast to the traditions that you were taught, either by an oral statement or by a letter of ours.

2 Thessalonians 3:6 — We instruct you, brothers, in the name of (our) Lord Jesus Christ, to shun any brother who conducts himself in a disorderly way and not

according to the tradition they received from us.

Titus 1:7-9

The presiding elder has to be irreproachable since he is God's representative: never arrogant or hot-tempered, nor a heavy drinker or violent, nor avaricious; but hospitable and a lover of goodness; sensible, upright, devout and self-controlled; and he must have a firm grasp of the unchanging message of the tradition, so that he can be counted on both for giving encouragement in sound doctrine and for refuting those who argue against it.

To forsake Tradition is to forsake Scripture, since Scripture is part of Tradition. I've studied religion for many years. Studying the development of Judaism and Christianity from the ancient past has strengthened my faith. If the Bible were all neatly wrapped up like a present I would doubt my faith more. I would cry more often, "I believe! Help my unbelief!" (Mark 9:24). But the Bible tells of the development of the faith of the Jews and Christians in exquisite detail. I find this fascinating from a faith perspective. As the Apostle Paul once remarked, "Faith is the realization of what is hoped for and evidence of things not seen" (Hebrews 11:1). The more I study the Bible, the more I am convinced of its universal theological eternal truths. Remember, the Bible contains scientific errors and historical errors because the Bible is neither a science textbook nor a history textbook. Rather, the Bible contains no theological errors because the Bible is a theology textbook. By studying other religions, I have become more and more aware of the truth of C.S. Lewis's remark, "Most religions are vague prophetic distortions of the one true God and his Messiah." By studying the development of the Jewish and Christian faiths in the tumultuous mix of numerous other surrounding religions, I've developed an even greater appreciation for the uniqueness that is the Bible.

Similarly, by studying numerous other religious figures from history, I have developed an even greater appreciation for the uniqueness of Jesus Christ. I am first and foremost a student of Jesus the Christ who is my rabbi, my rebbe, my teacher, my lover, my husband, my saviour, my messiah, my brother, my God. Jesus is the bread that came down from heaven. Other religious figures have also made impacts on the history of humanity, so I have studied them and have concluded that Jesus is similar in many ways but unique in many ways as well. Other mystery religions of the period speak of a god who dies and is buried in the soil whence fruit arises, so that believers consume the fruit/food that is the resurrected god. Syncretistically, Christianity took this idea and applied it to Jesus. Ancient myths are like prophecies of the coming true faith. Other people of the ancient world had creation myths, and when the Jews were exiled to Babylon, they encountered some of these myths and asked, "Hey, why don't we have a creation myth?" So they wrote one that was uniquely Jewish. God blessed this interpretation of the creation myth motif[63] and made it holy because it more accurately than any other myth reflected the truth about the mystery of creation. The Genesis creation myth is not about how the universe was created but why the universe was created, and this pleased God who is usually more interested in why than how about many things including worship. In other words, why we worship is just as significant as how we worship. We worship in spirit and truth. God hears all prayers. Many people are more concerned with the how than the why. Christianity is concerned with both. That is why in the Catholic Church we pray "for those whose faith is known to God alone."

I am a strong Catholic with an intellectual taste for religious faith, and I do not deny my religious fervor. Every member of the Body of Christ is part of the greater whole (i.e., the whole is greater than the sum of its parts). I'm willing to discuss my beliefs and my faith intelligently, but I do not say, "You must agree with me or you go to hell." I do not think God judges us on the basis of the accuracy of our orthodoxy. God will judge us by our faith and works, and we'll be sheep or goats, although I have consecrated my heart to the Immaculate Heart of Mary, meaning I obey Mary's one command in the New Testament, to wit, "Do whatever [Jesus Christ] tells you to do" (John 2:5), so that I rely for my salvation exclusively upon the

---

[63] A motif in folklore is a recurring character, situation, event, or theme; a theme is the dominant idea of a literary work.

grace of Jesus Christ. I do not believe the Doctrine of Limited Atonement. I believe Jesus is universal. I believe the message of Jesus is universal and must apply to extraterrestrials as well as inhabitants of the Earth or it is meaningless.

I had a high school English teacher named Mrs. Levy, an Orthodox Jew, who knew the New Testament backwards and forwards because, she claimed, without an understanding of the Bible, Old Testament and New Testament, it is almost impossible to understand the vast majority of Western literature. Mrs. Levy treated us like individuals and encouraged us to study the various literary works of our respective religions because, she said, "I want you to be able to discuss and defend what you believe intelligently." I have always respected and admired her for that, not to mention being grateful. She introduced me to Augustine and Thomas Aquinas, and I, by the way, introduced her to Maimonides. I was interested in the Jewish view of creation, and Maimonides wrote an interesting book on the subject, and I shared it with my teacher in obedience to Galatians 4:6: "One who is being instructed in the word should share all good things with his instructor." Like Mrs. Levy, I want people with whom I converse, particularly my own students, to be able to discuss and defend what they believe intelligently.

I am not proselytizing per se in this book, although, if, by reading this book, some come to have faith in Christ, then I think that that is a good thing. I just explain what I believe and let the chips fall where they may. I believe that we should evangelize by behaving ethically, and only after practicing that for many years should we have the audacity to try to convert people with words. I try to convert people by acting like a Christian. As C.S. Lewis once remarked, "I intend to live as like a Narnian as I can even if there is no Narnia." I intend to believe that extraterrestrials are children of God just like we are even if, in my lifetime, we do not discover or encounter inhabitants from other worlds.

Eugene A. Laverdiere, S.S.S. wrote a section in the New American Bible for Catholics entitled "Literary Forms of the Bible" in which he writes the following on page 1465:

> The first eleven chapters of *Genesis* are much closer to mythical forms of writing. Myth, in this case, must not be understood to mean that the events told were fictional or

untrue. A myth is a profoundly true statement which speaks to universal aspects of life and reality. It is a statement whose meaning rises above time and space. Although biblical myths were influenced by other mythical statements of the ancient world, they are used by the biblical writers to express history's relationship to God. They point to history's origins at the moment of the world's creation. They speak of the beginnings where history touches eternity, and, therefore, to moments which cannot be historically described. Myth is thus essential to biblical faith. We do the Scriptures a serious injustice if we read myth as though it were history. Such a tendency must be resisted along with the opposite tendency to read biblical history as though it were mythical. By reading the early chapters of *Genesis* with sensitivity to poetic symbol and imagery, we can easily avoid such temptations.

Let's try a profane example. I heard a scientist on television telling a story once about Galileo. He said one day Galileo was in church attending mass and he saw a light fixture (a candle or lamp, I suppose) swinging back and forth high above him across the pews. Galileo began to time the swings of the larger lamps and the smaller lamps and noticed that they took the same amount of time to swing back and forth. The scientist remarked, "It must have been a very dull sermon." From this observation, nevertheless, Galileo deduced that gravity causes objects to fall at the same rate regardless of their size. He later tested his theory atop the Leaning Tower of Pisa in which he dropped a large and small object and asked someone on the ground to see whether they hit the ground at the same time. They did. The rest is history.

Now, do you believe that Galileo really made these observations during a dull sermon at Mass or do you think it's just a story designed to teach a scientific truth? Do you think Newton was really hit by an apple? Does it really matter? In other words, does your belief or unbelief in the actual reality of the incidents adversely affect your understanding of scientific explanations? Does it adversely affect your ability to repeat Galileo's experiment and arrive at the same conclusion? I don't know about you, but, for me, the answer is "No." I understand the science behind the story and the literal truth of the story is irrelevant. Similarly, the myth of creation in the Bible is designed to teach theological truth; whether the story is literally true or not is irrelevant. The theological truth cannot really be described in words but teaches us to understand that God is the Creator of the universe, however he managed it, and that he cares about his creation and his creatures, especially us and any other inhabitants of other worlds he may have created.

Appendix A.

Listing of Certain Authors of Category 5

Category 5:   Incarnation Unique To Earth Applies Universally to both Human Beings and Inhabitants of Other Worlds

Category 5 authors include Immanuel Kant; Edward Young; C.S. Lewis (20th century); Clergyman Andreas Ehrenberg (d. 1726); rector Johan Schudt (1664 – 1722); Hymnologist David Schober (1696 – 1778); James Beattie (1735 – 1803); Beilby Porteus (1731 – 1808), bishop of Chester and subsequently of London; George Adams (1750 – 1795); Barthold Heinrich Brockes (1680 – 1740); Andrew Fuller (1754 – 1815), a Baptist minister; Rev. Edward Nares (1762 – 1841); Comte Joseph de Maistre (1754 – 1821); John Herschel, the famous son of the famous astronomer William Herschel; Sir William Rowan Hamilton (1805 – 1865); Samuel Noble (1779 – 1853); Ellen White of the Seventh Day Adventists; Rev. Thomas Rawson Birks (1810 – 1883); Hugh Miller (1802 – 1856); Rev. Josiah Crampton (1809 – 1883); Rev. Charles Louis Hequembourg in 1859; Camille Flammarion (1842 – 1925), a Frenchman; Abbe Francois Moigno (1804 – 1884); Pierre Corbet in an 1894 essay; Theophile Ortolon (b. 1861); Johann Ebrard (1818 –1888); Aubrey de Vere (1814 – 1902), a Catholic poet; Rev. Edwin T. Winkler (1823 – 1883); Rev. George Mary Searle (1839 – 1918), a Catholic; Januarius De Concilio (1836 – 1898); and Wolfhart Pannenberg (German theologian). Clergyman Andreas Ehrenberg (d. 1726), whose pseudonym was Geierbrand Haraneus, and rector Johan Schudt (1664 – 1722) both note the difficulty inherent in how any discovery of inhabitants of other worlds affects the atonement (Crowe 34). Hymnologist David Schober (1696 – 1778) attempts a reconciliation of the problem of inhabitants of other worlds with the Christian doctrine of redemption (Crowe 34).

Appendix B:

Saint Thomas Aquinas

The following sections are taken from the Summa Theologica of Saint Thomas Aquinas, translated by the Fathers of the English Dominican Province (1947). It is taken from the following website: www.sacred-texts.com/chr/aquinas/summa/index.hmt, which has the following notice: "This is St. Thomas' encyclopedia-length work on Catholic theology. This translation, considered of high quality, is in the public domain in the United States due to lack of copyright renewal, as required by law at the time." The sections below are taken specifically from: http://www.sacred-texts.com/chr/aquinas/summa/sum005.htm. It is from the Treatise on the One God: QQ[2]-26.

THE EXISTENCE OF GOD (THREE ARTICLES)

Because the chief aim of sacred doctrine is to teach the knowledge of God, not only as He is in Himself, but also as He is the beginning of things and their last end, and especially of rational creatures, as is clear from what has been already said, therefore, in our endeavor to expound this science, we shall treat: (1) Of God; (2) Of the rational creature's advance towards God; (3) Of Christ, Who as man, is our way to God.

In treating of God there will be a threefold division, for we shall consider: (1) Whatever concerns the Divine Essence; (2) Whatever concerns the distinctions of Persons; (3) Whatever concerns the procession of creatures from Him.

Concerning the Divine Essence, we must consider: (1) Whether God exists? (2) The manner of His existence, or, rather, what is NOT the manner of His existence; (3) Whatever concerns His operations---namely, His knowledge, will, power.

Concerning the first, there are three points of inquiry:

(1) Whether the proposition "God exists" is self-evident?

(2) Whether it is demonstrable?

(3) Whether God exists?

Whether the existence of God is self-evident?

Objection 1: It seems that the existence of God is self-evident. Now those things are said to be self-evident to us the knowledge of which is naturally implanted in us, as we can see in regard to first principles. But as Damascene says (De Fide Orth. i, 1,3), "the knowledge of God is naturally implanted in all." Therefore the existence of God is self-evident.

Objection 2: Further, those things are said to be self-evident which are known as soon as the terms are known, which the Philosopher (1 Poster. iii) says is true of the first principles of demonstration. Thus, when the nature of a whole and of a part is known, it is at once recognized that every whole is greater than its part. But as soon as the signification of the word "God" is understood, it is at once seen that God exists. For by this word is signified that thing than which nothing greater can be conceived. But that which exists actually and mentally is greater than that which exists only mentally. Therefore, since as soon as the word "God" is understood it exists mentally, it also follows that it exists actually. Therefore the proposition "God exists" is self-evident.

Objection 3: Further, the existence of truth is self-evident. For whoever denies the existence of truth grants that truth does not exist: and, if truth does not exist, then the proposition "Truth does not exist" is true: and if there is anything true, there must be truth. But God is truth itself: "I am the way, the truth, and the life" (Jn. 14:6). Therefore "God exists" is self-evident.

On the contrary, No one can mentally admit the opposite of what is self-evident; as the Philosopher (Metaph. iv, lect. vi) states concerning the first principles of demonstration. But the opposite of the proposition "God is" can be mentally admitted: "The fool said in his heart, There is no God" (Ps. 52:1). Therefore, that God exists is not self-evident.

I answer that, A thing can be self-evident in either of two ways: on the one hand, self-evident in itself, though not to us; on the other, self-evident in itself, and to us. A proposition is self-evident because the predicate is included in the essence of the subject, as "Man is an animal," for animal is contained in the essence of man. If, therefore the essence of the predicate and subject be known to all, the proposition will be self-evident to all; as is clear with regard to the first principles of demonstration, the terms of which are common things that no one is ignorant of, such as being and non-being, whole and part, and such like. If, however, there are some to whom the essence of the predicate and subject is unknown, the proposition will be self-evident in itself, but not to those who do not know the meaning of the predicate and subject of the proposition. Therefore, it happens, as Boethius says (Hebdom., the title of which is: "Whether all that is, is good"), "that there are some mental concepts self-evident only to the learned, as that incorporeal substances are not in space." Therefore I say that this proposition, "God exists," of itself is self-evident, for the predicate is the same as the subject, because God is His own existence as will be hereafter shown (Q[3], A[4]). Now because we do not know the essence of God, the proposition is not self-evident to us; but needs to be demonstrated by things that are more known to us, though less known in their nature---namely, by effects.

Reply to Objection 1: To know that God exists in a general and confused way is implanted in us by nature, inasmuch as God is man's beatitude. For man naturally desires happiness, and what is naturally desired by man must be naturally known to him. This, however, is not to know absolutely that God exists; just as to know that someone is approaching is not the same as to know that Peter is approaching, even though it is Peter who is approaching; for many there are who imagine that man's perfect good which is happiness, consists in riches, and others in pleasures, and others in something else.

Reply to Objection 2: Perhaps not everyone who hears this word "God" understands it to signify something than which nothing greater can be thought, seeing that some have believed God to be a body. Yet, granted that everyone understands that by this word "God" is signified something than which nothing greater can be thought, nevertheless, it does not therefore follow that he understands that what the word signifies exists actually, but only that it exists mentally. Nor can it be argued that it actually exists, unless it be admitted that there actually exists something than which nothing greater can be thought; and this precisely is not admitted by those who hold that God does not exist.

Reply to Objection 3: The existence of truth in general is self-evident but the existence of a Primal Truth is not self-evident to us.

Whether it can be demonstrated that God exists?

Objection 1: It seems that the existence of God cannot be demonstrated. For it is an article of faith that God exists. But what is of faith cannot be demonstrated, because a demonstration produces scientific knowledge; whereas faith is of the unseen (Heb. 11:1). Therefore it cannot be demonstrated that God exists.

Objection 2: Further, the essence is the middle term of demonstration. But we cannot know in what God's essence consists, but solely in what it does not consist; as Damascene says (De Fide Orth. i, 4). Therefore we cannot demonstrate that God exists.

Objection 3: Further, if the existence of God were demonstrated, this could only be from His effects. But His effects are not proportionate to Him, since He is infinite and His effects are finite; and between the finite and infinite there is no proportion. Therefore, since a cause cannot be demonstrated by an effect not proportionate to it, it seems that the existence of God cannot be demonstrated.

On the contrary, The Apostle says: "The invisible things of Him are clearly seen, being understood by the things that are made" (Rom. 1:20). But this would not be unless the existence of God could be demonstrated through the things that are made; for the first thing we must know of anything is whether it exists.

I answer that, Demonstration can be made in two ways: One is through the cause, and is called "a priori," and this is to argue from what is prior absolutely. The other is through the effect, and is called a demonstration "a posteriori"; this is to argue from what is prior relatively only to us. When an effect is better known to us than its cause, from the effect we proceed to the knowledge of the cause. And from every effect the existence of its proper cause can be demonstrated, so long as its effects are better known to us; because since every effect depends upon its cause, if the effect exists, the cause must pre-exist. Hence the existence of God, in so far as it is not self-evident to us, can be demonstrated from those of His effects which are known to us.

Reply to Objection 1: The existence of God and other like truths about God, which can be known by natural reason, are not articles of faith, but are preambles to the articles; for faith presupposes natural knowledge, even as grace presupposes nature, and perfection supposes something that can be perfected. Nevertheless, there is nothing to prevent a man, who cannot grasp a proof, accepting, as a matter of faith, something which in itself is capable of being scientifically known and demonstrated.

Reply to Objection 2: When the existence of a cause is demonstrated from an effect, this effect takes the place of the definition of the cause in proof of the cause's existence. This is especially the case in regard to God, because, in order to prove the existence of anything, it is necessary to accept as a middle term the meaning of the word, and not its essence, for the question of its essence follows on the question of its existence. Now the names given to God are derived from His effects; consequently, in demonstrating the existence of God from His effects, we may take for the middle term the meaning of the word "God".

Reply to Objection 3: From effects not proportionate to the cause no perfect knowledge of that cause can be obtained. Yet from every effect the existence of the cause can be clearly demonstrated, and so we can demonstrate the existence of God from His effects; though from them we cannot perfectly know God as He is in His essence.

Whether God exists?

Objection 1: It seems that God does not exist; because if one of two contraries be infinite, the other would be altogether destroyed. But the word "God" means that He is infinite goodness. If, therefore, God existed, there would be no evil discoverable; but there is evil in the world. Therefore God does not exist.

Objection 2: Further, it is superfluous to suppose that what can be accounted for by a few principles has been produced by many. But it seems that everything we see in the world can be accounted for by other principles, supposing God did not exist. For all natural things can be reduced to one principle which is nature; and all voluntary things can be reduced to one principle which is human reason, or will. Therefore there is no need to suppose God's existence.

On the contrary, It is said in the person of God: "I am Who am." (Ex. 3:14).

I answer that, The existence of God can be proved in five ways.

The first and more manifest way is the argument from motion. It is certain, and evident to our senses, that in the world some things are in motion. Now whatever is in motion is put in motion by another, for nothing can be in motion except it is in potentiality to that towards which it is in motion; whereas a thing moves inasmuch as it is in act. For motion is nothing else than the reduction of something from potentiality to actuality. But nothing can be reduced from potentiality to actuality, except by something in a state of actuality. Thus that which is actually hot, as fire, makes wood, which is potentially hot, to be actually hot, and thereby moves and changes it. Now it is not possible that the same thing should be at once in actuality and potentiality in the same respect, but only in different respects. For what is actually hot cannot simultaneously be potentially hot; but it is simultaneously potentially cold. It is therefore impossible that in the same respect and in the same way a thing should be both mover and moved, i.e. that it should move itself. Therefore, whatever is in motion must be put in motion by another. If that by which it is put in motion be itself put in motion, then this also must needs be put in motion by another, and that by another again. But this cannot go on to infinity, because then there would be no first mover, and, consequently, no other mover; seeing that subsequent movers move only inasmuch as they are put in motion by the first mover; as the staff moves only because it is put in motion by the hand. Therefore it is necessary to arrive at a first mover, put in motion by no other; and this everyone understands to be God.

The second way is from the nature of the efficient cause. In the world of sense we find there is an order of efficient causes. There is no case known (neither is it, indeed, possible) in which a thing is found to be the efficient cause of itself; for so it would be prior to itself, which is impossible. Now in efficient causes it is not possible to go on to infinity, because in all efficient causes following in order, the first is the cause of the intermediate cause, and the intermediate is the cause of the ultimate cause, whether the intermediate cause be several, or only one. Now to take away the cause is to take away the effect. Therefore, if there be no first cause among efficient causes, there will be no ultimate, nor any intermediate cause. But if in efficient causes it is possible to go on to infinity, there will be no first efficient cause, neither will there be an ultimate effect, nor any intermediate efficient causes; all of which is plainly false. Therefore it is necessary to admit a first efficient cause, to which everyone gives the name of God.

The third way is taken from possibility and necessity, and runs thus. We find in nature things that are possible to be and not to be, since they are found to be generated, and to corrupt, and consequently, they are possible to be and not to be. But it is impossible for these always to exist, for that which is possible not to be at some time is not. Therefore, if everything is possible not to be, then at one time there could have been nothing in existence. Now if this were true, even now there would be nothing in existence, because that which does not exist only begins to exist by something already existing. Therefore, if at one time nothing was in existence, it would have been impossible for anything to have begun to exist; and thus even now nothing would be in existence---which is absurd. Therefore, not all beings are merely possible, but there must exist something the existence of which is necessary. But every necessary thing either has its necessity caused by another, or not. Now it is impossible to go on to infinity in necessary things which have their necessity caused by another, as has been already proved in regard to efficient causes. Therefore we cannot but postulate the existence of some being having of itself its own necessity, and not receiving it from another, but rather causing in others their necessity. This all men speak of as God.

The fourth way is taken from the gradation to be found in things. Among beings there are some more and some less good, true, noble and the like. But "more" and "less" are predicated of different things, according as they resemble in their different ways something which is the maximum, as a thing is said to be hotter according as it more nearly resembles that which is hottest; so that there is something which is truest, something best, something noblest and, consequently, something which is uttermost being; for those things that are greatest in truth are greatest in being, as it is written in Metaph. ii. Now the maximum in any genus is the cause of all in that genus; as fire, which is the maximum heat, is the cause of all hot things. Therefore there must also be something which is to all beings the cause of their being, goodness, and every other perfection; and this we call God.

The fifth way is taken from the governance of the world. We see that things which lack intelligence, such as natural bodies, act for an end, and this is evident from their acting always, or nearly always, in the same way, so as to obtain the best result. Hence it is plain that not fortuitously, but designedly, do they achieve their end. Now whatever lacks intelligence cannot move towards an end, unless it be directed by some being endowed with knowledge and intelligence; as the arrow is shot to its mark by the archer. Therefore some intelligent being exists by whom all natural things are directed to their end; and this being we call God.

Reply to Objection 1: As Augustine says (Enchiridion xi): "Since God is the highest good, He would not allow any evil to exist in His works, unless His omnipotence and goodness were such as to bring good even out of evil." This is part of the infinite goodness of God, that He should allow evil to exist, and out of it produce good.

Reply to Objection 2: Since nature works for a determinate end under the direction of a higher agent, whatever is done by nature must needs be traced back to God, as to its first cause. So also whatever is done voluntarily must also be traced back to some higher cause other than human reason or will, since these can change or fail; for all things that are changeable and capable of defect must be traced back to an immovable and self-necessary first principle, as was shown in the body of the Article.

Bibliography

Aquinas, Saint Thomas. *Summa Contra Gentiles*. CD: *Writings of the Saints: Volume V.* Produced by Chris Tesch.

Aquinas, Saint Thomas. *Summa Theologica.* CD: *Writings of the Saints: Volume II.* Produced by Chris Tesch.

Aquinas, Saint Thomas. *Commentary on Aristotle's "On the Heavens" (Aristotelis libros de caelo et mundo, generatione et corruptione, meteorologicorum expositio* (Rome, 1952)).

Aquinas, Saint Thomas. *Thomas Aquinas: Selected Writings.* Edited and translated by Ralph McInerny. New York: Penguin Books, 1998.

Archelaus: *The Acts of the Disputation with the Heresiarch Manes (a Fragment of the Same Disputation).* Logos Software: The Early Church Fathers.

Asimov, Isaac. *Extraterrestrial Civilizations.* New York: Crown Publishers, Inc., 1979.

Ashkenazi, M. "Not the Sons of Adam: Religious Responses to ETI." *Space Policy,* 8/4: 341-349. 1992.

Anonymous. Personal email to author, 26 September 2010. The author of the email prefers to remain anonymous..

Author unknown. "The Rael Thing." Earth Island Journal, Spring 98, Vol. 13 Issue 2, p 3.

Balducci, Corrado, Monsignor. "Vatican Acknowledges ET Presence." www.gvnr.com/85/editorial.htm.

Blish, James. *A Case of Conscience.* New York and Canada: The Ballantine Publishing Group, a division of Random House, Inc., 1958.

Brewster, Sir David. *More Worlds Than One: The Creed of the Philosopher and the Hope of the Christian.* London: John Murray, Albe Marle Street, 1862.

Brook, John H. "Natural Theology and the Plurality of Worlds: Observations on the Brewster-Whewell Debate." *Annals of Science,* 34 (1977), 221 – 286.

Buridan, John. "Quaestiones super libris quattuor de caelo et mundo." Cited by Dick, *Plurality of Worlds* 29).

Burkes, Joseph, MD. "Church Dialog" in 5th World Journal, Contact Forum 2000.1, pages 10 – 11. 1999.

Cairns, David. "Thomas Chalmers's Astronomical Discourses: A Study in Natural Theology." *Scottish Journal of Theology*, 9 (1956), 410 – 421.

Cannell, A. and C. Domb, eds. *Challenge: Torah Views on Science and Its Problems.* 2nd edition. New York: n.p., 1978.

Chalmers, Thomas, D.D. *A Series of Discourses on the Christian Revelation, Viewed in Connection with the Modern Astronomy.* New York: American Tract Society, n.d.

Clarke, Arthur C. *The Exploration of Space.* New York: Harper & Brothers, 1951.

Coyne, Rev. Dr. George V., S.J. *The Many Worlds and Religion.* Keynote Speech at INSAP II Conference, Malta: 9 January 1999.

Croswell, Ken. "No news from Alpha Centauri (yet)." *New York Times*, 7/26/96, Vol. 145 Issue 50500 p A29.

Crowe, Michael J. *The Extraterrestrial Life Debate, 1750 -- 1900.* Dover Publications, May 1999. ISBN: 048640675X.

Crowe, Michael J., ed. *The Extraterrestrial Life Debate: Antiquity to 1915: A Source Book.* Notre Dame, Indiana: University of Notre Dame Press, 2008.

Cumont, Franz. *Astrology and Religion among the Greeks and Romans.* New York: Dover Publications, Inc., 1960.

Davies, P.C.W. *Are We Alone? The Philosphical Implications of the Discovery of Extraterrestrial Life.* Basic Books, August 1996. ISBN: 0465004199.

Davis, Charles. "The Place of Christ." *Clergy Review*, n.s., 45 (1960), 707 – 718.

Davis, Jimmy H. and Harry L. Poe. *Designer Universe: Intelligent Design and the Existence of God.* Nashville, Tennessee: Broadman and Holman Publishers, 2002.

Davis, John Jefferson. "Search for Extraterrestrial Intelligence and the Christian Doctrine of Redemption." *Science and Christian Belief*, 9 (1997), 21 – 34.

De Fontenelle, Bernard Le Bovier. *Conversations on the Plurality of Worlds.* Translated by H. A. Hargreaves. University of California Press, August 1990. Originally published in 1686. ISBN: 0520071719.

Delano, Kenneth J. *Many Worlds, One God.* Hicksville, NY: Exposition Press, 1977. ISBN: 0682486442.

Deutsch, Otto Erich. *Schubert: A Documentary Biography*, translated by Rich Bloom. London: J.M. Dent, 1946.

De Chardin, Teilhard. *The Phenomenon of Man*. Translated by Bernard Wall. New York and London: William Collins Sons & Co., Ltd., and Harper & Row Publishers, Incorporated, 1959.

De Unamuno, Miguel. *Tragic Sense of Life*. Translated by J. E. Crawford Flitch. New York: Dover Publications, Inc., 1954.

DeWohl, Louis. "Religion, Philosophy, and Outer Space." *America*, 24 July 1954, 420-21.

Dick, Steven J. *The Biological Universe: The Twentieth-century Extraterrestrial Life Debate and the Limits of Science*. Cambridge University Press, 15 February 2001. ISBN: 0521799120.

Dick, Steven J. *Cosmotheology: The New Universe and Its Theological Implications*. A sermon by Steven J. Dick Sunday 18 March 2001. Copyright 2001 Steven J. Dick and the Unitarian Universalists of Sterling. www.uusterling.org/sermons/2001/sermon%202001-03-18.htm.

Dick, Steven J. *Life on Other Worlds: The Twentieth-century Extraterrestrial Life Debate*. [Note: This book appears to be an abridged and updated version *of The Biological Universe*.]

Dick, Steven J., ed. *Many Worlds: The New Universe, Extraterrestrial Life & the Theological Implications*. Philadelphia and London: Templeton Foundation Press, 2000.

Dick, Steven J. *Plurality of Worlds: The Origins of the Extraterrestrial Life Debate from Democritus to Kant*. Cambridge University Press, August 1984. ASIN: 0521319854.

Downing, David C. *Planets in Peril: A Critical Study of C.S. Lewis's Ransom Trilogy*. Amherst: Univ. of Massachusetts Press, 1992.

Fitzgerald, R. *The Complete Book of Extraterrestrial Encounters: The Ideas of Carl Sagan, Eric von Daniken, Billy Graham, Carl Jung, John C. Lilly, John G. Fuller, and Many Others*. New York: Collier Books, 1979.

Frankfort, Henri and Mrs. H.A. Frankfort and John A. Wilson and Thorkild Jacobsen. *Before Philosophy: The Intellectual Adventure of Ancient Man*. Baltimore, Maryland: Penguin Books, 1946.

Frye, Northrop. *The Great Code: The Bible and Literature*. New York: Harcourt, Brace & Company, 1981.

Galloway, Allan D. *The Cosmic Christ*. New York, 1951.

George, Marie I. "The Catholic Faith, Scripture, and the Question of the Existence of Intelligent Extra-terrestrial Life" in *Faith, Scholarship, and Culture in the 21st Century*, edited by Alice Ramos and Marie I.

George. Washington: The Catholic University of America Press, 2002. Website: www.unav.es/cryf/georgemaritain.html.

Greeley, Andrew. Personal email exchanges with the author.

Heeren, Fred. *Show Me God: What the Message from Space is Telling Us about God.* Wonders That Witness Volume 1. Wheeling, IL: Day Star Productions, 1997.
ISBN: 1885849524.
[Note: Ross Pavlac says on his web page: This is a bit of an odd duck, sort of like the stuff in Walker Percy's *Lost in the Cosmos.* *Show Me God* is a non-fiction book about the evidences for God based on various constants and values in the universe being necessary for life to exist. The short story is included at the beginning of the book to show an all-too-possible version of what might happen if the SETI project ends up finding life out there, but not the kind of intelligent life they were expecting.]

Heeren, Fred. "Home Alone in the Universe?" *First Things: A Monthly Journal of Religion & Public Life*, Mar 2002 Issue 121, p 38.

Hesburgh, Theodore. Foreward. *The Search for Extraterrestrial Intelligence.* NASA. SP-419. WASHINGTON, D.C., 1977. Morrison Report of SETI, c. 1975-1976. Morrison, P. and J. Billingham and J. Wolfe, eds.
[Note: Source of quote is *The Biological Universe* by Steven J. Dick page 511: Theodore Hesburgh was the President of Notre Dame University: "As a theologian, I would say that this proposed search for extraterrestrial intelligence (SETI) is also a search of knowing and understanding God through His works -- especially those works that most reflect Him. Finding others than ourselves would mean knowing Him better."]

Hyman, Arthur and James J. Walsh. *Philosophy in the Middle Ages.* Indianapolis: Hackett Publishing Company, 1974.

Kaiser, Christopher. "Extraterrestrial Life and Extraterrestrial Intelligence." *Reformed Review,* 51 (1997 – 1998), 77 – 91.

Kaplan, Rabbi Aryeh. World Wide Web: www.innernet.org.il/archives/extract.htm. Extracted with permission from "The Aryeh Kaplan Reader" published by ArtScroll/Mesorah Publications Ltd., Brooklyn, New York, January 2002 edition.

Lamm, Rabbi Norman. *Faith and Doubt – Studies in Traditional Jewish Thought.* New York Ktav 1971. [Note: Chapter 5 is entitled: "The religious implications of extra-terrestrial life."]

La Peyrere, Isaac de. *Men Before Adam or A Discourse upon the twelfth, thirteenth, and fourteenth Verses of the Fifth Chapter of the Epistle of the Apostle Paul to the Romans By which are prov'd That the first Men were created before Adam.* London: Early English Books Online, www.proquest.com, 1656.

Leslie, John, ed. *Modern Cosmology & Philosophy.* New York: Prometheus Books, 1998.

Levine, Al. Personal email exchanges with the author, 26 July 2003.

Levine, Faye. "Qualities of the Golem." http://atomick.net/fayelevine/pk/golem/pk007.php. First published: 06-15-2000. Last modified: 04-29-2006.

Lewels, Francisco Joe, Ph.D. "The Vatican and UFOs: Can Theology Accept an Alien Presence?" *Contact Forum: The Journal of the Fifth World.* May-June 1998, Volume 6, Issue 3. Pages 24-28.

Lewis, C.S. *Out of the Silent Planet.* New York, NY: Scribner, 1938.

Lewis, C.S. *Perelandra.* New York, NY: Scribner, 1944.

Lewis, James. R., ed. *The Gods Have Landed: New Religions from Other Worlds.* New York: State University of New York Press, 1995.

McColley, Grant and H.W. Miller, "Saint Bonaventure, Francis Mayron, William Vorilong and the Doctrine of a Plurality of Worlds." *Speculum,* 12 (1937), 386 – 389.

Michaud, Michael. *Contact with Alien Civilizations: Our Hopes and Fears about Encountering Extraterrestrials.* New York, New York: Copernicus Books, 2007.

Miller, Lisa. "If we're not alone." *Wall Street Journal -- Eastern Edition,* 01/01/2000, Vol. 235 Issue 1, p R50.

Miller, Walter. *A Canticle for Leibowitz.* New York: Harper & Row, 1959.

Milne, E. A. "The Second Law of Thermodynamics: Evolution." *Modern Cosmology and the Christian Idea of God.* Oxford, 1952. [Note: Discusses the problem of the Incarnation of Christ on other planets.]

Murphy, George L., Ph.D. "Intelligent Design as a Theological Problem." www.elca.org/faithandscience/covalence/covalence_vol4_no2.pdf. Volume IV, Number 2 "Summer Reading" Issue Second Quarter, 2002.

Newman, Robert C. *The Biblical Firmament: Vault or Vapor?* Hatfield, Pennsylvania: Interdisciplinary Biblical Research Institute, 2000.

O'Malley, William J. "Carl Sagan's Gospel of Scientism." *America, 144* (Feb. 7, 1981), 95 – 98.

O'Meara, Thomas F. *Christian Theology and Extraterrestrial Intelligent Life.* Theological Studies, 00405639, Mar 99, Vol. 60, Issue 1.

Parrinder, Patrick. "Detached, planet, no neighbors." *Times Higher Education Supplement*, 1/14/94 Issue 1106, p13.

Peters, Rev. Dr. Ted. "Exo-Theology: Speculations on Extra-Terrestrial Life." World Wide Web: www.contactsupport.net/exo1.html.

Phalan, J. M. "Men and Morals in Space." *America* 113 (9 October 1965), 405-7.

Plotinus. *Enneads.* Oaks.nvg.org/sa1ra6.html.

Polkinghorne, John. *Quarks, Chaos, and Christianity.* London: Triangle Press, 1994.

Proctor, Richard A. *Other Worlds Than Ours: the Plurality of Worlds Studied under the Light of Recent Scientific Researches.* Akron, Ohio: The Werner Company, 1870.

Ramm, Bernard. *The Christian View of Science and Scripture.* Grand Rapids, Michigan: William B. Eerdmans Publishing Company, 1954.

Runes, Dagobert D., ed. *Dictionary of Philosophy: Ancient-Medieval-Modern.* Ames, Iowa: Littlefield, Adams, & Co., 1960.

Russell, Robert John and William R. Stoeger, S.J., and George V. Coyne, S.J., eds. *John Paul II on Science and Religion: Reflections on the New View from Rome.* The Vatican: Vatican Observatory Publications, 1990.

Seife, Charles. "Gimme that E.T. Religion." *Science Now*, 03/02/2000, p 3.

Simek, Rudolf. *Heaven and Earth in the Middle Ages: The Physical World before Columbus.* Translated by Angela Hall. Woodbridge: The Boydell Press, 1992.

Sitchin, Zecharia. "Sitchin and Vatican Discuss ETs." World Wide Web: www.sitchin.com. *5th World Journal.* (Formerly: *Contact Forum*) 2000.2 Pages 29-30.

Smyth, Marina. *Understanding the Universe in Seventh-Century Ireland.* Woodbridge: The Boydell Press, 1996.

Strange, James F. "Some Observations from Archaeology and Religious Studies on ETI." World Wide Web: it.utsi.edu/~spsr/articles/someobservations.html. University of South Florida, 1994.

Tanzella-Nitti, Giuseppe,ed. "Extraterrestrial Life" in *Interdisciplinary Encyclopedia of Religion and Science.* www.disf.org/en/Voci/65.asp, 7-22-2003.

Tartar, Donald E. "Looking for God and Space Aliens." *Free Inquiry*, Summer 2000, Vol. 20 Issue 3, p 38.

Tarter, Jill C. "SETI and the Religions of the Universe." Presented at the Many Worlds: The New Universe and Its Implications for Theology Symposium. Sponsored by the John Templeton Foundation, Nassau, The Bahamas (November 22-24, 1998).

Unamuno, Miguel de. *The Tragic Sense of Life.* Originally published in 1913, Spain, under the Spanish title *Del Sentimiento Tragico de la Vida.* The Gutenberg Project etext: http://www.gutenberg.org/catalog/world/readfile?fk_files=119564.

Vanderkam, James C. *An Introduction to Early Judaism.* Grand Rapids, Michigan: William B. Eerdmans Publishing Company, 2001.

Wallace, Alfred Russell. *Man's Place in the Universe: A Study of the Results of Scientific Research in Relation to the Unity or Plurality of Worlds.* New York: McClure, Phillips & Co., 1903.

Westermann, Claus. *Creation.* Philadelphia: Fortress, 1974.

Whewell, William. *The Plurality of Worlds.* Boston: Gould and Lincoln, 1856.

Wiker, Benjamin D. "Alien Ideas: Christianity and the Search for Extraterrestrial Intelligence." World Wide Web: www.crisismagazine.com/november2002/feature7.htm.

Wilkinson, David. *Alone in the Universe? Aliens, the X-Files and God.* Downers Grove, Illinois: InterVarsity Press, 1997.

Wojcik, Daniel. *The End of the World as We Know It: Faith, Fatalism, and Apocalypse in America.* New York and London: New York University Press, 1997.

Wolf-Chase, Grace, Ph.D. "One Scientist's Thoughts on the Theological Implications of the Existence of Extraterrestrial Life." World Wide Web: www.elca.org/faithandscience/covalence/covalence_vol4_no2.pdf. Volume IV, Number 2 "Summer Reading" Issue Second Quarter, 2002.

World Wide Web: www.ou.org/torah/ti/5760/vayeitzei60.htm. [Note: Jewish discussion of four levels of interpretation of Scripture.]

Zabilka, Ivan L. *Nineteenth Century British and American Perspectives on the Plurality of Worlds: A Consideration of Scientific and Christian Attitudes.* University of Kentucky doctoral 31dissertation, 1980.

Cynthia Anne Miller Smith

CPSIA information can be obtained at www.ICGtesting.com
Printed in the USA
LVOW101947290212

271009LV00020B/295/P

9 781936 533022